HEARTLAND

HEARTLAND

THE COOKBOOK

Judith Fertig

Location Photography by Jonathan Chester
Food Photography by Ben Pieper

Andrews McMeel
Publishing, LLC
Kansas City • Sydney • London

11 12 13 14 15 SDB 10 9 8 7 6 5 4 3 2 1

ISBN: 978-1-4494-0057-6

Library of Congress Control Number: 2010929351

Location Photography: Jonathan Chester
Food Photography: Ben Pieper
Design: Julie Barnes and Holly Ogden
Food Stylist: Tina Stamos
Assistant Food Stylists: Richard Garcia and Daniel Trefz

www.andrewsmcmeel.com

Attention: Schools and Businesses

Andrews McMeel books are available at quantity
discounts with bulk purchase for educational, business,
or sales promotional use. For information, please
write to: Special Sales Department, Andrews McMeel
Publishing, LLC, 1130 Walnut Street, Kansas City,
Missouri 64106.

For my family and friends, who put the "heart" in Heartland.

CONTENTS

ACKNOWLEDGMENTS

Heartland has been a labor of love right from the start.

I'd like to thank everyone who made this project so deliciously fun, incredibly interesting, and amazingly heartfelt. First off, thank you to publisher Kirsty Melville, editor Jean Lucas, art director Julie Barnes, marketing and public relations guru Tammie Barker, and all the team at Andrews McMeel for such a wonderful hands-on opportunity, made possible by the best literary agent on the planet, Lisa Ekus. Then, thank you to photographer Jonathan Chester, who was as brilliant capturing Berkshire pigs in Iowa as he was penguins in Antarctica. Food photographer Ben Pieper and stylist Tina Stamos did a fabulous job, as well.

A big thank-you to Justin Rashid of American Spoon Foods in Michigan, Jonathan Justus of Justus Drugstore in Missouri, Tory Miller of L'Etoile in Wisconsin, Kathy and Herb Eckhouse of La Quercia in Iowa, and Sarah Hoffman and John Spertus of Green Dirt Farm in Missouri for being generous with their time in helping me tell the stories behind the food and guiding Jonathan Chester to the photos that help illustrate them.

Thank you, also, to the foodies, farmers, restaurant owners, chefs, Slow Food members, and food artisans who helped point the way: Allen and Mary Schrag, Alvin Brensing, and Frank Reese in Kansas; Jude Becker, Seed Savers Exchange, and Joyce Lock in Iowa; Jenny Britton Bauer and Fred and Linda Griffith in Ohio; Jasper Mirabile, Jane Zieha, Ted Habiger, the Saint Louis Culinary Society, and the Kansas City Barbeque Society in Missouri; John and Dorothy Priske and the Wisconsin Milk Marketing Board in Wisconsin; Wes Jarrell and Lesley Cooperband, Sarah Stegner, Susan Goss, Andrew Zimmerman, Norm Dinkel Jr., and Weber in Illinois; and Nola Gentry, Larry Oates, and Ron Harris in Indiana.

There are still, thankfully, many Heartland writers who continue to put into words what we think and feel about where we live. My thanks for the quotes in this book go to Willa Cather, Paulette Jiles, Marilyn Kluger, Kit Kiefer, Garrison Keillor, Carrie Young, Elizabeth Landeweer, Ruth Suckow, W. P. Kinsella, Justin Isherwood, Nancy Horan, Carl Sandburg, Clementine Paddleford, Lauren Chapin, Conrad Richter, Louise Erdrich, Susan Power, Laura Ingalls Wilder, and Adam Z. Horvath.

I greatly appreciate everyone who provided recipe inspiration or helped me develop and test the recipes in this book: Nick and Jessica Fertig, Sarah Fertig, Julie Fox, Karen Adler, Mary Ann Duckers, Dee Barwick, Frank Stitt, Peter Golaszewski, Harlan "Pete" Peterson, and Lindsay Laricks. Thank you to Jenny Britton Bauer, Christopher Elbow, Vicki Johnson, and Roxanne Wyss for generously allowing me to use their recipes.

And finally, thanks to all the Heartland folks who were so giving of their expertise as we all write the next culinary chapter in the place we call home.

INTRODUCTION

"The horizon was like a perfect circle, a great embrace, and within it lay the cornfields, still green, and the yellow wheat stubble, miles and miles of it, and the pasture lands where the white-faced cattle led lives of utter content," wrote Willa Cather in "The Best Years."

Among those fortunate enough to have been born and raised in the Midwest, this is how we think of it. The Heartland holds us, comforts us, makes us stand up straight. Even if we leave, it still claims a place in our hearts.

The Heartland, or Midwest, is the center section of the United States, which also happens to be its agricultural core. According to geographer James Shortridge, "The Midwest is America's pastoral face, etched into our consciousness as a permanent physical location, despite the presence of industrial cities," which are accepted, nonetheless, as exceptions to the rule.

You hear the Heartland in the rustle of golden, ripening wheat in the Dakotas. You see it in the mysterious deep green gloom as you wander into an Indiana cornfield. You taste it in the sweet corn, slathered with butter. You smell it in hickory smoke.

The term *Middle West* first appeared in print in 1880 to describe the Kansas/Nebraska region. It was subsequently shortened to *Midwest* and the area enlarged to include all twelve of the current Midwestern states—Ohio, Indiana, Michigan, Illinois, Iowa, Wisconsin, North Dakota, South Dakota, Minnesota, Missouri, Kansas, and Nebraska—by 1910.

Today, the geography of the Midwest or Heartland consists of broad river valleys, marsh, rolling prairie, thick forest, great lakes, Flint Hills, Badlands, and savannahs—all specific *terroirs* or microclimates good for growing certain crops or raising certain livestock. Broad river valleys, with sandy or loamy soil, produce wonderful melons, squash, sweet corn, and pumpkins. Swampy marshlands like the Sandhills of Nebraska attract the annual migration of cranes and other waterfowl, but they also provide rangeland for beef cattle. Rolling prairie is a natural grassland, so grasses like wheat, sorghum, oats, and rye do well from central Ohio through to western Kansas; grasslands to the north—especially in northern Iowa, southern Wisconsin, and eastern Minnesota—get more rainfall and have thus become dairy country. Northern forests in Wisconsin, Michigan, and Minnesota offer hardwoods like maple, oak, and hickory that feed the barbecue lover's need for smoky flavor—and charcoal. The Great Lakes teem with fresh fish like lake perch, walleye pike, chub, and whitefish, but they also offer the perfect climate—on the eastern shore of Lake Michigan—for stone fruits like cherries and apricots. The Flint Hills and Badlands feature rocky soil and hardy prairie grasses and lots of room to roam for herds of beef

cattle and bison. Oak savannahs or lightly forested grasslands compose most of what is now Illinois and Iowa—where the farmer's trinity of corn, soybeans, and hogs are right at home.

The Heartland also includes big cities like Chicago, Illinois; St. Louis, Missouri; Detroit, Michigan; and Minneapolis/St. Paul, Minnesota. It encompasses cities that are more like big small towns, such as Milwaukee, Wisconsin; Kansas City, Missouri; Indianapolis, Indiana; Des Moines, Iowa; Cleveland and Cincinnati, Ohio. There are also historic small towns with courthouse squares and iconic architecture—the white-painted farmhouse west of the Mississippi and the log cabin east of it.

The Heartland is known for small towns, family farms, hard workers, "let's all get along" values, and that "have a good day" type of friendliness. A recent study by Cambridge University produced a "personality map" of the United States. It's not surprising that most of the top 10 states in the sociable, energetic, enthusiastic, warm, compassionate, cooperative, dutiful, responsible, and self-disciplined areas were in the Midwest. As Garrison Keillor, a Minnesota native, drily explains: "We are a modest people with much to be modest about, self-effacing, anxious to efface ourselves and not wait for others to do the job."

The Heartland is united in believing, like Dorothy in *The Wizard of Oz* (written by Midwesterner Frank L. Baum), that what's really important in life is no farther than "your own backyard " and that "There's no place like home."

Some people believe that rhubarb symbolizes that backyard idea, but I'll get to that later. Heartlanders feel strongly about home. That's what underlines this passage from Paulette Jiles's *Enemy Women*, about a young Missouri woman wrongly imprisoned during the Civil War. The night before she and her sisters have to flee their home, Adair looks at the log cabin quilt her deceased mother had made, with the red square "hearth" in the center of each "cabin":

"The hearths were all velvets of varying reds. Carmine, scarlet, a garnet, a deep rose. Adair ran her dirtied fingers over the piecings in the vagrant light. There was a beautiful silk repeated over and over on the shadow side, which was dark brown with a figure in garnet that might have been the face of a clock. Adair spread her hand over one of the blocks as if over her home with its red velvet fire in the heart of her family, both living and dead."

Many other Heartland authors have written of their love for the land, the people, the place—a number of them are represented in the pages of this book. Somehow, living in the Heartland—despite all the jokes about the weather, how we don't take to trends quickly, how we're too nice—makes you realize what's really important in life.

Midwesterners have a grounded sense of who they are because they're still close to the land. Many families are only a generation or two removed from the family farm, and they still feel that summer is not summer without canning tomatoes or making homemade preserves. Outlying farms surround most metropolitan areas, and Midwesterners know they don't have to go far to breathe a little fresh air and be out in the country. They never really left their roots.

All of this is reflected in the Heartland kitchen, where dishes hark back to the farmhouse kitchen, take their cues from comfort, add a twist of ethnic heritage, and yet still celebrate what's fresh in the garden or foraged from the wild.

In the dozen years since I wrote *Prairie Home Cooking*, a lot has happened in the Heartland. Second only to the California/Oregon/Washington region, the Midwest now has thirty-three Slow Food chapters, which have helped educate the public about local foods, farmers' issues, and the whole farm-to-table idea.

Artisan food purveyors have also increased, as Heartland farmers and artisan producers make the choice for quality over quantity and take the concept of "value-added" products—making higher-priced butter from cream, for example—a step further. "For a while, Iowa went away from making food for people to making food for animals or food for cars—ethanol," says

Herb Eckhouse, co-owner with wife, Kathy, of La Quercia, a highly praised artisan producer of prosciutto, guanciale (jowl bacon), and pancetta outside Des Moines, Iowa. Now Iowa is home to farmer Jude Becker of Dyersville, who breeds the heritage Berkshire pigs that become what the *New York Times* has called "the great novel" of La Quercia prosciutto—or end up center of the plate at Mario Batali's Babbo and Lidia Bastianich's Felidia in New York City or Alice Waters's Chez Panisse in Berkeley, California.

When I wrote *Prairie Home Cooking*, there were no artisan bakeries in the Kansas City area; now there are four. Microbreweries were just getting started; now there are microdistilleries like Rehorst in Milwaukee making small-batch vodka and gin—make sure you try a Garden Gimlet (page 125) made with Rehorst vodka. Vosges (Chicago, Illinois) and Christopher Elbow (Kansas City, Missouri) chocolates have come into being during that time, as well as La Quercia cured meats and Jeni Britton Bauer's signature ice creams in Columbus, Ohio.

Tastier heritage breeds of turkey, chicken, and pork are now raised in the Heartland, mainly in Kansas, Minnesota, Wisconsin, and Iowa, and are featured on restaurant menus throughout the country. Order heritage poultry or meat (see Resources, page 266), and then make Pan-Roasted Chicken Breasts with Tarragon Creamed Corn (page 204), Smoke-Roasted Pork Shoulder with Sooey Sauce (page 188), or Roast Heritage Turkey with Pancetta-Roasted Brussels Sprouts (page 215) and taste how delicious they are.

Foraged foods (wild foods like elderflowers and elderberries, native persimmons, mulberries, wild greens, black walnuts, and hickory nuts), once a necessity, now lend a certain locavore cachet to high-style restaurant menus. Once you take a bite of Crackly-Top Hickory Nut Cake (page 252), you'll be right out there foraging too—or having Ray's Hickory Nuts (see Resources, page 266) do it for you.

Grilling and barbecuing keep growing in popularity, with Heartlanders transferring their love of cold-smoked cheese and sausages to hot smoking and planking on the grill. Give Heartland grocery store deli meats and cheeses a wonderful and easy flair with Brewpub Cheese and Charcuterie on a Plank (page 108)—you'll be amazed at how wonderful they taste. Or slather a steak with a regional grilling paste, as in the Morel Grilled Rib-Eye recipe (page 195)—and sear it over the coals for a memorable meal.

Midwesterners used to depend on their pantries to see them through the winter months (as the novels of Willa Cather so movingly describe), so canning and bottling were very important. A scene in Cather's *My Antonia*, when Jim Burden visits Antonia's farm after being gone for many years, illustrates her love for and fascination with the bottled and canned treasures assembled in colorful rows. As Antonia's children show Jim the pantry/root cellar, "Nina and Jan, and a little girl named Lucie, kept shyly pointing out to me the shelves of glass jars. They said nothing, but, glancing at me, traced on the glasses with their finger-tips the outline of the cherries and strawberries and crabapples within, trying by a blissful expression of countenance to give me some idea of the deliciousness."

Preserving is still about capturing summer's bounty, but it's also about having signature ingredients on hand, such as char-grilled onions, smoked garlic and tomatoes, infused creams, sauces, unique jams and jellies, pies, barbecue sauces and rubs, and flavored butters in the kitchen cupboard, refrigerator, or freezer.

Heritage districts still abound and are as popular as ever, many of them known for specialty baked goods. Lindsborg, Kansas, has two main Swedish festivals every year—Midsommerdag in June and Saint Lucia Day (and a Swedish bake sale) in December. German Village, near Columbus, Ohio, features sausage and beer *hauses* as well as a local, seasonal bakery that specializes in Christmas cookies—there's a line of customers out the

door every year. Germans—and non-Germans alike—enjoy Friday fish frys in Milwaukee. Festivals and church suppers are still turning points in the year. In small towns along the Ohio/Indiana border, summertime means the Fried Chicken Dinner Trail, with fried chicken dinners ending with homemade pie at different churches each weekend right up until Labor Day.

Many beloved Midwestern desserts are centuries old, brought by settlers from Europe, adapted to what grows here, and still popular: sugar cream pie, hickory nut cake, Swedish gingersnaps, Scandinavian cheesecake-like desserts, native persimmon pudding, and Shaker lemon pie.

Yet Heartlanders, like everybody else, are busy. And this book reflects that reality. If we want to eat well, from farm to table, we have to make the cooking process work for us, not against us. So, throughout *Heartland*, you'll see new methods and dishes that the farm wife of yesteryear would have saluted. Farmhouse Butter (page 7), formerly churned laboriously, is now made in the food processor. Breads that used to require kneading and monopolized the day can now be made with a no-knead/one-bowl dough that respects your schedule. Try Clover Honey Challah (page 85) and you'll realize that you can be free from the tyranny of yeast dough! Homemade preserves used to rely on a chancy test drip of syrup, but Strawberry Spoon Fruit (page 27), Sour Cherry Preserves (page 29), and Red Haven Peach Chutney (page 18) can now be made with simpler methods. Cheese soufflés benefit not only from Heartland farmstead cheese but also from a no-fail recipe—I promise. Versatile cake batters—in yesteryear, you'd have a different batter for each type of cake—now turn out bundt, layer, and loaf cakes or cupcakes.

And in this book, leftovers are a good thing. When you purposefully cook for leftovers, you'll have ready-made ingredients for other dishes like Minnesota Wild Rice Soup (page 163), Haymaker's Hash (page 48), or Hunter's Pie (page 210). Cook once, eat several times!

This book is about ingredient-centered food and is a testament to the fact that if you grow, raise, or buy quality foods, you don't have to do a lot to them to make them taste great. You'll see this refrain throughout *Heartland*.

And as Herb Eckhouse of La Quercia says, "We have to get away from the idea that making food is work instead of pleasure. Making the food is part of the fun."

So, let's step into the Heartland kitchen.

"THE PANTRY NEXT TO OUR KITCHEN in the farmhouse had a look of delicious plenty," Marilyn Kluger writes in *The Midwestern Country Cookbook: Recipes and Remembrances from a Traditional Farmhouse*. The book recalls her 1930s childhood in southern Indiana, before electricity eventually reached rural communities after World War II and the era she describes came to an end. "Its pine-sheathed walls were lined with sturdy shelves that sagged gently under the weight of sparkling jars of garden vegetables, fruits, and jellies, the overflow from the cellar. Deep covered bins for pastry flour, bread flour, sugar, and cornmeal stood along one wall. On the table under the window were flat pans filled with fresh tomatoes from the garden or potatoes from the cellar, baskets of brown-shelled eggs, shiny tin pails of leaf lard, and earthenware crocks brimming with cream-topped milk. On the windowsill bloomed rose geraniums with their scented leaves, and blue-flowered chives."

My grandparents lived in a late Victorian, shotgun-style house with one room behind the other. One of its fascinations for my sister and me was the pantry, a small room no bigger than a closet off the kitchen that had a wonderful, spicy smell. In the built-in cabinet in the tongue-and-groove paneled pantry, my grandmother kept her kitchen essentials: flour, sugars, and salt; herbs and spices; homemade canned goods; tins of crackers and cookies; shortening and oil; homemade dried noodles in bags; dried beans; potatoes and onions. Eggs and milk were kept in the refrigerator, and shortening had replaced lard, but neighbor Mrs. Seebohm's spicy homemade ketchup still joined jars of watermelon pickle, blackberry jelly, and strawberry preserves.

Perhaps *treasure* is not the term that comes to mind when one thinks of those preserved foods that used to grace Sunday or holiday Midwestern dinner tables. But treasure it was. And treasure it should be. Foods that the homemaker had "put up" for the winter months represented months of hard work and considerable culinary skill—her most translucent watermelon pickles, little jeweled crabapples, the sunniest corn relish flecked with red and green peppers; or the brandy-laced mincemeat that won farm wife Melissa Frake a blue ribbon—and made the cranky judge tipsy—in the 1945 movie *State Fair*.

Willa Cather, who immortalized the people and kitchens of the Great Plains in novels such as *My Antonia* and *O Pioneers!*, remembered the treasures she had seen and tasted in her hometown of Red Cloud, Nebraska. Even though she moved away to New York City, in 1934 she requested preserved foods from her Red Cloud friends and family to be sent as gifts to her city friends, rather than buying the inferior foodstuffs of the metropolis.

Today, the Heartland pantry is still a place of culinary possibility, where the bounty of the garden, orchard, farm, or hunter's or forager's trip becomes an artisan food. In farmer's lingo, what you create from these raw materials is "value-added." Butter becomes the highest form of cream. Syrups and preserves make the most of garden or wild plants.

Instead of pleasing judges, today's makers of gourmet preserved foods want to please customers' palates with everything from Caramel Pecan Apple Butter from Blackberry Hill Farms in Rich Hill, Missouri, to Grannie's Garden Tangy Tomato Jam from Two Cookin' Sisters in Brookston, Indiana (see Resources, page 266).

Today's pantry also looks a little different from the jar-lined shelves of yesteryear. It might not be a separate room or even a storage area off the kitchen. But it lives in your freezer or refrigerator or on your kitchen shelves.

Most people today don't preserve foods because they have to, but because they want to. Pantry foods you make taste better than what you can buy, pure and simple. You can easily go out and buy good canned tomatoes, but Smoke-Roasted Tomato Sauce (page 16) for pasta—a frozen asset—delivers the taste of summer year round. You can easily go out and buy butter, but when you make Farmhouse Butter (page 7) and taste it, you might decide that it's the only butter to serve with artisan bread.

The methods now used to preserve foods or make an artisan product are also different than in years past. The food processor replaces the butter churn, the refrigerator and freezer the need for canning, the slow cooker the long watchfulness needed for something simmering on the stove. What endures, however, is good, old-fashioned flavor.

In this chapter, you'll find ways to make the most of signature Heartland foods in every season—Farmhouse Butter (page 7) and Smoked Goat Cheese (page 14) in the spring; Sour Cherry Preserves (page 29), Red Haven Peach Chutney (page 18), and fresh-tasting syrups in the summer; smoked foods and duck confit in the fall; and Bacon-Infused Vodka (page 37) for winter.

"The first sight of Sophie Lundstrom's dinner table always made me gasp! It completely filled the long narrow dining room, whose south windows opened out on a sunporch beyond which one could see miles of snow-covered prairies reflecting the sun. Places were laid for fourteen with white china on a white damask tablecloth. There was no color on the table at all except a luscious ribbon of translucent jellies, relishes, and preserves that ran down the length of the table and caught up the sun— like a feast spread out in the snow. In the center was a glorious crown tomato aspic, and streaming down on either side were grape and chokecherry jellies, rhubarb jam and plum preserves, pickled beets, spiced crabapples, and watermelon pickles."

—CARRIE YOUNG IN *NOTHING TO DO BUT STAY: MY PIONEER MOTHER*, ABOUT HER MOTHER'S HOMESTEADING DAYS IN NORTH DAKOTA

"No sloven can make good butter. The one thing to be kept in mind, morning, noon and night, is neatness, neatness, neatness. The milking should be done in the cleanest place that can be found, and the cows should be kept as clean as possible. . . . If there is cream enough each day, it should, of course, be churned. . . . The best plan is to churn as soon as it becomes slightly acid."

—*BUCKEYE COOKERY AND PRACTICAL HOUSEKEEPING*

FARMHOUSE BUTTER **EACH BUTTER MAKES ABOUT 1½ CUPS**

Churning cream into butter—and, very often, selling it for extra money—was once the province of farm wives. Now, it's an easy way to get the best butter you've ever tasted to go with homemade or artisan breads. Here it is in two styles: sweet cream that is just that and the slightly tangier salted cultured butter.

Sweet Cream Butter

2 cups heavy cream

1 Line a sieve with a single layer of cheesecloth and place the sieve over a bowl. Pour the cream into the work bowl of a food processor and process for about 5 minutes. The cream will go, in stages, from liquid to whipped cream to thick whipped cream to a solid mass of butter that separates from the milky liquid or whey.

2 Transfer the butter to the cheesecloth-lined sieve and press the butter with a wooden spoon to release more of the whey. When the butter does not release any more whey, scoop the butter from the sieve and cover in plastic wrap. Use right away, keep covered in the refrigerator for up to 1 month, or freeze indefinitely.

Salted Cultured Butter

2 cups heavy cream

2 tablespoons sour cream

¼ teaspoon kosher or sea salt

1 In a medium bowl, whisk the cream and sour cream together. Cover with plastic wrap and let sit at room temperature for 4 to 24 hours. Refrigerate for 2 hours.

2 Make the butter as above, and then scoop the butter from the sieve into a bowl. Mix the salt into the butter with a fork. Use right away, keep covered in the refrigerator for up to 1 month, or freeze indefinitely.

In the African-American pioneer town of Nicodemus, Kansas, "We used to have a little song we sang when we was churning butter," Pearlena Moore remembers:

"Come, butter, come.
Mama wants you come,
Baby wants you come,
Come, butter, come."

HOME-RENDERED LARD **MAKES ABOUT 3 CUPS**

Why render your own lard? Good question. Lard used to be bad. Now lard is good again—at least the home-rendered kind. Most commercially available lard is made from any and all pork fat and is partially hydrogenated, resulting in a sort of musky flavor. Home-rendered lard starts with leaf lard, the hard white fat that surrounds the kidneys, so called because a thin membrane causes it to curl inward like a long leaf. The hardest part of making lard is finding leaf lard. A good butcher or grocery store that carries natural or organic meat should be able to order it for you. The rendering process is easy, but it takes a bit of time. After you trim and cut the fat into small pieces, you'll want to render it slowly so that it can be used for both making pastry and frying (if the lard gets too brown, it could make your lard pie crust taste like pork roast). I use the slow cooker, which does the rendering work without too much attention from the cook. Herb and Cathy Eckhouse of La Quercia in Norwalk, Iowa, render their lard in a 250°F oven. Either way works well. You'll end up with pale golden lard that turns creamy white when chilled. If you like, freeze some of the lard in premeasured portions in ice cube trays or freezer bags to use for pie crust. Use the cracklings in soups, salads, or cornbread—they taste like toasted sesame seeds.

2 pounds leaf lard in 1 piece, membrane trimmed and fat cut into 1-inch pieces

1 Place the chopped fat in a 2-quart slow cooker and turn it to the Low setting. Cover and let render for 8 to 12 hours, or until most of the fat has melted.

2 Line a funnel with a coffee filter or cheesecloth and place the funnel in the top of a clean, widemouthed quart jar. Ladle the hot fat into the lined funnel until only the small pieces of unrendered fat or cracklings are left in the bottom of the cooker. Set the jar of lard aside to cool at room temperature.

3 Turn the cooker to High and let the cracklings cook until they turn medium brown, stirring occasionally. Transfer the cracklings to a plate and let cool.

4 Cover the jar of lard and store in the refrigerator, where it will keep indefinitely. Place the cracklings in a storage container in the refrigerator and use within 1 month.

A TUB OF LARD

According to an ad in a 1906 issue of *Pearson's Magazine*, Armour's Simon Pure Leaf Lard was sold in 3-, 5-, and 10-pound pails. "The lard that shows a deeply wrinkled and 'wavy' top, when the pail is opened, is the pure leaf lard," the ad proclaims, "the best lard to use for fine cooking." At that time, Armour & Company had sites in Chicago, South Omaha, Sioux City, Kansas City, East St. Louis, and Fort Worth.

CHAR-GRILLED ONIONS AND PEPPERS
MAKES ABOUT 6 CUPS

Use your summer kitchen—the grill outdoors—to grill and then put up onions and peppers when they're plentiful in summer. Then use them for dips, soups, omelets, and flatbreads through the year. By the time they're past their 6 months in the freezer, you can grill a fresh crop. Package and then freeze them in quart-size freezer bags for easier use.

12 red or Bermuda onions, peeled and cut into 1-inch slices

12 red, yellow, and/or orange bell peppers

Canola oil, for brushing

1 Prepare a medium-hot fire in your grill.

2 Thread several onion slices, lollipop-style, onto skewers. Brush the onion slices and whole peppers with oil.

3 Char-grill the vegetables, turning several times, until they have good grill marks and have charred somewhat and softened, about 15 minutes for the onions and 10 minutes for the peppers. When cool enough to handle, remove the onions from the skewers. Cut each pepper into quarters lengthwise and stem, seed, and skin them. If you like, finely chop the vegetables. Portion the onions and peppers separately into quart-size freezer bags and freeze for up to 6 months.

THE SMOKE PANTRY

Smoke is the flavor that unites Heartlanders, no matter their ethnic origin.

In the Goosetown section of New Ulm, Minnesota, in 1882, dozens of simple wood frame houses stood amidst the outbuildings that allowed families from the German/Czechoslovakian border a measure of independence. Beside the lush gardens, chicken coops, fenced hog yards, cow stalls, tool sheds, and outhouses, there would also be a smokehouse. Rectangular in shape with domed roof and a side chimney, the brick smokehouse was fired up in the fall after the hogs were butchered.

When the embers from the hickory logs were just right, the hams and sides of bacon, previously rubbed with salt and spices to draw out moisture, were hung from the rafters on metal hooks and smoked for days. Sausages and cheeses were also smoked to help preserve them during the winter.

Now that slow-smoked barbecue is so popular, we've rediscovered the secret that our Midwestern ancestors knew—that a little wood smoke can make even everyday foods taste wonderful. In addition to the barbecue capitals of Kansas City and St. Louis, big cities and small towns celebrate the European art of cured meats, from hickory- or apple-smoked bacon to "cottage ham" (cured and smoked pork butt, also known as bauernschinken), Great Lakes fish smoked over maple wood, hickory-smoked salt, smoked Wisconsin cheeses, smoked nuts, and even Chicago's Vosges chocolate made with smoked salt and smoked porter from O'Fallon Brewery in O'Fallon, Missouri.

For a hint of smoky flavor in soups, stews, flavored butters, sauces, or dips, keep Double-Smoked Bacon (page 45), Smoked Goat Cheese (page 14), Smoke-Roasted Tomato Sauce (page 16), and Smoke-Roasted Pork Shoulder (page 188) on hand in the freezer. Keep liquid smoke flavoring in your refrigerator and hickory-smoked salt in your kitchen cabinet.

SMOKED GOAT CHEESE MAKES 8 OUNCES

This has become one of the staples at our house. I use it crumbled over salads or pasta, stuffed into cherry tomatoes, spread on a sandwich with roasted chicken and baby greens, stirred into soups, or blended with cream cheese for a dip. If you like, use a fresh Heartland chèvre such as Capriole from Greenville, Indiana; Donnay Dairy in Kimball, Minnesota; or Prairie Fruits Farm in Champaign, Illinois. You will need 1 to 2 cups of apple, hickory, pecan, or other hardwood chips for this.

8 ounces fresh goat cheese or cream cheese in a log

Canola oil, for brushing

1 Prepare a medium-heat indirect fire in your grill, with the fire on one side and no fire on the other.

2 Place the goat cheese in a disposable aluminum pan and brush the cheese with canola oil.

3 For a charcoal grill, scatter 1 to 2 cups wood chips on the charcoal; for a gas grill, place the chips in a smoker box or an aluminum foil packet poked with holes near a gas burner. When you see the first wisp of smoke from the chips, place the pan of goat cheese on the indirect or no-heat side of the grill and close the lid. Smoke for 1 hour, or until the cheese has a burnished appearance and a smoky aroma. Store the smoked cheese in the refrigerator for up to 1 month.

VARIATION: To smoke garlic, trim about ½ inch from the top and bottom of a whole head of garlic. Brush with canola oil, place in a disposable aluminum pan, and proceed from step 3. Smoke for about 45 minutes, until the garlic is soft when you squeeze it and it has a smoky aroma. Store in the refrigerator for a few days or in the freezer for up to 3 months.

Smoked Goat Cheese and Smoke-Roasted Tomato Sauce ▶

SMOKE-ROASTED TOMATO SAUCE MAKES ABOUT 4 CUPS

In the late 1970s, my husband and I bought a fixer-upper house in Loveland, Ohio. Built in 1875 in a Carpenter Gothic style, it had wide front and side porches, a center hallway with a carved wood staircase, and a separate outbuilding in the backyard—a summer kitchen. This would have been the place where the family canned garden "stuff" or prepared their meals to keep the heat out of the house. Today, our summer kitchens are on the deck or patio, around the grill. So why not rethink canning tomatoes indoors? Why not smoke-roast some of those tomatoes into sauce to eat now, freeze, or can? That way, you'll have a taste of vine-ripe tomatoes and the smokiness of the grill, even when the "summer kitchen" is covered in snow. Serve this with Farmhouse Egg Pasta (page 24), use it as a lasagna sauce, transform it into Smoke-Roasted Tomato Soup (page 159), or spoon it over anything grilled. You will need about 1 cup of apple, cherry, hickory, oak, or pecan wood chips.

3 pounds tomatoes (any variety)

3 cloves garlic, peeled

2 tablespoons olive oil

Fine kosher or sea salt and freshly ground black pepper

1 Prepare an indirect fire in your grill, with the fire on one side and no fire on the other.

2 Meanwhile, halve the tomatoes and pack them in a disposable aluminum pan. Mix the garlic with the olive oil in a small bowl and drizzle over the tomatoes. Season to taste with salt and pepper.

3 For a charcoal grill, scatter the wood chips on the charcoal; for a gas grill, place them in a smoker box or an aluminum foil packet poked with holes near a gas burner. When you see the first wisp of smoke, place the pan of tomatoes on the indirect or no-heat side of the grill and close the lid. Smoke-roast for 35 to 45 minutes, until the tomatoes are soft, just beginning to brown, and have a smoky aroma.

4 Puree the tomatoes and garlic in a food processor along with the juices in the pan. Use right away, or freeze in quart-size freezer bags for up to 3 months.

NOTE: To can this sauce, ladle into 2 hot, sterilized pint jars, leaving about ½ inch headspace. Wipe any excess from the rims and seal the jars according to the manufacturer's directions. Process the jars in a boiling water bath for 10 minutes. Remove from the canner. Over the next hour or two, you'll hear the jar lids "pop" as they become vacuum sealed. To test whether a jar is sealed, simply press in the middle of the metal jar lid. If it gives, the jar is not sealed. If the jar is sealed, it will keep in a cool, dark place for at least 1 year. Jars that are not sealed—or that you open—will keep, refrigerated, for about 1 week.

NOTE: For an indoor method, roast the tomatoes in a 350°F oven for 35 minutes. Add 1 teaspoon of liquid smoke when you puree them.

NOTE: For Vodka Cream Sauce for pasta, warm the tomato sauce and add 2 tablespoons Bacon-Infused Vodka (page 37). Bring to a simmer, and then add 2 tablespoons heavy cream.

RED HAVEN PEACH CHUTNEY

MAKES 7 HALF-PINT JARS

My food stylist friend Vicki M. Johnson grew up on a farm near Russell, Kansas, and was known as one of the "plucky Merz girls." She still has a big garden and loves to put up preserves like this one—so addictive you'll have to hide it, even from yourself. Delicious on bread, with pork or chicken, over a soft cheese for an appetizer, or straight out of the jar, this chutney can be kept in the refrigerator for up to a year or canned for longer storage. It's slow to set up, so allow 3 to 4 days before you use it—if you can wait that long.

4 cups pitted, peeled, and chopped ripe Red Haven or other fresh peaches (about 3 pounds)

½ cup cider vinegar

¼ cup freshly squeezed lemon juice

1 cup dried cherries or sweetened dried cranberries

⅓ cup chopped onion

1 teaspoon grated fresh ginger

¼ cup chopped crystallized ginger

1 teaspoon ground cinnamon

½ teaspoon ground allspice

1 tablespoon fine kosher or sea salt

1 (1¾-ounce) package powdered fruit pectin

4¼ cups granulated sugar

¾ cup packed light brown sugar

SUGGESTED PEACH VARIETIES:
Red Haven, Cresthaven, Harrow's Beauty, and Reliance

1   Heat a large pot of water until just boiling. Add 7 half-pint jars with their rings and lids. Keep warm in the water, but do not boil.

2   In a large saucepan, combine the peaches, vinegar, lemon juice, dried cherries, onion, fresh and crystallized ginger, cinnamon, allspice, and salt over medium-high heat. Sprinkle the pectin on top of the mixture and stir to combine. When the mixture comes to a full boil, stir in the sugars. Bring to a boil again and cook for 5 minutes, stirring constantly. Remove from the heat and let cool for 10 minutes, skimming off any foam that rises to the top.

3   Using tongs, remove the jars from the water. Ladle the chutney into the prepared jars, wipe the rims dry, and seal. Over the next hour or two, you'll hear the jar lids "pop" as they become vacuum sealed. To test whether a jar is sealed, simply press in the middle of the metal jar lid. If it gives, the jar is not sealed. If the jar is sealed, it will keep in a cool, dark place for at least 1 year. Jars that are not sealed—or that you open—will keep, refrigerated, for up to 1 year.

TWENTY-FIRST-CENTURY HOMESTEADING

In 1862, President Lincoln signed the Homestead Act, which opened up large portions of the Midwest for settlement. The land was free to anyone who would file an application, make improvements on the land, and file for a title. This act led to the settlement of more than 60 different ethnic groups in Kansas alone—and stirred the melting pot once again. But some environmental historians claim that the massive influx of farmers changing the landscape contributed to the Dust Bowl—the severe erosion of prairie soils in the 1930s.

Now, a new wave of homesteaders aims to reclaim agricultural land with organic practices and careful husbandry. Wes Jarrell and Leslie Cooperband are among them. In 2003, they left their "urban and academic life" in Madison, Wisconsin, for the Champaign/Urbana area of Illinois to start Prairie Fruits Farm & Creamery.

"We have begun to transform the landscape from cash grain agriculture to diversified perennial fruit trees and berries, goat pastures, hayfields and prairie," they write. "In 2004, we planted over 350 fruit trees and 600 berry plants and purchased our first four Nubian goats (three does and one buck)."

They graze their herd of Nubian and La Mancha goats on grass and alfalfa. The milk from their goats goes into making farmstead goat cheese, ranging from fresh chèvre to a unique Blazing Star Banon—an all-Illinois soft ripened goat cheese wrapped in sycamore leaves from their farm and soaked in an Illinois Chambourcin wine.

Their fruit season starts with strawberries in May, and moves on to raspberries plus red and white currants in early June and black currants, more raspberries, gooseberries, and cherries in late June. From late July through August come the peaches—Reliance with floral and apricot flavors, Sweet Sixteen, Red Haven, Harrow's Beauty, White Lady, Elberta, and Belle of Georgia—and blackberries. In early fall, it's apple and pear time.

Jarrell and Cooperband, like other successful twenty-first-century homesteaders, are good at marketing too. They take their cheeses and produce to the local Urbana market as well as to the Green City Market in Chicago. Their farm dinners, held on weekends during the summer and featuring Chicago chefs, regularly sell out. See Resources, page 266, for more information.

CRISP REFRIGERATOR DILL PICKLES **MAKES 2 PINT JARS**

Gourmet burger restaurants like Blanc Burger + Bottles in Kansas City, Missouri, take the elements of the classic burger and make them as good as possible: quality beef, brioche buns, aiolis in place of mayonnaise, and house-made crispy-sweet pickles like these. The secret ingredients for the crispest pickles are 5-inch *very firm* baby or pickling cucumbers and a grape leaf stuffed in the bottom of the pickle jar. Grape leaves contain a little alum, which contributes to the crunchy texture of the pickles. I use wild grape leaves, as they grow on the side of my house, but any grape leaf will work. You can find large bunches of dill with seed heads at farmer's markets or grocery stores. Northeast Social, a casual farm-to-fork eatery in Minneapolis, serves pickled chard stems with a mustard aioli as a new take on the old-fashioned appetizer relish dish; see below on how to pickle Swiss chard stems.

1 cup water

1 cup white vinegar

1 cup sugar

1½ teaspoons salt

2 grape leaves (optional)

1 pound pickling or baby cucumbers, ends trimmed and quartered lengthwise

8 cloves garlic, peeled

2 teaspoons black peppercorns

2 seed heads fresh dill, with some of the stalk

SUGGESTED CUCUMBER VARIETIES:
Bush Pickle, which can be grown in a container, or the heirloom Snow's Fancy Pickling cucumber from Chicago

1 Combine the water, vinegar, sugar, and salt in a saucepan and bring to a boil over medium-high heat. Stir until the sugar and salt dissolve. Let cool to room temperature.

2 Stuff a grape leaf, if desired, in the bottom of each clean pint jar. Pack in the cucumber spears. Divide the garlic and peppercorns between the jars. Stuff a large dill seed head into the center of the jar. Pour the cooled liquid over the mixture, making sure everything is completely covered with liquid. Seal the jars and refrigerate for 24 hours before using. Keep refrigerated for up to 1 year. The flavor will continue to develop over time.

NOTE: Tiny haricots verts, steamed until crisp-tender and rinsed under cold water, also taste delicious pickled this way. Or pickle the stems from Swiss chard—again, steam until crisp-tender, and then pack in jars with the flavorings and brine and refrigerate.

"In July, Mr. and Mrs. started to feel they'd set something in motion back there that was getting out of hand, and now, late July and August, the glacier is moving in on them for good. The pressure cooker has been running full blast for days, Ralph is out of Kerr lids, but vegetables still fill up the fridge, the kitchen counter—quarts of tomatoes have been canned, still more tomatoes move in. The Mister reaches for the razor in the morning, he picks up a cucumber. Pick up the paper, underneath it are three more zucchini. They crawled in under there to get some shade, catch a few Zs, maybe read the comics. Pumpkins are moving in to live with them. At night they check the bed for kohlrabi. Turn out the lights, they hear rustling noises downstairs: a gang of cauliflower trying the back door."

—GARRISON KEILLOR IN *LAKE WOBEGON DAYS*

FARMHOUSE EGG PASTA **MAKES ABOUT 1 POUND**

Fresh egg pasta is an essential in a Heartland kitchen. No matter your ethnic background, you'll make something wonderful with it, whether rolled out and cut or stuffed. From Russian-Mennonite vareniki to Polish pierogi to Italian ravioli, good fresh pasta is a must. Use it fresh or dry it for egg noodles. Fresh pasta will cook to al dente in a few minutes, while dried noodles will take 12 to 15 minutes.

2 cups unbleached all-purpose flour, plus more for dusting

1 teaspoon fine kosher or sea salt

3 large eggs, beaten

1. On a flat surface or in the work bowl of a food processor, combine the flour and salt. By hand, make a well in the center and add the beaten eggs. With a fork, start stirring the egg mixture, mixing in a little bit of the flour as you go. Using your hands and a dough scraper or pancake turner, squeeze the dough together, scraping up flour bits to add to the dough, until you have a smooth ball of dough. In the food processor, add the beaten eggs and pulse to combine, then process until the dough forms a mass, about 1 minute.

2. Turn the dough out onto a floured surface and knead for 5 minutes, or until smooth and elastic. Cut the dough in half. Form it into 2 disks, cover with plastic wrap, and let rest at room temperature for 30 minutes.

3. To roll by hand, dust a work surface and a rolling pin with flour. Sprinkle the dough with flour and brush off excess with a pastry brush. The pasta dough should feel soft and elastic, but not sticky. Roll out each disk until the pasta is so thin you can almost see through it, about 1/16 inch. Then cut into the desired shapes. To use a pasta machine, cut the disk into 4 pieces, and flatten each piece. Sprinkle with flour and brush off excess with a pastry brush. Feed each piece into the pasta machine set at the thickest setting. When all the pieces have been rolled through, adjust the machine to a thinner setting, feed the sheets of pasta into the machine, and roll through again. Sprinkle with flour and brush off excess with a pastry brush as needed to keep the dough from sticking. Keep rolling the pasta at thinner and thinner settings until you can almost see through it, about 1/16 inch. If necessary, cut the sheets in half for a more manageable process.

4. Use right away, freeze, or dry. To freeze, lay the pieces, side by side, on parchment paper. Starting with a short side, roll the parchment paper and noodles up into a cylinder. Place the cylinder in a plastic freezer bag, seal, and freeze for up to 3 months. To dry, lay the pieces on wire racks for several hours, until dry. Pack dried pasta into plastic storage bags and keep for up to 1 month at room temperature.

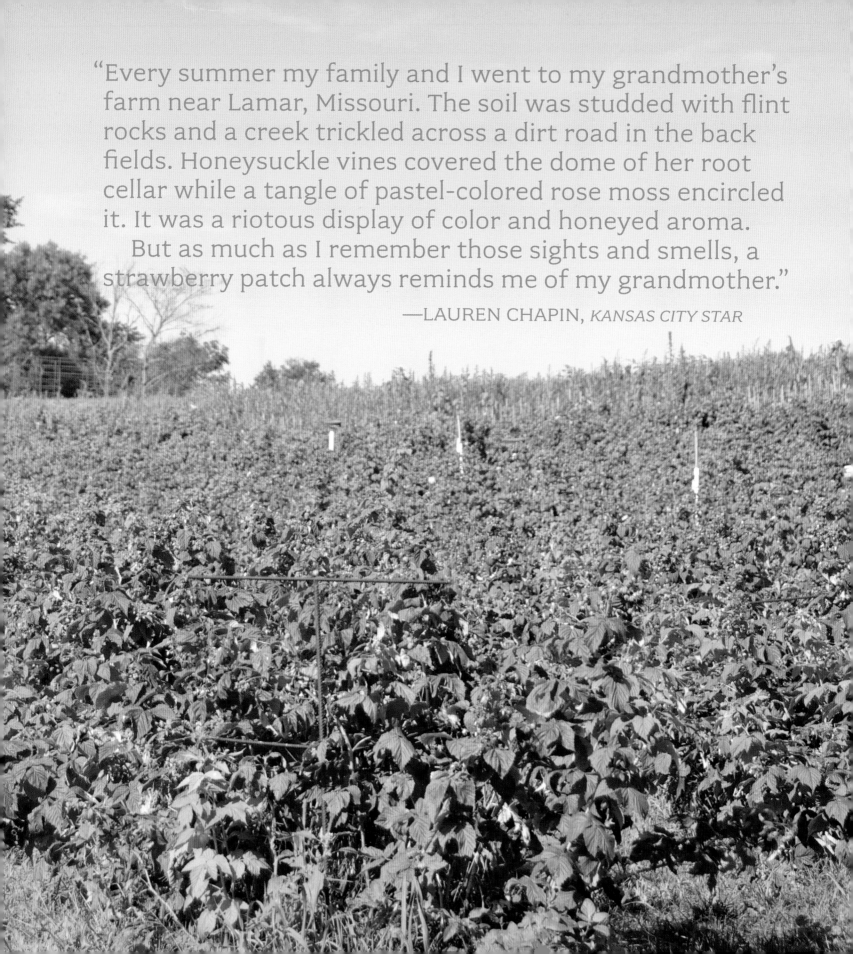

"Every summer my family and I went to my grandmother's farm near Lamar, Missouri. The soil was studded with flint rocks and a creek trickled across a dirt road in the back fields. Honeysuckle vines covered the dome of her root cellar while a tangle of pastel-colored rose moss encircled it. It was a riotous display of color and honeyed aroma.
   But as much as I remember those sights and smells, a strawberry patch always reminds me of my grandmother."

—LAUREN CHAPIN, *KANSAS CITY STAR*

SPOON-ABLE STRAWBERRY PRESERVES **MAKES 4 CUPS**

When Mary Todd Lincoln lived in a two-story Federal-style house in Springfield, Illinois, her June social calendar revolved around strawberries. In a letter to her friend Hannah Shearer on June 26, 1859, she describes the height of strawberry season: "For the last two weeks, we have had a continual round of strawberry parties, this last week I have spent five evenings out. . . ." *So many strawberries, so little time* must have been the thinking back then. Spoon fruit, or softly set preserves, is still made by American Spoon Foods in Michigan and by home cooks like Charlotte Flichler of Strawberry Point, Iowa. I've added a touch of rosewater, which is available in small bottles at Asian markets and gourmet shops. This old-fashioned flavoring gives this fruit a taste like the tiniest, most aromatic *fraises des bois*. Serve these soft-set preserves spooned over cheesecake, pound cake, or ice cream; on homemade bread; or simply by the spoonful.

4 cups (about 1½ pounds) fresh strawberries, hulled and halved

2 tablespoons freshly squeezed lemon juice

4 cups sugar

1 teaspoon rosewater

1   Place the strawberries in a large saucepan over medium-low heat. Pour the lemon juice over the berries and sprinkle with the sugar. Stir to blend with a wooden spoon. Bring the mixture to a full boil, then cook for exactly 8 minutes. Watch the saucepan carefully to make sure the mixture does not boil over. If you boil the mixture longer than 8 minutes, you may end up with preserves and not spoon fruit.

2   Remove the mixture from the heat and stir in the rosewater. Transfer the mixture to a glass or ceramic bowl. Let cool for 15 minutes, then cover with plastic wrap and leave at room temperature for 24 hours.

3   When the berries have plumped and the mixture has thickened to a syrup-like consistency, transfer to clean glass jars with lids. Cover and keep in the refrigerator for up to 3 months.

QUINCE PRESERVES MAKES 4 CUPS

In late fall, a bowl of knobby yellow quinces can perfume a room with a sweet, apple-like scent. In north-central Ohio, near Wooster, quince trees with golden fruit clinging to bare branches bring a kind of poetry to Amish farmsteads. Quinces also work a kind of magic in this recipe. When their juices and peels cook with sugar, the syrup turns a deep ruby red. With a pineapple-like flavor, quince is a delicious accompaniment to ice cream, pound cake, pancakes and waffles, or French toast.

4 large quinces, peeled, quartered, and cored (reserve the peels and cores)

Juice of 1 lemon

4 cups sugar

1 vanilla bean

1   Place the quince peels, cores, and quarters in a large saucepan with enough water to cover. Bring to a boil, then turn down the heat and simmer for 10 to 15 minutes, or until the water turns red. Transfer the quince quarters to a separate plate and reserve. With a slotted spoon, remove the peels and cores and discard.

2   Add the lemon juice, sugar, and vanilla bean to the cooking water and bring to a boil. Lower the heat to a simmer. Cut the quince quarters into smaller slices and return them to the cooking water. Simmer, uncovered, until the quinces are softened and the syrup is a deep red, about 20 minutes. Serve warm or cold. Or pack into clean jars with lids, making sure the fruit is covered with the syrup. Secure the lids and refrigerate for up to 1 year.

SOUR CHERRY PRESERVES   MAKES ABOUT 3 CUPS

I always buy my sour Montmorency cherries from a jelly and preserve vendor at the farmer's market near my home. Beautifully red, plump, and already pitted and frozen, these cherries are reliably fabulous. Although sour cherry trees dot the Midwest, the best sour cherries are from Michigan, where they grow to be the plumpest and juiciest, thanks to the Great Lakes microclimate. One trick, if you pick your own sour cherries: To keep their plump shapes, freeze whole cherries and then pit them frozen. Use a candy thermometer to monitor the temperature of the cherries as they cook. Use Sour Cherry Preserves on cheesecake or pound cake, as a tart filling, over ice cream, or on good bread.

4 cups pitted fresh or thawed frozen sour cherries

2 cups sugar

Juice of ½ lemon

½ teaspoon almond extract

1   Heat the cherries and sugar in a large saucepan over medium-high heat. Attach a candy thermometer to the interior side of the pan. Cook, stirring occasionally as the cherries begin to bubble and release their juices; the cherries will continue to bubble and rise higher in the pan. Keep cooking until the mixture reaches 220°F and has reduced to a preserves-like consistency, about 20 minutes. Remove from the heat and stir in the lemon juice and almond extract.

2   Transfer half of the mixture to a food processor and pulse into a jam with flecks of cherry. Combine in a bowl with the whole cherries from the pan. Divide among clean glass jars with lids, let cool, and secure the lids. Store in the refrigerator for up to 1 year.

Raspberries
$4.00/Pint

Easy freezer
Jam Recipe

I.Q.F.
(Individually Quick Frozen)

40# Box
pitted & Frozen

$60.00

Ask @ counter
Mont...

A MAP OF
SECTION
MICHIGAN

Sweet
Cherries
$4.50/quart
$12.00/3 quarts
$35.00/Lug (20#)

Queen Mary Lonn Trapp
1951

National
Cherry
Festival

Cherry BBQ
&
Yankee Barbecue
BBQ
$7

NORTHERN FRUITLANDS

When forager meets chef, great things can happen. In the late 1970s, Justin Rashid was living in northern Michigan. A friend of his was a waitress at The River Café in New York, where Larry Forgione was a chef looking for fresh Midwestern morels. Forgione called to ask if Rashid could get some for him. "Sure," Rashid said. "I've been picking morels since I was 13 years old." Morels led to berries and orchard fruit—and eventually making artisan fruit preserves, from a recipe that Forgione supplied.

What makes fruit grown on the eastern side of Lake Michigan so delicious? "The weather fronts come in from the west over the deep lake," says Rashid. "So the lake becomes a climate modifier. In the spring, the first warm breezes blow over the ice on the lake and are cooled down, delaying the progress of blossoming until the risk of frost has largely passed." Then, as summer comes in, hot winds blow over the cool lake and are tempered again, "delaying the development of fruit so it has more character," says Rashid. In the fall, cold winds from Canada are gentled by the summer-warmed lake, extending the growing season. In winter, a deep blanket of snow keeps the trees insulated from the worst of the cold. "Were it not for the lake, you couldn't grow fruit this far north on a commercial scale," he says.

The soils built up from old sand dunes are sandy, loamy, and glacial. "The trees develop expansive root systems, a great anchor to stand up to the winds. Moisture from the lake brings trace minerals," he adds.

Farmers use the topography to plant fruit trees where they'll do best—sweet fruits at the top of the ridge, tart fruits below.

Rashid is partial to preserves made from Montmorency cherries, heirloom Rubel blueberries, and Harlayne apricots, which are hand-pitted and peeled. But his favorite variety comes from Red Haven peaches. The Red Haven peach "ripens unevenly" and can't be mechanically peeled, but "it's the peachiest peach there is," he says.

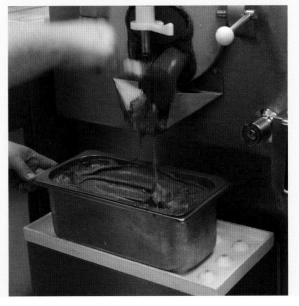

WISCONSIN CRANBERRY JAM
MAKES ABOUT 2 CUPS

I love the tart, fresh berry flavor of this easy and versatile jam, which is delicious with whipped cream on waffles, as a coffee cake filling, spooned over ice cream, or spread on toast. It might surprise you to learn that cranberries are a species native to Wisconsin, with commercial production beginning around 1860 near Berlin, in the central part of the state. Growers simply dug ditches around existing cranberry vines to create marshes. Cranberries blossom in late June or early July on low-growing, trailing, woody evergreen vines. Bees help pollinate the flowers so the fruits will form, which ripen until harvest in September and October.

12 ounces fresh cranberries

¾ cup sugar

1 tablespoon water

1 (10-ounce) package unsweetened frozen strawberries

Freshly squeezed lemon juice (optional)

1 Combine the cranberries, sugar, and water in a medium saucepan over medium-high heat and bring to a boil. Cook, stirring occasionally, until the cranberries start to pop and bubble up, 5 to 7 minutes. Add the strawberries and cook until thawed.

2 Transfer half of the mixture to a food processor and pulse into a jam with flecks of cranberry. Combine in a bowl with the whole berries from the pan. Taste, then add lemon juice, if desired. Divide among clean glass jars with lids, let cool, then secure the lids. Store in the refrigerator for up to 1 year.

BLACKBERRY–LAVENDER SYRUP
MAKES ABOUT 1½ CUPS

A few dried lavender buds from your garden or a health food store add depth and interest to this easy-to-make syrup. Drizzle this over Lemon–Ricotta Pancakes (page 50), yogurt, or ice cream. Or use it to make Summer in a Jar (page 261) or A Trio of Snow Cones (page 264).

1 cup sugar

¾ cup water

1 teaspoon dried lavender buds

1 cup blackberry jam

Freshly squeezed lemon juice

1 In a large, microwave-safe glass measuring cup, combine the sugar, water, and lavender. Microwave on high power until the sugar dissolves, 3 to 4 minutes. Whisk in the blackberry jam. Let the mixture steep for 20 to 30 minutes.

2 Season to taste with lemon juice, strain the mixture into a bowl, and let cool. Use right away, or store in a covered glass jar in the refrigerator for up to 2 weeks.

FRESH HERB SYRUP

MAKES ABOUT 1 CUP

For this recipe, use the freshest, most aromatic tender herb you can find, such as basil, mint, or lemon balm. Use this fresh-tasting syrup to make a Garden Gimlet (page 125), Porch Swing Lemonade (page 127), or A Trio of Snow Cones (page 264), or drizzle it over fresh cantaloupe, berries, or peaches.

1 cup sugar

¾ cup water

½ cup packed fresh, aromatic herb leaves (see above), coarsely chopped

1 In a large, microwave-safe glass measuring cup, combine the sugar, water, and herbs. Microwave on high power until the sugar dissolves, 3 to 4 minutes. Let the mixture steep for 20 to 30 minutes.

2 Strain the mixture into a bowl and let cool. Use right away, or store in a covered glass jar in the refrigerator for up to 2 weeks.

ROSY RHUBARB SYRUP

MAKES ABOUT 3 CUPS

Rhubarb, also known by the old-fashioned term *pie plant*, was an established garden plant in the Heartland by the mid-nineteenth century. One of the favorite heirloom varieties is Queen Victoria, which is the only variety you can grow reliably from seed. The only problem with perennial rhubarb is that sometimes you have too much of a good thing and it ends up being more woody than tender. That's when you make this recipe. Rhubarb syrup is a pretty pink color, tart yet sweet, and is delicious over pancakes, French toast, or fresh fruit, or in lemonade or a Farm Girl Cosmo (page 125). You can also make Rosy Margaritas with 1 cup Rosy Rhubarb Syrup, ½ cup tequila, the juice of 1 lime, and all the ice you want.

4 cups chopped fresh or thawed frozen rhubarb

1 cup water

2 cups sugar

Juice of 2 lemons

1 Place the rhubarb and 1 cup water in a saucepan over medium-high heat and bring to a boil. Lower the heat to medium-low, cover, and cook the rhubarb until tender and pulpy, about 10 minutes.

2 Strain out the rhubarb pulp, reserving the juice. Measure the juice and add enough water to equal 2 cups. Return the liquid to the saucepan over medium-high heat and stir in the sugar. Bring to a boil and cook until the sugar dissolves, about 8 minutes. Remove from the heat, stir in the lemon juice, and let cool. Strain again, then pour into clean glass jars with lids or bottles. Refrigerate for up to 1 month.

"Rhubarb is a metaphor for finding happiness in your own backyard."

—FROM *A PRAIRIE HOME COMPANION* RADIO PROGRAM

"My mother churned her own butter, rendered her own lard, made her own bread, and canned whatever she could clean out of the summer's parched garden. She always had rhubarb. . . ."

—FROM CARRIE YOUNG'S MEMOIR OF HER MOTHER, CARRINE GAFJKEN, WHO HOMESTEADED 160 ACRES IN NORTH DAKOTA BY HERSELF, IN *NOTHING TO DO BUT STAY: MY PIONEER MOTHER*

BACON-INFUSED VODKA MAKES 2 CUPS

Apple- or hickory-smoked bacon—or even Double-Smoked Bacon (page 45)—slowly flavors vodka to make signature drinks like a Bacon Blood Mary (page 131) and memorable pasta sauces. Use both good-quality bacon and vodka.

1 to 2 slices smoked bacon

2 cups vodka

1   Cook the bacon in a small skillet over medium heat until it is almost crisp.

2   While the bacon is still warm, pour the vodka into a pint jar, add the bacon, and screw on the lid. Let steep in a cool, dry place for a few days. Remove the bacon. Over time, you may see some congealed bacon fat in the vodka, but just shake the jar to blend it all together.

CARAMELIZED ONIONS MAKES ABOUT 2 CUPS

Wouldn't it be wonderful to have caramelized onions on hand for pizzas, sandwiches, appetizers, and more? Well, with this easy slow-cooker recipe, you can. Adapted from a recipe by Kathryn Moore and Roxanne Wyss, these caramelized onions can be refrigerated for up to 1 week or frozen for up to 6 months.

4 large yellow onions, peeled and thinly sliced

2 tablespoons olive oil

2 tablespoons unsalted butter

Salt and freshly ground black pepper

1   Combine the onions, olive oil, and butter in a slow cooker. Cover and cook on high for 6 to 8 hours, or until the onions have turned medium brown and have wilted.

2   Season to taste with salt and pepper. Let cool, then store in sealable plastic containers and refrigerate for up to 1 week or freeze for up to 6 months.

FLYOVER COUNTRY DUCK CONFIT SERVES 4 TO 6

Mallard and teal ducks, Canada geese, and other waterfowl take to the skies in autumn, heading south via the Mississippi Corridor. Oxbow rivers, placid lakes, and stubble fields of wheat and corn provide welcome refuge. Fall is also the time to make this rich, hearty, can't-leave-it-alone preserved food. The French method of salting and then slow-cooking fowl in fat renders a tender, succulent result. Whether you use domestic or wild fowl for confit, you can save the breast for the entrée, and then turn the thighs, legs, hearts, and gizzards into confit. You can also prepare the duck breast as confit, once you get hooked. Heartland chefs use duck confit in many ways—as a simple appetizer, sizzled in its own fat and served over greens for a cold weather salad, or taken off the bone and shredded for a soup garnish or fried with potatoes for breakfast hash. The great thing about duck confit is that you can make it in a slow cooker and then keep the confit in the refrigerator for 1 month or frozen for up to 1 year. I also provide instruction for making this in the oven.

4 duck legs with thighs

4 duck wings, trimmed

⅓ cup coarse kosher or sea salt

2 teaspoons freshly ground black pepper

4 cloves garlic, coarsely chopped

3 large sprigs thyme, coarsely chopped

3 bay leaves, coarsely chopped

2 cups canola oil, plus more if needed

1 Rub the duck pieces all over with salt and put them in a baking dish. Sprinkle the duck with the pepper and any remaining salt and top with the garlic, thyme, and bay leaves. Cover with plastic wrap and refrigerate for 1 to 2 days (the longer you let it marinate, the more flavorful it will be).

2 If preparing in the oven, preheat the oven to 300°F.

3 Remove the duck and wipe off all the accumulated salt and juice with paper towels. Place the duck pieces, skin side down, in a large nonstick skillet and brown over low heat until the fat begins to render, 15 to 20 minutes. (For wild duck, you may need to add some of the canola oil to the pan.) Remove the duck pieces and place them in a slow cooker or a covered casserole dish. Deglaze the pan with the canola oil, stirring to loosen any browned bits, then pour over the duck. If necessary, add more canola oil so that the duck pieces are just covered by the oil.

4 Cook on high in the slow cooker or in the oven for 2 hours, or until the duck is fall-off-the-bone tender.

5 Let cool, then place the duck pieces in a plastic storage container and completely cover with the cooking oil. Seal and store in the refrigerator for up to 1 month, where the confit will develop even more flavor. You can also wrap and freeze the confit for up to 1 year.

6 To serve the confit, simply wipe off excess fat and brown the duck pieces in a skillet until the skin is crisp and the meat is warmed through. Serve the pieces whole, or remove the meat from the bones and shred with the crispy skin.

CHAPTER 2 | RISE AND SHINE | BREAKFAST AND BRUNCH

CINCINNATIAN CAROLE COTTRILL REMEMBERS growing up in a Polish

neighborhood and going to church on Easter Saturday for the blessing of the food. "We would bring all of our Easter breakfast goods in baskets to be blessed, just like everyone else in the church," she says. "At just the right time, everyone would carefully unfold the napkins that enclosed the food in the baskets as the priest gave the blessing. The wonderful aromas that filled the church are indescribable."

Today, many of those traditions are still strong. In the Polish section of Chicago, along Milwaukee Avenue, you can buy butter formed into the traditional lamb shape at small mom-and-pop ethnic groceries. Bakeries full of almond babkas, *mazurek* (the Polish Easter cake) with dried fruit and nuts, *chruscik* or fried pastries dusted with powdered sugar, and poppy seed coffee cake produce their own indescribable aromas.

A typical Polish Sunday feast is like a breakfast buffet all day. Dishes with eggs and ham, the butter lamb, and special breads and pastries underscore the theme of rebirth—of the spirit and of the land. That's what breakfast is supposed to do—revive you after a night's sleep and get you ready for the day ahead.

When Midwesterners mainly lived on farms, breakfasts had to be hearty to fuel the body for a day of physical labor—milking cows, feeding livestock, mucking out stalls, planting and harvesting. Breakfasts of sourdough biscuits, salt pork and gravy, and fried potatoes sustained the Ingalls family throughout their *Little House on the Prairie* days.

Today, most Heartlanders plow through their e-mail rather than fields, so breakfast has changed, too. It's more about flavor than fuel. Now that free-range eggs, dry-cured and double-smoked bacon, artisan sausage, and wheat berries ready to grind into flour are more readily available, a farm-to-fork breakfast is a big reason to get up in the morning.

Try making your own breakfast sausage—it's easy and much like making meat loaf. Or double-smoke flabby grocery store bacon for more body and better flavor. Make a delicious whole-grain cereal in the slow cooker for a healthy, no-fuss meal the next morning. Sling a new kind of hash with leftover Smoke-Roasted Pork Shoulder (page 188), drizzled with Sooey Sauce, and watch it disappear. Scramble eggs with a few ethnic flavorings—paprika for Hungarians, sautéed bread crumbs for Germans, fresh herbs and cheese for the French, and sausage for Croatians—that can change with the season or your shopping trip. Whip up a batch or two of pancakes made with freshly ground wheat, sweet potato puree, or ricotta cheese. Dollop them with Farmhouse Butter (page 7) and drizzle with a good syrup, and you've got a great start to the day. For brunch, bake a Persimmon Bread Pudding (that's also good for dessert; page 54) and finish it off with Warm Cider Caramel sauce (page 55).

Rise and shine!

BRINGIN' HOME THE BACON

Supermarket bacon is wet cured—meaning it's submerged in salty water with liquid smoke and other flavorings added. All that added water means that flabby supermarket bacon shrinks and spatters when you cook it.

Real bacon is firmer, dry cured and cold smoked over smoldering hardwoods like hickory or apple. When you cook it, it doesn't shrink much and doesn't spatter. The fat has a translucence that you don't get in supermarket bacon. And the flavor? Ahhhhh.

These Heartland purveyors make wonderful bacon, so bring it on home. (See Resources, page 266, for more information.)

CLAUS' GERMAN SAUSAGE & MEAT; INDIANAPOLIS, INDIANA—Claus' bacon is double-smoked over white oak. If you don't get to his butcher shop early, the double-smoked bacon could be sold out. Luckily, you can order it online.

LA QUERCIA; NORWALK, IOWA—Herb and Kathy Eckhouse have been experimenting with American-style slab bacon smoked over applewood, called Pancetta Americano. It's voluptuous—sort of the curvy girl of bacon next to the waif-like grocery store stuff—and fabulous.

NUESKE'S; WITTENBERG, WISCONSIN—Applewood-smoked, this dry-cured bacon has an irresistible aroma and flavor and is a favorite of chefs.

DOUBLE-SMOKED BACON **MAKES 1 POUND**

If you can't find double-smoked bacon in your area, here is an easy way to make it yourself—even from grocery store bacon. All you need is a grill, fuel for that grill, and 2 cups of hardwood chips, chunks, or sticks—preferably hickory, apple, or oak. If you have a charcoal grill, you might want to soak the chips in water before scattering them on the coals; use dry chips for a gas grill. You'll be smoking the bacon, not cooking it (hence the bed of ice), so double-smoke a batch, and then wrap and refrigerate it until you're ready to fry it for breakfast. If some of the bacon gets cooked along the way, no worries. Double-smoked bacon also makes a wonderful BLT.

1 pound smoked bacon, slab or in slices

1 Prepare a medium indirect fire in your grill, with a fire on one side and no fire on the other.

2 Arrange a layer of ice on the bottom of a large (about 10 by 8 inches) disposable aluminum pan. Place a second aluminum pan on top and add the bacon in one piece (do not separate slices).

3 Scatter ½ cup of water-soaked wood chips on the charcoal or place ½ cup dry wood chips in a smoker box or an aluminum foil packet poked with holes near a gas burner on a gas grill. When you see the first wisp of smoke from the chips, place the doubled pan of bacon on the indirect or no-heat side of the grill and close the lid.

4 Smoke for 1½ to 2 hours, adding more wood chips every 30 to 45 minutes, until the bacon has a smoky aroma and a burnished appearance. The bacon will keep for up to 2 weeks—if it lasts that long!

FARMHOUSE BREAKFAST SAUSAGE **SERVES 10 TO 12**

If you can make a meat loaf, you can make a signature breakfast sausage, a fact not lost on Heartland sausage makers like Jones in Wisconsin or Bob Evans in Ohio, which started out as mom-and-pop businesses, formed at the kitchen table. Buy 3 pounds of pork butt marbled with fat, and ask your butcher to coarsely grind it for you; you want some fat in the sausage so it will be tender and moist. Traditional pork breakfast sausage is also flavored with dried sage and black pepper; however, using fresh sage, rolling the sausage log in pepper, and grilling it makes it all taste fresher and better.

3 pounds coarsely ground pork butt

1 tablespoon finely minced fresh sage

1 tablespoon finely minced fresh Italian parsley

1 tablespoon fine kosher or sea salt

1 teaspoon freshly ground black pepper, plus more for coating

½ teaspoon red pepper flakes

1 clove garlic, minced

1 In a large bowl, gently combine all the ingredients, using your hands. Divide the mixture into 4 parts. Roll each portion into a long roll about 1½ inches in diameter. Wrap in plastic and refrigerate overnight to allow the flavors to blend.

2 Prepare a medium-hot fire in a grill. Unwrap each roll and coat with more black pepper.

3 Grill until all sides are nicely browned and an instant-read thermometer inserted in the center of a roll registers 160°F, about 12 minutes. To serve, slice each roll into portions.

NOTE: You can wrap and freeze the uncooked sausage for up to 6 months. You can also slice and pan-fry the sausage until done.

NOTE: To add a kiss of smoke, use 1 cup hickory or applewood chips while grilling. For a charcoal grill, soak the chips first for 30 minutes. Then drain and scatter the chips on the hot coals. For a gas grill, place the wood chip—filled smoker box or aluminum foil packet over direct heat. When you see the first wisps of smoke, put the sausage on the grill and close the grill lid. Open every 4 minutes to turn the sausage, and then quickly close the grill lid again.

GOT MILK FROM GRASS-FED COWS?
A cold glass of milk is a great way to start your day. And when that milk has a fuller, richer flavor from grass-fed cows (compared to most grocery store milk from assembly-line cows), it will wake you right up.

Some Heartland dairy farmers have decided to bottle and market their own products instead of joining huge cooperatives. These microdairies produce hormone-free milk from cows that graze on grassy pastures. Why do it the old-fashioned way again? Dairy products from grass-fed cows have more omega-3 than those from grain-fed cows—as well as more flavor (see Resources, page 266, for more information).

CLOVER CLOVE DAIRY; Atkinson, Nebraska

GRASS POINT FARMS; Thorpe, Wisconsin

RADIANCE DAIRY; Fairfield, Iowa

SHATTO MILK COMPANY; Osborn, Missouri

TRADERS POINT CREAMERY; Zionsville, Indiana

HAYMAKER'S HASH **SERVES 4 TO 6**

"Make hay while the sun shines" is an aphorism that Midwesterners take to heart. When you have a long day of chores or yard work, make this dish for breakfast. Haymaker's Hash is not only delicious but it's also thrifty, another virtue in which Midwesterners take pride. Use leftover baked potatoes, if you like, and leftover shredded meat. I love the combination of Smoke-Roasted Pork Shoulder and the fried potatoes, drizzled with sharp-tasting Sooey Sauce to wake you up. Serve with eggs any way you like them for a really hearty breakfast.

2 large baking potatoes or 1 pound new potatoes, cooked

2 tablespoons Home-Rendered Lard (page 10) or canola oil

1 large onion, chopped

2 cups shredded or finely chopped cooked meat (such as Smoke-Roasted Pork Shoulder, page 188)

½ cup Sooey Sauce (page 189)

1 Chop the potatoes, skins and all. Heat the lard in a large skillet and sauté the onion and potatoes until well browned, about 15 minutes. Stir in the shredded meat and cook until warmed through.

2 Serve drizzled with the sauce.

FEATHERWEIGHT WHOLEWHEAT PANCAKES **MAKES 12 TO 14 PANCAKES**

People who grew up in wheat-farming communities throughout the Great Plains often reminisce about the wonderful flavor of breads and pancakes made with freshly ground grain. And no wonder—freshly ground wholewheat flour, with the bran and germ, has a deliciously nutty flavor. Farm kitchens had hand-cranked grain mills that ground wheat berries to a very coarse flour. Electric grain mills for the home kitchen such as the Wonder Mill or attachments to stand mixers will grind the wheat as coarse or as fine as you like. Buy hard red winter wheat berries in the bulk section of the grocery or health food store; grind them into flour at stores that have a grain mill or at home. Then, make these pancakes. With Farmhouse Butter (page 7) and maple syrup, they're heaven. I like to make extra pancakes on weekends and then microwave them during the week for a fast homemade breakfast.

2 cups wholewheat flour (preferably freshly ground)

1 teaspoon baking soda

3 tablespoons sugar

½ teaspoon salt

2 large eggs, beaten

¼ cup white vinegar

1¾ cups whole milk

¼ cup canola oil

1 Sift the flour, baking soda, sugar, and salt together in a small bowl. In a large bowl, combine the eggs, vinegar, milk, and oil. Whisk the dry ingredients, a little at a time, into the egg mixture until you have a smooth batter.

2 Lightly grease a griddle or cast-iron skillet. Pour the batter from a large spoon or ¼ cup measuring cup onto the griddle. Turn the pancakes when the underside is browned—before the telltale bubbles burst through the upper surface. Turn and brown the other side. Keep the pancakes warm until all are done, and serve immediately.

LEMON-RICOTTA PANCAKES WITH BLACKBERRY-LAVENDER SYRUP

MAKES 12 TO 14 PANCAKES

Heartlanders of many ethnic origins keep a type of fresh cheese in their refrigerators. German families are fond of cottage cheese, Italians of ricotta, Eastern Europeans of dry-curd cottage cheese. You can use any of these in this pancake recipe. The drier the cheese, the thicker the batter, though. Substitute vanilla extract for the lemon zest and serve these fluffy but substantial pancakes with Red Haven Peach Chutney (page 18), Wisconsin Cranberry Jam (page 32), or your favorite maple syrup, or go out on a limb and try Indiana shagbark hickory syrup (see Resources, page 266).

2 cups unbleached all-purpose flour

2 teaspoons baking powder

½ teaspoon salt

2 large egg yolks

1½ cups whole milk

1 cup ricotta cheese, cottage cheese, or dry-curd cottage cheese

1 teaspoon freshly grated lemon zest

2 large egg whites

1 cup Blackberry-Lavender Syrup (page 32) or syrup of your choice

Fresh blackberries, for garnish

1 In a large bowl, whisk the flour, baking powder, and salt together. Whisk in the egg yolks, milk, cheese, and lemon zest until well blended. In a separate bowl, beat the egg whites with a stand mixer until medium peaks form. With a rubber spatula, fold the egg whites into the batter, going around the perimeter of the bowl with the spatula and then making several slices across it. Repeat the process until you can't see streaks of egg whites.

2 Heat a large nonstick skillet or griddle over medium-high heat. Add a little butter to the pan. Use a ¼-cup measuring cup to drop the batter onto the hot skillet, smoothing each pancake out to a 6-inch diameter. Cook until bubbles start to rise to the top of the pancake, then flip and cook a minute or two longer. Keep the finished pancakes warm in a casserole dish with a lid while you make the rest.

3 Serve warm, drizzled with the blackberry syrup and sprinkled with fresh blackberries.

WINTERBERRY BREAKFAST PUDDING SERVES 4

Like a rice pudding, but better for you, this starts with whole-grain wheat berries, which you can find in bulk at health food stores and better grocery stores. With a little lemon, vanilla, and blueberry, you've got a delicious dish to get you started in the morning. You can also make this in the slow cooker overnight on the low setting, so that it's ready when you get up.

1 cup hard red winter wheat berries

2 cups whole milk

¼ cup sugar or honey

1 teaspoon vanilla extract

1 teaspoon freshly grated lemon zest

2 cups frozen blueberries

Blueberry or lemon yogurt, for garnish

1 In a large saucepan, combine the wheat berries, milk, and sugar over medium-high heat. Bring to a boil, then lower the heat and simmer, covered, until the wheat berries are al dente, about 45 minutes.

2 Stir in the vanilla, lemon zest, and berries and simmer for 10 minutes longer, or until the berries have warmed.

3 Serve hot in bowls and top with the yogurt.

NOTE: For a slow-cooker version, combine the wheat berries, milk, and sugar on the low setting. Cover and let cook overnight. Stir in the vanilla, lemon zest, and berries and cook until warmed through.

CRANBERRY-PEAR COMPOTE MAKES ABOUT 4 CUPS

Keep cranberries in the freezer so that you can make this easy dish any time of year.

12 ounces fresh cranberries

1 tablespoon water

¾ cup sugar

2 large ripe pears, peeled, cored, and chopped

1 teaspoon almond extract

Combine the cranberries, water, and sugar in a medium saucepan over medium-high heat and bring to a boil. Cook, stirring occasionally, until the cranberries start to pop and bubble up, 5 to 7 minutes. Add the pears and cook until warmed through, then add the almond extract. Serve warm.

BAKED EGGS WITH PROSCIUTTO AND ASIAGO CREAM **SERVES 4**

Make French press coffee. Slice the Clover Honey Challah (page 85). Arrange wedges of Indiana melon and bowls of fresh berries on the breakfast table. Then elegantly drape ramekins with Heartland prosciutto. Crack in farm-fresh eggs. Drizzle with a little cream and sprinkle with grated Wisconsin Asiago. Bake to a perfect sizzle. Now you're awake.

4 to 8 slices prosciutto

4 large eggs

4 tablespoons half-and-half or heavy cream

¼ cup grated Asiago cheese

Freshly ground black pepper

4 cups boiling water

1 Preheat the oven to 375°F. Line 4 ramekins with prosciutto so the bottom and sides are almost completely covered and some prosciutto drapes over the sides. Cut the prosciutto to fit better if necessary. Crack an egg into each prepared ramekin. Drizzle 1 tablespoon half-and-half on top of each egg and sprinkle each with 1 tablespoon cheese. Season with pepper.

2 Arrange the ramekins in a 9-inch square baking pan and carefully pour in the boiling water until it reaches halfway up the ramekins.

3 Bake for 10 to 12 minutes, or until the whites are set and the yolk is done to the desired firmness. The eggs will continue to cook after you remove them from the oven, so underbake them slightly. Serve immediately. Eat the eggs right out of the ramekins with a knife and fork.

PERSIMMON BREAD PUDDING
WITH WARM CIDER CARAMEL

SERVES 12 TO 16

Is this a brunch dish—or a dessert? Just for autumn or any time of year? You be the judge. In my opinion, this luscious bread pudding baked in a springform pan is delicious at any meal all year long. It looks great on a cake pedestal and can be made ahead, so it's perfect for entertaining. If you can get your hands on native persimmon pulp, go for it. If not, use canned pumpkin or pureed squash or sweet potato. I love the cake spice mixture from Penzeys Spices in Milwaukee, Wisconsin, but you can also use pumpkin pie spice. The Warm Cider Caramel is an easy sauce that is ready in minutes.

4 large eggs

4 large egg yolks

¾ cup granulated sugar

2 cups whole milk

1 cup heavy cream

1 teaspoon vanilla extract

2 cups native persimmon pulp or 1 (15-ounce) can pumpkin (not pie filling)

1 teaspoon cake spice or pumpkin pie spice

¼ teaspoon fine kosher or sea salt

20 (½-inch-thick) slices Clover Honey Challah (page 85) or other soft but firm bread

¼ cup pecans, chopped (optional)

¼ cup packed dark brown sugar

1 Preheat the oven to 325°F. Butter the inside of a 10-inch springform pan and wrap the outside with aluminum foil. Set the springform pan in a roasting pan.

2 In a large bowl, whisk the eggs, egg yolks, and granulated sugar together until smooth. Whisk in the milk, cream, vanilla, persimmon, cake spice, and salt. Dip the bread slices, one by one, in the egg mixture and arrange in an overlapping pattern that rises in the center in the prepared pan. You will use about half of the egg mixture for the slices. Carefully pour the remaining custard over the slices and let rest at room temperature for 30 minutes.

3 Make a water bath by pouring about 3 cups hot tap water in the roasting pan so that the water comes about halfway up the sides of the springform pan. Bake for 45 minutes.

4 Combine the pecans and brown sugar. Remove the bread pudding from the oven and sprinkle this mixture on top. Return the bread pudding to the oven and bake for 15 minutes longer, or until a toothpick inserted in the center comes out clean. Lift the pan out of the water bath and let cool in the pan for 20 minutes. Then carefully peel back the aluminum foil and remove the sides.

Warm Cider Caramel

⅔ cup packed light or dark brown sugar

3 tablespoons cornstarch

2 cups apple cider

6 tablespoons heavy cream

3 tablespoons unsalted butter

¼ teaspoon coarse kosher or sea salt

5 For the caramel sauce, whisk the brown sugar and cornstarch together in a large saucepan. Press out any lumps with your fingers. Stir in the cider and cook over medium-high heat, whisking constantly, until large bubbles form around the perimeter of the pan and the sauce thickens, 10 to 12 minutes. Remove from the heat and whisk in the cream, butter, and salt. Serve drizzled over the bread pudding.

WILD ABOUT PERSIMMON

A wild orange fruit that ripens in the fall, the native persimmon (*Diospyros virginiana*) ranges across the southern half of the Midwest. When not fully ripened, the fruit has a bitter, tannic flavor. But when it's so ripe it falls off the tree, a persimmon has a sweet, mild flavor much like winter squash and pumpkin. The small round fruits are full of seeds that are fiddly to remove, so they're not commercially viable. But a cottage industry of foragers and retired folks gather and process the fruits, selling persimmon pulp to those in the know. When I go to KitchenArt in West Lafayette, Indiana, to teach cooking classes, I get my secret stash of persimmon pulp from a local forager there. You just have to ask.

Or go to a festival. Mitchell, Indiana, in scenic Brown County, has hosted a persimmon festival in late September since 1946, where you can enjoy a ham, bean, and cornbread dinner with a grand finale of homemade persimmon pudding. Taylorville, Illinois, hosts their one-day persimmon party in early November.

For all things persimmon, see Resources, page 266.

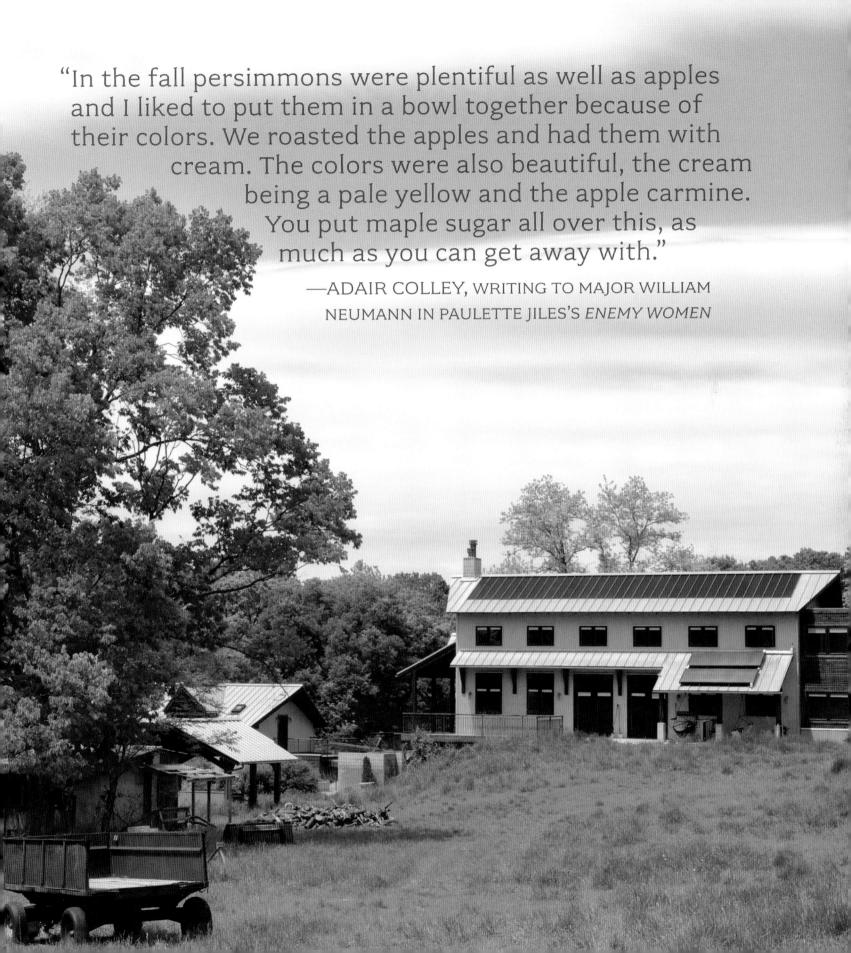

"In the fall persimmons were plentiful as well as apples and I liked to put them in a bowl together because of their colors. We roasted the apples and had them with cream. The colors were also beautiful, the cream being a pale yellow and the apple carmine. You put maple sugar all over this, as much as you can get away with."

—ADAIR COLLEY, WRITING TO MAJOR WILLIAM NEUMANN IN PAULETTE JILES'S *ENEMY WOMEN*

SWEET POTATO WAFFLES WITH WHIPPED ORANGE BUTTER

MAKES ABOUT 6 LARGE WAFFLES OR 12 PANCAKES

Pioneers in Missouri and Kansas used sweet potato plants to help break up the prairie soil in their gardens. This recipe uses the same tuber to break up the monotony of ho-hum pancakes. With a boost of color and vitamins A and C from sweet potatoes, these waffles are delicious any time of year. Topped with a dollop of fluffy orange butter, the waffles don't really need syrup. But go ahead if you must. This batter also makes delicious pancakes. The butter is also good on Farmhouse Yeast Rolls (page 88) or Clover Honey Challah (page 85).

2 cups unbleached all-purpose flour

1 tablespoon baking powder

½ teaspoon fine kosher or sea salt

½ cup packed brown sugar

½ teaspoon ground cinnamon

⅛ teaspoon ground ginger

1¼ cups milk

⅓ cup sorghum syrup or molasses

½ cup cooked or canned sweet potato or pumpkin puree (not pie filling)

1 large egg

Whipped Orange Butter

½ cup (1 stick) unsalted butter, softened

1 teaspoon freshly grated orange zest

1 tablespoon granulated sugar

1   In a medium bowl, combine the flour, baking powder, salt, brown sugar, cinnamon, and ginger. Add the milk, sorghum, pumpkin, and egg. Whisk until smooth.

2   Bake in a waffle iron according to the manufacturer's directions. Baking time will vary with the consistency of the batter and your preference for browning.

3   For the butter, place the butter, orange zest, and sugar in the bowl of a stand mixer and whip until light and fluffy. Serve with the waffles. The butter will keep, covered, in the refrigerator for up to 1 week.

RISE AND SHINE BREAKFAST CASSEROLE **SERVES 8**

You can never have too many breakfast casserole recipes for a holiday or family get-together. This one features some of the Heartland's best: bacon, Wisconsin cheddar, and farm-fresh eggs. Assemble this dish the night before you want to serve it, and then pop it into the oven while you brew the coffee. Serve with fresh fruit or Cranberry-Pear Compote (page 51).

6 cups French bread, cut into ¾-inch cubes

2 cups shredded cheddar cheese

6 slices smoked bacon, cooked until crisp and crumbled

1½ cups cooked and crumbled breakfast sausage or diced cooked ham

3 cups whole milk

6 large eggs, beaten

3 tablespoons chopped fresh Italian parsley

1 teaspoon dry mustard

½ teaspoon freshly ground black pepper

¼ teaspoon onion powder

1 Butter a large casserole or baking dish and toss the bread, cheese, bacon, and sausage together in it. In a large bowl, whisk the milk, eggs, parsley, mustard, pepper, and onion powder together. Pour over the bread mixture. Cover and refrigerate for at least 8 hours and up to 24 hours.

2 Preheat the oven to 350°F.

3 Bake for 35 to 45 minutes, until puffed and browned. Let stand for 5 minutes before cutting and serving.

HEARTLAND SCRAMBLE SERVES 4

A free-range egg is like a blank page of good paper on which to write your culinary "story." Is it about your Italian/German/Dutch family? Your trip to the farmer's market last weekend? Use this recipe as your outline, and then fill it in with your details.

¼ cup prosciutto pieces or crumbles; cooked and crumbled Italian, Polish, or breakfast sausage; or flaked Apple-Smoked Trout (page 177) or other smoked fish

¼ cup scallions, chopped

¼ cup shredded fontina, pecorino, cheddar, or brick cheese

4 large eggs, beaten

1   Heat a large nonstick skillet over medium-high heat. Add the prosciutto and scallions and stir for 2 minutes, or until the scallions are starting to brown a little. Sprinkle the cheese over the mixture. When the cheese begins to melt, pour in the eggs and scramble, stirring, until the eggs are cooked.

2   Portion onto plates and serve hot.

SAVORY WILD MUSHROOM STRUDEL

MAKES 2 STRUDELS TO SERVE 12 TO 16

This strudel is delicious as a brunch dish, a substantial appetizer, a side dish for a game dinner, or a meatless main course. Use equal parts domestic and wild mushrooms or vary the proportion as you wish.

Filling

1 pound white mushrooms

1 pound wild mushrooms

6 tablespoons (¾ stick) unsalted butter

½ cup minced scallions

1 teaspoon fresh thyme, or ½ teaspoon dried thyme leaves

2 (8-ounce) packages cream cheese

Kosher or sea salt and freshly ground white pepper

SUGGESTED MUSHROOM VARIETIES: morel, cremini, chanterelle, oyster, cèpe, and/or baby bella

Pastry

8 sheets frozen strudel or filo dough (22 by 16 inches)

¾ cup (1½ sticks) melted unsalted butter

Bread crumbs, for sprinkling

Sprigs of thyme, for garnish

1 Preheat the oven to 400°F. Line a large baking sheet with parchment paper and set aside.

2 For the filling, mince the mushrooms. Place them in a clean kitchen towel and squeeze to remove excess moisture. Melt the butter in a large skillet over medium-high heat and sauté the mushrooms, scallions, and thyme until the liquid has evaporated, 8 to 10 minutes. Stir in the cream cheese, season to taste with salt and pepper, and remove from the heat.

3 For the pastry, spread a sheet of strudel dough on a damp towel, with the short end horizontal to you. Brush the pastry with melted butter and sprinkle with bread crumbs. Repeat with the second and third sheets, stacking them on top of the first sheet. Add the fourth sheet and brush with butter, but do not sprinkle with crumbs. Spoon half of the mushroom mixture along the short end of the dough, leaving a 2- to 3-inch border at three sides. Fold in the sides; then, using the edge of the towel, roll into a jelly roll. Repeat the process for a second strudel. Place the strudels on the prepared baking sheet.

4 Bake until browned, about 20 minutes. To serve, let cool slightly, then cut into slices with kitchen shears. Garnish whole strudels or slices with sprigs of fresh thyme. The strudel can be made and baked ahead, stored in the refrigerator or freezer overnight, and then reheated in the oven.

STRUDEL TOWNS

Slice into a flaky strudel and you'll see swirls of featherlight pastry enclosing a filling of sweet fruit or savory vegetables. *Strudel* is German for "whirlpool," and it is made up of layers of thin dough rolled into a log around a filling and baked until it turns a crispy golden brown. It is one of those foods that triggers thoughts of home and family. Perhaps that's why Eastern European settlers brought the pastry to the Midwest, where strudel shops abound. "Strudel seems to hook people," says strudel fanatic, cookbook author, and Slow Food member Linda Griffith, of Cleveland. "It's the memories of special family occasions."

CLEVELAND, OHIO—Try the savory cabbage or the sweet poppy seed strudel at Lucy's Sweet Surrender.

CHICAGO, ILLINOIS—Try the praline pecan, cherry and cheese, or poppy seed strudel in a sweet yeast dough at Dinkel's Bakery (www.dinkels.com).

EAGAN, MINNESOTA—Try the savory brat and kraut or the sweet pear and ginger strudel from Ruhland's Strudel (www.thestrudelhaus.com).

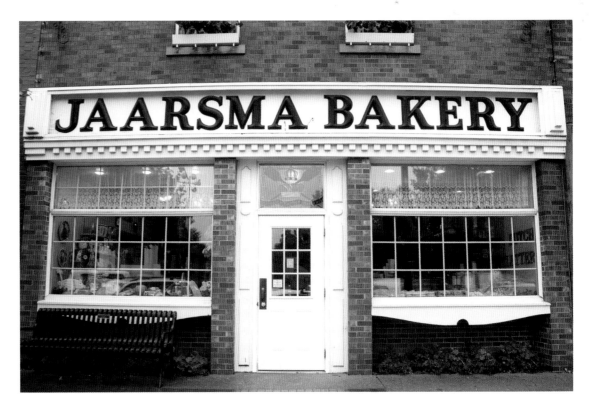

CHAPTER 3 | THE HEARTLAND BREADBASKET | BREADS

RECENTLY, WHEN I WAS at the Iowa Summer Writer's Workshop, I paused to look down at the sidewalk and read a passage from Ruth Suckow's 1929 novel *The Kramer Girls* that was etched into a bronze relief: "She loved being able to know that country was all around her and that any moment she could reach it . . . and stand and let great sunny silence sink into her whole being, not just into her mind."

That's exactly how I feel. Like many Midwesterners, I always like to think I'm not too far from the wide-open spaces that speak to my ancestral farm roots. My great-grandparents came from farming families in Germany, the Netherlands, and Ireland. One great-grandpa became a flour salesman, and another turned his home into a bakery during the Depression.

Since I gave up hilly southern Ohio for the rolling prairie of Kansas, I mark the year by how the wheat grows. Although I live in a Kansas suburb of Kansas City, Missouri, I'm not that far from wheat fields. In fact, I can drive for 15 or 20 minutes and see the dry stubble give way to bright green wheat grass in the fall. Or on a brilliant June day, I can marvel at how the chartreuse wheat looks against a brilliant blue sky.

When you buy a bag of all-purpose flour, this is where it comes from, even if it's milled to certain specifications and packaged by King Arthur or other well-known brands.

We have the unusual combination of the Santa Fe Railroad and the Russian Mennonites to thank for turning the Great Plains into the nation's breadbasket. In the 1870s, the railroad wanted to make sure that their newly laid tracks had built-in customers. Pacifist Russian Mennonites in the Ukraine needed to find a new place to farm their winter wheat, as they were soon going to be forced into the armed service. So, in a match made in bread heaven, the Russian Mennonites came to Kansas with bags of Turkey red winter wheat seeds, a variety of wheat perfectly suited to the prairie *terroir*.

Today, wheat fields stretch from Kansas through the Dakotas. So it's only natural that the baking tradition is strong in the Midwest, especially in places settled by Germans, Austrians, Hungarians, Czechs, and Scandinavians. Each community takes pride in its unique baked goods—yeasty coffee cakes in Cincinnati, strudels in Chicago, ethnic breads of all kinds, moist muffins and scones, and the cinnamon roll—courtesy of Swedish bakers—that unites us all.

In the late nineteenth century, good flour was hit-and-miss, as each community with water power ground its own grain. As electrical power replaced water to run the mills, wheat flour became more standardized. Today, Hudson Cream Flour, from regional wheat milled at Stafford County Flour Mills in south-central Kansas, is now recognized as one of the finest all-purpose flours. Artisan bread baking and precision flour milling, thanks to the expertise of Kansas State University's milling and baking researchers, continue to thrive.

And so does home baking in this part of the country. From a homemade bun for your hamburger at a local diner to Farmhouse Yeast Rolls (page 88) on the Sunday dinner table, Heartlanders still recognize that the aroma of bread baking in the oven signals "relax—you're home" like nothing else. This chapter features two no-knead yeast doughs that the farm wife of yesteryear would have loved—Clover Honey Dough (page 80) and Caraway Rye Dough (page 96). These easy doughs let you control the bread baking process, not the other way around.

WHITE LADIES

When the crude log cabin or sod house gave way to a white Victorian farmhouse, it meant the Heartland family was settled, and the wilderness was turning into civilization.

Such marks of civilization are evident in rural communities throughout the Midwest. Some of these Victorian farmhouses have pretentious Gothic windows as portrayed in Grant Wood's *American Gothic* house in Eldon, Iowa. Others proclaim an ethnic heritage, as evidenced by the light blue trim and elegant scrolled gingerbread found on "white ladies" favored by Swedish builders in Lindsborg, Kansas.

Poet Justin Isherwood, who lives and farms in Plover, Wisconsin, knows these white farmhouses well: "They were Victorians, standing like Victorians must; straight, unflinching, haughty-eyed; they were what the land needed. They were to agriculture, to landscape, prairie and field what the log cabin had been to the pioneer. More sophisticated than logs, genteel yet fortress-like, girdled, braced, whale-boned Victorians, with a touch of lace. . . .

"They calmed the farmstead, smoothed its hair, petted its forehead, gentled the frantic stray sheds, clucked and nuzzled the raw ends into a self-protective circle, a pack of mutually dependent animals against the emptiness of land. I was raised by a white lady and so was everybody I knew. . . ."

MISSOURI SKILLET CORNBREAD

MAKES 1 (10-INCH DIAMETER) BREAD

In the forested hills and bluffs of Missouri, gristmills were one of the signs of settlement along waterways with names like Shoal River, Big Indian Creek, Elk River—or the Mighty Mississip. Falling water powered the wooden water wheels, turning the big mill stones that, in turn, ground local shelled corn, brought to the miller in sacks that held two bushels each. As pay, the miller took one-sixth of the corn, which he fed to his hogs or ground for his own use in dishes like this one. With wood-grilled, fresh-caught fish or a juicy pork chop, this cornbread is a wedge of heaven.

1½ cups stone-ground yellow cornmeal

½ cup unbleached all-purpose flour

1 tablespoon baking powder

1 teaspoon salt

1 large egg

1 cup whole milk

4 slices smoked bacon

4 scallions, finely minced

4 tablespoons (½ stick) unsalted butter, melted

1 Position an oven rack in the center of the oven and preheat the oven to 450°F.

2 In a large bowl, whisk the cornmeal, flour, baking powder, and salt together. In a small bowl, whisk the egg and milk together. Stir the egg mixture into the dry mixture until well blended. Set aside.

3 Fry the bacon in a 10-inch cast-iron skillet over medium-high heat until crispy. Transfer the bacon to paper towels to drain and add the scallions to the skillet. Sauté the scallions for 1 minute, then transfer to the cornmeal batter. Crumble the bacon into fine pieces. Stir the crumbled bacon and melted butter into the batter, then spoon the batter into the hot skillet.

4 Immediately, wearing oven mitts, place the skillet on the middle rack of the oven. Bake until golden and a toothpick inserted in the center comes out clean, about 10 minutes. Let cool slightly before cutting.

NOTE: Turn leftover cornbread into croutons for Prairie Panzanella (page 147) or other salads. Cut the cornbread into ¾-inch cubes, spread on a baking sheet, and toast in a 350°F oven until the edges turn golden, about 10 minutes. Let cool, and store in an airtight container for up to 2 weeks or freeze for up to 3 months.

"The sun shines, the rain falls, and the dry kernel becomes plump and sends forth a sprout, and low, the first green leaf: The scent of a field of growing corn is honey-sweet, a trifle musky. You can hear the cornstalks grow. On a warm summer night the corn talks. It cracks its knuckles and seems to chuckle to itself."

—ELIZABETH LANDEWEER, KANSAS CITY, MISSOURI

WHEAT HARVEST

It's late June. Allen and Mary Schrag, along with their son Paul, are making sure the huge combine and the wheat truck are in good order at their farm in Halstead, Kansas. The Schrags' silo is almost empty, ready for this year's crop of wheat berries or kernels, soon to come. Grown daughters Rhiannon, Beth, and Amanda will come in tomorrow to help. Wheat harvest is a family affair.

Wheat-farming Mennonites who migrated from the Netherlands to Germany and then on to the Ukraine, the first Schrags came to Kansas in 1873 when the railroads were offering free land to farmers. That this free land was on either side of the railroad tracks was no fluke—railroad executives wanted a ready-made market for their services.

These Mennonite farmers brought huge sacks of Turkey red winter wheat to the prairie because it had done so well on the Russian steppes.

Today, Kansas hard red winter wheat is still planted by drilling it into the ground in October, avoiding summers that can be too hot and dry or too rainy. By November, urged on by autumn rains, the brilliant green wheat shoots up like blades of grass, upon which cattle can graze. With the first cold snap, the wheat goes into a dormant phase but stays green all winter. From March through June, aided by spring rains, the wheat starts growing again. By April, it is 6 inches high. By late May or early June, it's chartreuse green and knee-high. When ready to harvest, the wheat is about several feet tall and golden.

"Every year is a surprise," says Allen. "Wheat is hard to predict."

What's not difficult to predict is the weather. It's usually hot—sometimes 100°F. The heat churns up violent storms, often with hail. Wheat farmers tell horror stories of watching a whole year's worth of work flattened in minutes.

So the pressure is on to get the wheat harvested and safely stored in the silo as quickly as possible. When the sun has burned any moisture off the wheat, the harvest begins. Allen and Paul drive the combine, while Mary follows with the truck. The combine cuts the wheat, sucks and separates the kernels into a storage chamber, and blows the wheat straw out on the field. When the storage chamber is full, the wheat truck pulls alongside the combine and the wheat is pumped into the dump truck. The truck then goes to the grain elevator on the Schrags' farm, where it dumps the wheat onto the floor, to be taken by a motorized system into the silo. And then it starts all over again—all day long, all week long, until all 2,000 acres have been harvested.

When darkness finally falls and everything is quiet, it will still be a night of restless sleep until the harvest is all in. No storms. No hail. Good news—so far. "Wheat harvest is a lot of stress," admits Allen. "But while it's a business, it's also our way of life."

PUMPKIN PATCH MUFFINS MAKES 12 MUFFINS

With a golden color, a soft and moist crumb, and a spicy streusel topping, these muffins were a hit at my cookbook club—I'm doubly blessed in having wonderful friends who are also fabulous cooks! This recipe is from my friend Roxanne Wyss, a home economist/cookbook author/recipe developer extraordinaire. I love these addictive muffins for breakfast, lunch, or dinner. To make these from fresh pumpkin, buy several small sugar or pie pumpkins—before Halloween—at the market, then roast, puree, and freeze enough to use in dishes both savory and sweet (see page 221).

Streusel Topping

½ cup (1 stick) unsalted butter, softened

½ cup granulated sugar

¾ cup unbleached all-purpose flour

¼ teaspoon salt

½ teaspoon ground cinnamon

1 Preheat the oven to 400°F. Line 12 muffin cups with paper liners or lightly grease the muffin pan.

2 For the streusel, combine all the ingredients in a medium bowl, rubbing the butter in with your fingers until the mixture is crumbly. Gently squeeze bits of the mixture together to form larger pieces of streusel. Set aside.

3 For the muffins, stir the melted butter and pumpkin together in a medium bowl, then stir in the yogurt, eggs, and vanilla until smooth. In a large bowl, sift the flour, baking powder, cinnamon, ginger, allspice, cloves, nutmeg, and salt together, then stir in the sugars. Stir the pumpkin mixture into the flour mixture until just combined. Spoon or scoop the batter into the prepared muffin cups and top with the streusel mixture.

4 Bake for 16 to 19 minutes, or until a toothpick inserted in the center comes out clean. Let the muffins cool in the pan for 5 minutes to allow the streusel to set, then remove from the pan.

Muffins

½ cup (1 stick) unsalted butter, melted and slightly cooled

¾ cup roasted and pureed or canned pumpkin (not pie filling)

½ cup yogurt or sour cream

2 large eggs

1 teaspoon vanilla extract

2 cups unbleached all-purpose flour

2 teaspoons baking powder

1 teaspoon ground cinnamon

½ teaspoon ground ginger

¼ teaspoon ground allspice

¼ teaspoon ground cloves

¼ teaspoon ground nutmeg

½ teaspoon salt

½ cup brown sugar

½ cup granulated sugar

SUGGESTED PUMPKIN VARIETIES:
Amish Pie, Green-Striped Cushaw, Cornfield

PUMPKIN PATCHES

Deep black loam mixed with sand and hot summers are ideal for growing pumpkins in:

MORTON, ILLINOIS—where 5,000 acres of Dickinson Select pumpkins are grown for Libby's canned pumpkin—85 percent of the world's canned pumpkin. Their pumpkin festival starts in mid-September and includes a pumpkin chuckin' contest.

CIRCLEVILLE, OHIO—Since 1903, a pumpkin festival has been held in October. Over a 4-day period, more than 23,000 pumpkin pies and 100,000 pumpkin doughnuts are sold, as well as pumpkin cookies, burgers, taffy, ice cream, waffles, fudge, milk shakes, and soups.

NO-KNEAD CLOVER HONEY DOUGH

MAKES BREADS, COFFEE CAKES, OR ROLLS TO SERVE 24 TO 32

Can bread dough be a pantry staple? Yes, if you consider your refrigerator as "pantry." With a bowl of this versatile made-ahead dough on hand, you'll be already halfway to yeasty breads, rolls, and coffee cakes. Busy Heartland farm wives in the early part of the twentieth century had two yeast dough recipes they used regularly. One was for bread and one was for dinner rolls, cinnamon rolls, and coffee cakes. This streamlined approach made life easier for them, and it can still make things easier for us today. Plus, there's also another way to streamline bread baking. Adding more liquid to a dough eliminates the need to knead. You can simply stir the dough together, keep it in the refrigerator for up to 3 days, and bake when you're ready. So why not have a baking day, and then wrap and freeze your wares for up to 3 months?

A Danish dough whisk features a mitten-shaped metal mixing end on a wooden handle and makes short work of mixing any dough. Measuring is an important step to assure that your bread turns out right, so follow thedirections exactly. Use this dough to make Berry Pickin' Coffee Cake (page 95), Cider-Glazed Cinnamon Rolls (page 89), Clover Honey Challah (page 85), or Farmhouse Yeast Rolls (page 88).

6½ cups bread flour, plus more for dusting

2 tablespoons instant or bread machine yeast

1½ tablespoons fine kosher salt

1 cup clover or other amber honey

¼ cup vegetable or canola oil

2 large eggs

Warm water (about 100°F)

1 Spoon the flour into a measuring cup, level with a knife or your finger, then dump the flour into a 16-cup mixing bowl.

2 Add the yeast and salt to the flour. Stir together with a wooden spoon or a Danish dough whisk. Mix the honey, oil, and eggs together in a 4-cup measuring cup. Add enough warm water to reach the 4-cup mark and stir together. Pour the honey mixture into the flour mixture, stir to combine, then beat for 40 strokes, scraping the bottom and the sides of the bowl, until the dough forms a lumpy, sticky mass.

3 Cover with plastic wrap and let rise at room temperature (72°F) for 2 hours, or until the dough has risen to about 2 inches below the rim of the bowl and has a spongelike appearance.

4 Use that day or place the dough, covered with plastic wrap, in the refrigerator for up to 3 days before baking. If you like, write the date on the plastic wrap so you know the bake-by date for your dough.

"Moonlight butters the whole Iowa night. Clover and corn smells are thick as syrup."

—W. P. KINSELLA, *SHOELESS JOE*

CLOVER HONEY BOULES

MAKES 2 (12-INCH) ROUND LOAVES

Like two prairie harvest moons, these round loaves can be bewitching with their yeasty aroma and homemade flavor. With a tender and moist custard crumb, this bread is delicious as toast or sliced for sandwiches.

1 batch No-Knead Clover Honey Dough (page 80)

Unbleached all-purpose flour, for dusting

1   To bake into 2 round loaves, preheat the oven to 350°F and line 2 baking sheets with parchment paper. Divide the dough in half on a floured surface. Coax the dough into a round shape and place each round on the prepared baking sheets. Pinch any seams closed, cover with kitchen towels, and let rest at room temperature for 40 minutes.

2   Bake for 40 to 42 minutes, or until the crust is a shiny, medium brown and an instant-read thermometer inserted in the center of the loaf registers at least 190°F. Transfer to a wire rack to cool. Enjoy right away with Farmhouse Butter (page 7), or let cool, wrap, and freeze for up to 3 months. Freeze any leftover or stale bread to use in bread puddings.

"Everywhere the grain stood ripe and the hot afternoon was full of the smell of the ripe wheat, like the smell of bread baking in the oven."

—WILLA CATHER, *O PIONEERS!*

CLOVER HONEY CHALLAH

MAKES 1 (14-INCH) BRAIDED LOAF

Light, tender challah, a bread served on the Jewish sabbath and Rosh Hashanah, is made without dairy products, so it can be served with a meal containing meat to adhere to kosher dietary rules. In major metropolitan areas, many bakeries make challah a weekend staple. No matter your religious preference, this airy, tender bread is as easy to eat as it is to make.

½ batch No-Knead Clover Honey Dough (page 80)

Unbleached all-purpose flour, for dusting

1 large egg mixed with 1 tablespoon water, for egg wash

Sesame or poppy seeds, for sprinkling (optional)

1 Line a baking sheet with parchment paper.

2 To form the loaf, transfer the dough to a floured surface. Working the dough as little as possible, use a rolling pin to roll the dough into a large rectangle, dusting with flour as necessary. Fold the dough in half, turn a quarter turn, and roll out again. Repeat three more times. With your hands, form the dough into a cylinder. With a dough scraper, divide the dough into 3 equal portions. Transfer the dough portions to a floured surface and dust very lightly with flour. Flour your hands. Working the dough as little as possible and adding flour as necessary, roll each portion into a 16-inch-long rope. Lay the ropes out vertically, parallel to each other and close but not touching. Braid the ropes together snugly, starting from the top. Lift each rope and pass it over or under one of the others in sequence. Tuck the ends under to form an oblong loaf about 14 inches long. Carefully transfer the loaf to the prepared baking sheet.

3 Cover with a tea towel and let rest at room temperature for 40 minutes.

4 Meanwhile, preheat the oven to 350°F. Carefully brush the loaf with the egg wash. Sprinkle with the seeds.

5 Bake for 40 to 42 minutes, or until the crust is a shiny, medium brown and an instant-read thermometer inserted in the center of the loaf registers at least 190°F. Transfer to a wire rack to cool. Enjoy right away with Farmhouse Butter (page 7), or let cool, wrap, and freeze for up to 3 months.

NOTE: Leftover challah (as if!) makes excellent French toast or bread pudding.

THE MILLER'S TALE

Once the wheat is harvested and goes into storage at the co-op, then what? That's just when the miller's tale begins. "Wheat that's harvested in June won't even be processed until September," says Alvin Brensing, the octogenarian head of the Stafford County Flour Mill in Stafford, Kansas. Dressed in his standard gear of plaid shirt, Western-style belt and buckle, and cowboy hat, Brensing still comes into work. The milling business, after all, has been his life.

"Wheat has to age a little before we can mill it," he says. And that process begins with tempering the wheat—first cleaning, and then tempering the wheat berries with a little water to boost the moisture content up to about 16 percent. This makes for easier removal of the outer bran layer from the inner germ at the bottom of the kernel and the endosperm at the top. Because the germ contains fat, it can cause the flour to go rancid if left in. Most of the flour comes from the starchy endosperm.

Brensing buys local red winter wheat to first store, and then mill into Hudson Cream Flour, a short patent flour that is so finely sifted that 100 pounds of wheat kernels translate into only 62 pounds of this top-grade all-purpose flour; 28 pounds get sifted out to become animal feed, while another 10 pounds get sifted into "clear flour," a low-grade flour often added to spice blends.

Because wheat varies in protein content from field to field, blending wheats to get the right protein content also takes place before milling. Protein in flour means the presence of tough, elastic, rubbery gluten. Bread flour has a higher protein level, with the gluten working with yeast to raise the bread dough. Cake flour has a low protein level because cakes need a finer texture and so rely on eggs to raise the batter. All-purpose flour like Hudson Cream has a medium protein level, and it can be used with either additional gluten and yeast to make bread or with eggs to make cookies and cakes. To arrive at Hudson Cream's 11 percent protein content or the 11½ to 12 percent protein for the slightly lower-grade Diamond H flour, Brensing has to start with batches of wheat with 12½ to 13 percent protein.

Tempered and blended, the wheat kernels next travel through corrugated rollers to be cracked and separated. The bran and germ are removed, and the flour from the center or endosperm goes through several sifting processes, with the flour blown through silky woven netting

so fine that if you poured water into it, the water would bead up, not pour out. The sifting process is what separates Hudson Cream from other commercial millers like Pillsbury, Continental, or Archer Daniels Midland who don't sift as finely.

Along the way, a small pinch of malted barley flour gets added in, which helps the rising quality of the flour by converting some of the starch particles into malt sugar, according to Brensing. Some flour is bleached, but all flour bleaches naturally if left to age for 8 to 12 weeks, he says. Then the flour is bagged and each bag marked with the time and date.

The activity is nonstop, and there's a constant hum as well as a fine fog of flour dust in the air. The mill machinery goes 24 hours a day. Trucks drive in with deliveries and out with shipments. Millers from all over the world might stop by for a visit, perhaps as part of a milling and baking seminar at Kansas State University in Manhattan, to the north. Occasionally a rabbi from nearby Great Bend comes down to visit and approve the kosher flour that goes in green and orange packages to the East Coast. And then there are the McDonald's folks who buy Brensing's flour for their hamburger buns.

"We do the same things every day, but it's always different," Brensing says with a chuckle.

FARMHOUSE YEAST ROLLS MAKES 16 ROLLS

Feathery, yeasty dinner rolls are just minutes away when you have the dough already made in the refrigerator "pantry."

½ batch No-Knead Clover Honey Dough (page 80)

Unbleached all-purpose flour, for dusting

1 large egg mixed with 1 tablespoon water, for egg wash

1 Line a baking sheet with parchment paper.

2 To form the rolls, divide the dough in half with a serrated knife and a dough scraper. Transfer one half to a floured surface and dust very lightly with flour. Flour your hands. Working the dough as little as possible and adding flour as necessary, form the dough into a 16-inch-long cylinder. If the dough begins to stick to the surface, use the dough scraper to push the flour under the dough and scrape it up. Gently press and squeeze to form the dough into a solid cylinder. With a pastry brush, brush off any excess flour. With the dough scraper, slice the cylinder into 8 (2-inch) pieces. Cut each piece in half. Pinch the cut sides closed and coax into a seamless 2-inch round. Pinch any seams together. Repeat with the remaining dough.

3 Place the rolls about 1 inch apart on the prepared baking sheets. Cover with a kitchen towel and let rest at room temperature for 40 minutes.

4 Meanwhile, preheat the oven to 350°F. Brush the top of each roll with the egg wash.

5 Bake for 20 to 22 minutes, or until the rolls are domed, lightly browned, and an instant-read thermometer inserted in the center of a roll registers at least 190°F. Transfer to a wire rack to cool.

CIDER-GLAZED CINNAMON ROLLS   MAKES 16 ROLLS

Cinnamon rolls are true comfort food. Just the scent of them baking makes you feel good. If you like a more assertive cinnamon filling, use dark brown sugar and strong Vietnamese or Saigon cinnamon.

1 batch No-Knead Clover Honey Dough (page 80)

Unbleached all-purpose or bread flour, for dusting

Cinnamon Filling

4 tablespoons (½ stick) unsalted butter, softened

1 cup packed light or dark brown sugar

1 tablespoon ground cinnamon

Glaze

1 cup confectioners' sugar

2 tablespoons apple cider

1 Line a large baking sheet with parchment paper.

2 To form the rolls, divide the dough in half with a serrated knife and a dough scraper. The remaining dough in the bowl will deflate somewhat. Transfer each dough portion to a floured surface and dust very lightly with flour. Flour your hands. Working the dough as little as possible and adding flour as necessary, roll each portion into a 12 by 8-inch rectangle. Spread the filling over the dough, leaving a ½-inch perimeter. Starting with a short end, roll each piece of dough into an 8-inch cylinder with your hands. If the dough begins to stick to the surface, use the dough scraper to push the flour under the dough and scrape it up. With the dough scraper, slice each cylinder into 1-inch pieces.

3 Place the rolls, filling side up, in the prepared pan so that they are touching. Cover with a kitchen towel and let rest at room temperature for 1 hour.

4 Meanwhile, preheat the oven to 350°F.

5 Bake for 25 to 27 minutes, or until browned and an instant-read thermometer inserted in the center of the rolls registers at least 190°F. Transfer to a wire rack to cool.

6 For the glaze, whisk the sugar and cider together in a small bowl. Drizzle or spoon the glaze over the rolls when they are cool.

APRICOT-CREAM CHEESE STRUDEL

MAKES 2 (9 BY 5-INCH) STRUDELS

This is not the thin, flaky strudel made with filo dough. This is sweetened yeast dough strudel folded over a filling, as Dinkel's in Chicago has been doing for generations. I like to use Harlayne apricot preserves from American Spoon Foods in Michigan, but any good fruit preserves will be delicious.

½ batch No-Knead Clover Honey Dough (page 80)

Unbleached all-purpose flour, for dusting

Filling

One (8-ounce) package cream cheese, softened

½ cup sour cream

1 large egg

2 tablespoons sugar

1 teaspoon vanilla extract

1 cup good-quality apricot or other tart fruit preserves, such as Sour Cherry Preserves (page 29), blackberry, lingonberry, or strawberry

Almond Glaze

1 cup confectioners' sugar

½ teaspoon almond extract

3 tablespoons whole milk

1   Transfer the dough to a floured surface and dust very lightly with flour. Flour your hands. Using a dough scraper, divide the dough in half. Working the dough as little as possible and adding flour as necessary, roll each half into a 12-inch square. Wrap part of the dough over the rolling pin and transfer each half to a 9 by 5-inch loaf pan, fitting the dough into the length of the pan and letting the sides of the dough rest, draping over the sides of the pan.

2   For the filling, combine the cream cheese, sour cream, egg, sugar, and vanilla in the work bowl of a food processor and process until smooth. Pour half of the filling into each pan. Dollop ½ cup of preserves over the filling in each pan, then fold the sides over on top of the filling.

3   Cover with a kitchen towel and let rest at room temperature for 40 minutes.

4   Meanwhile, preheat the oven to 350°F.

5   When ready to bake, the dough will not have risen much, but will finish rising in the oven. Bake for 37 to 40 minutes, or until the crust has browned. Transfer to a wire rack to cool.

6   When the strudels are cool, whisk the glaze ingredients together in a small bowl and drizzle half the glaze over each strudel.

DRIED CHERRY SCONES **MAKES 12 SCONES**

Harlan "Pete" Peterson was one of the first Midwestern chefs to be nationally recognized for his regional cuisine—which included foraged foods—at his restaurant Tapawingo in Ellsworth, Michigan. From the 1980s onward, he championed the cause of wild leeks, morels, whitefish, local farms, and the fabulous fruit grown in the Upper Peninsula. I've adapted his recipe here. Serve these tender, flavorful scones with Farmhouse Butter (page 7) and Sour Cherry Preserves (page 29). Scones are best eaten the day they're baked, but you can wrap and freeze any leftovers for up to 3 months.

2 cups cake flour

2 cups unbleached all-purpose flour

4 teaspoons baking powder

½ cup granulated sugar

¼ teaspoon salt

½ cup (1 stick) unsalted butter, cut into small pieces, chilled

1 large egg, beaten

½ cup milk

½ cup sour cream

4 ounces (about ¾ cup) dried cherries, dried currants, or sweetened dried cranberries

Half-and-half, for brushing

Coarse granulated or sanding sugar, for dusting

1 Preheat the oven to 375°F. Line a baking sheet with parchment paper.

2 In the work bowl of a food processor, pulse together the flours, baking powder, sugar, and salt. Add the butter pieces, egg, milk, and sour cream and pulse again until the dough just comes together. Transfer the dough to a lightly floured surface and sprinkle the cherries on top. Using a dough scraper or a pancake turner, fold the dough over onto the cherries several times. Roll or pat the dough out to a 10-inch circle about 1 inch thick. With a large knife or a pizza wheel, cut the dough into 12 wedges. Carefully transfer each wedge to the prepared baking sheet, placing them 2 inches apart. Brush the tops with half-and-half and sprinkle with sugar.

3 Bake for 20 to 22 minutes, or until lightly browned on top. Serve warm.

OH, CHERRY

In the beginning, wild pin cherries and chokecherries flourished on the eastern shore of Lake Michigan. When European settlers came, they planted sour or Montmorency cherry trees, and they did well too. So well that by the early 1980s, farmer Don Nugent started experimenting with the annual glut of sour cherries in the Traverse City area.

And bingo—the sweetened dried cherry was born. It takes 8 pounds of fresh Montmorency cherries to make 1 pound of dried. Fresh cherries are first pitted and then frozen. Each 25-pound batch is capped with a 5-pound block of sugar. When the cherries are allowed to thaw, they produce lots of juice. And when they're slowly dried, they become infused with some of that sweetened juice and also retain their deep red color.

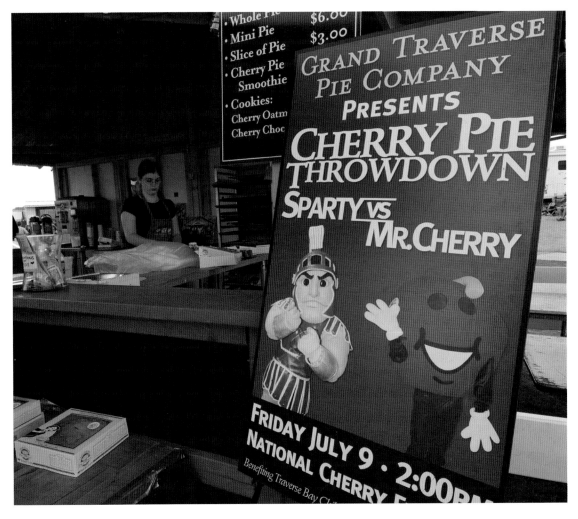

BACON, CHEDDAR, AND SCALLION SCONES

MAKES 12 SCONES

Make up a batch of these and freeze the leftovers (for up to 3 months), and you will have an on-the-go breakfast as a frozen asset.

2 cups cake flour

2 cups unbleached all-purpose flour

4 teaspoons baking powder

¼ teaspoon salt

½ cup (1 stick) unsalted butter, cut into small pieces, chilled

1 large egg, beaten

½ cup milk

½ cup sour cream

2 slices bacon, cooked crisp and crumbled

½ cup grated sharp cheddar cheese, plus more for sprinkling

¼ cup chopped scallions

Half-and-half, for brushing

1   Preheat the oven to 375°F. Line a baking sheet with parchment paper.

2   In the work bowl of a food processor, pulse together the flours, baking powder, and salt. Add the butter pieces, egg, milk, and sour cream and pulse again until the dough just comes together. Transfer the dough to a lightly floured surface and sprinkle the bacon, cheese, and scallions on top. Using a dough scraper or a pancake turner, fold the dough over onto the bacon mixture several times. Roll or pat the dough out to a 10-inch circle about 1 inch thick. With a large knife or a pizza wheel, cut the dough into 12 wedges. Carefully transfer each wedge to the prepared baking sheet, placing them 2 inches apart. Brush the tops with half-and-half and sprinkle with more cheese.

3   Bake for 20 to 22 minutes, or until lightly browned on top. Serve warm.

BERRY PICKIN' COFFEE CAKE MAKES 2 (8-INCH SQUARE) CAKES

I grew up in Cincinnati, Ohio, a great coffee cake town, as is Milwaukee and nearby Madison, Wisconsin. When I moved to Kansas, I had to learn to bake my own, as the "coffee cake Germans" didn't settle here. Making a yeast-risen coffee cake is easy if you already have the no-knead yeast dough prepared. Then you can make the cheesecake-like filling, dollop the coffee cake with your best and preferably homemade preserves, bake, and enjoy.

½ batch No-Knead Clover Honey Dough (page 80)

Unbleached all-purpose flour, for dusting

Filling

One 8-ounce package cream cheese, softened

½ cup sour cream

1 large egg

2 tablespoons sugar

1 teaspoon vanilla extract

1 cup good-quality tart fruit preserves, such as Sour Cherry Preserves (page 29), blackberry, lingonberry, apricot, or strawberry

Almond Glaze

1 cup confectioners' sugar

½ teaspoon almond extract

2 tablespoons whole milk

1 Transfer the dough to a floured surface and dust very lightly with flour. Flour your hands. Using a dough scraper, divide the dough in half. Working the dough as little as possible and adding flour as necessary, roll each half into a 10-inch diameter square. Wrap part of the dough over the rolling pin and transfer each half to an 8-inch square baking pan. Fit the dough into the bottom and up the sides of each pan.

2 Cover with a kitchen towel and let rest at room temperature for 40 minutes.

3 Meanwhile, preheat the oven to 350°F.

4 When ready to bake, the dough will not have risen much, but it will finish rising in the oven. About 5 minutes before baking, pat the dough up the sides of the pans again. For the filling, combine the cream cheese, sour cream, egg, sugar, and vanilla in the work bowl of a food processor and process until smooth. Pour half of the filling into each pan. Dollop ½ cup of the preserves over the filling in each pan.

5 Bake for 37 to 40 minutes, or until the crust has browned. Transfer to a wire rack to cool.

6 When the coffee cakes are cool, whisk the glaze ingredients together in a small bowl and drizzle half the glaze over each coffee cake.

NO-KNEAD SOUR CARAWAY RYE DOUGH

MAKES BREADS, FLATBREADS, OR ROLLS TO SERVE 24 TO 32

Like many Heartlanders, rye works hard. This grain is disease resistant and the hardiest of the cereal crops in the Dakotas, Nebraska, and Minnesota. Farmers plant winter rye, like winter wheat, by drilling seeds into the ground around September, and then they harvest in early summer. Rye is also a versatile crop, grown not only for the potential flour but also for holistic weed control, pasture for cattle during the winter months, and vodka. Quite a combo. Because rye is low in gluten, which is needed to develop the structure of bread, you use a combination of wheat and rye flours in rye bread dough. The rye bread flavor here comes from the caraway, the dark color from the cocoa powder, and gentle sourness from the yogurt. Beloved of Heartland families with northern European roots, this rye dough can be turned into flatbreads, loaves, and rolls. If you precisely follow all the steps, you'll have good success.

4½ cups bread flour, plus more for dusting

2 cups rye flour

2 tablespoons instant or bread machine yeast

1½ tablespoons fine kosher salt

¼ cup unsweetened cocoa powder

2 tablespoons caraway seeds

½ cup sorghum syrup or molasses

½ cup plain yogurt

1 Spoon the flours into a measuring cup, level with a knife or your finger, then dump the flours into a 16-cup mixing bowl.

2 Add the yeast, salt, cocoa powder, and caraway seeds to the flour. Stir together with a wooden spoon or Danish dough whisk. Mix the sorghum syrup, yogurt, and water together in a 4-cup measuring cup. Pour the molasses mixture into the flour mixture, stir to combine, then beat for 40 strokes, scraping the bottom and the sides of the bowl, until the dough forms a lumpy, sticky mass.

3 Cover with plastic wrap and let rise at room temperature (72°F) for 2 hours, or until the dough has risen to about 2 inches below the rim of the bowl and has a spongelike appearance.

4 Use that day or place the dough, covered with plastic wrap, in the refrigerator for up to 3 days before baking. If you like, write the date on the plastic wrap, so you know the bake-by date of your dough.

NO-KNEAD SOUR CARAWAY RYE BOULES
MAKES 2 (12-INCH) ROUND LOAVES

These dark and tangy round loaves taste delicious with fresh butter, herbed cream cheese, aged cheeses, or sausage.

No-Knead Sour Caraway Rye Dough (page 96)

All-purpose flour, for dusting

1 large egg, beaten

Coarse kosher or sea salt, fennel seeds, or nigella seeds, for sprinkling

1 To bake into 2 round loaves, line a baking sheet with parchment paper. Divide the dough in half on a floured surface. Coax the dough into a round shape and place each round on the prepared baking sheet. Pinch any seams closed, cover with kitchen towels, and let rest at room temperature for 40 minutes.

2 Meanwhile, preheat the oven to 350°F. Carefully brush the loaves with the egg. Sprinkle with the coarse kosher or sea salt, fennel seeds, and nigella (black onion) seeds.

3 Bake for 40 to 42 minutes, or until the crust is a shiny medium brown and an instant-read thermometer inserted in the center of the loaf registers at least 190°F. Transfer to a wire rack to cool. Enjoy right away with Farmhouse Butter (page 7), or let cool, wrap, and freeze for up to 3 months. Freeze any leftover or stale bread to use in savory bread puddings.

SOUR CARAWAY RYE BREAD MAKES 1 (14-INCH) LOAF

Can you whip up a batch of brownies from a mix? Sure you can. Well, those are the basic skills you need to make this savory, one-bowl, no-knead artisan bread, believe it or not. Follow the easy steps and you're on your way—without expensive equipment, lots of time, or baker's angst. Use instant or bread machine yeast, available in jars in the baking section, as it can simply be stirred into the flour. More moisture in the dough takes the place of kneading. And you'll know when your bread is done by taking its temperature (with an instant-read thermometer). What's even better, this dough follows your lead: You can bake right after the dough has risen or wait a couple of days. If only the rest of our lives worked like that. . . .

½ batch No-Knead Sour Caraway Rye Dough (page 96)

Unbleached all-purpose flour, for dusting

1 To form a bâtarde, transfer the dough to a floured surface and dust very lightly with flour. Flour your hands. Working the dough as little as possible and adding flour as necessary, form the dough into a 14-inch cylinder. Smooth the dough with your hands to form a soft, non-sticky skin. Pinch any seams together to prevent "blowouts" as the loaf bakes. Pinch each end into a point. Lightly flour any sticky places on the dough. The dough should feel soft and smooth all over, like a baby's skin (but with lumps from the caraway seeds), not at all sticky.

2 Line a baking sheet with parchment paper and place the dough on the baking sheet. Cover with a kitchen towel and let rest at room temperature for 40 minutes.

3 Meanwhile, position an oven rack in the center of the oven, and preheat the oven to 450°F. Place a broiler pan on the bottom rack of the oven.

4 When ready to bake, the dough will not have risen much, but it will finish rising dramatically in the oven. Using a serrated knife, make 5 evenly spaced diagonal slashes across and down the length of the dough, about 1 inch deep, exposing the moist dough under the surface. The slashes help the bâtarde bake more evenly, add an attractive pattern, and help prevent blowouts.

5 Place the baking sheet on the middle rack of the oven. Pull the lower rack out, pour about 2 cups of hot water into the broiler pan, and push the lower rack back in place. Bake for 27 to 29 minutes, or until the crust is a medium dark brown and an instant-read thermometer inserted in the center of the loaf registers at least 190°F. Transfer to a wire rack to cool.

"He gestured out toward the horizon, where a clear sky bordered prairie grasses as far as the eye could see. 'Eventually, I fell under the spell of that line out there. It was so simple: a huge block of blue on top of a block of gold prairie, and the quiet line between heaven and earth stretching endlessly. It felt like freedom itself to look at the horizon.'"

—FRANK LLOYD WRIGHT TO MAMAH BORTHWICK CHENEY,
IN NANCY HORAN'S *LOVING FRANK: A NOVEL*

GOLDEN ONION SOUR RYE ROLLS MAKES 16 ROLLS

This recipe makes artisan baking easy. A no-knead sour rye dough keeps in the refrigerator for up to 3 days until you're ready to bake. The big-flavor addition of sautéed seasoned onions stirs up in minutes. Baking at a high temperature and spraying the rolls with water during baking is a simple way to get a crisp and shiny crust. Enjoy these rolls hot from the oven with Farmhouse Butter (page 7), or use them for sandwiches—cheese, grilled brats or other sausages, shaved ham, or smoked turkey. When cooled, the rolls can be frozen for up to 3 months.

⅓ cup canola oil

2 large yellow onions, chopped

1 teaspoon freshly ground white pepper

1 teaspoon garlic salt

1 batch No-Knead Sour Caraway Rye Dough (page 96)

Unbleached all-purpose flour, for dusting

1 Heat the oil in a medium skillet over medium-high heat. Sauté the onions until translucent, 7 to 10 minutes. Season with the white pepper and garlic salt. Divide the mixture in half and set aside to cool.

2 Transfer the dough to a generously floured surface and generously dust with flour. Using a serrated knife and a dough scraper, cut the dough in half. Set one half aside. Flour your hands. Using the dough scraper, scrape half of the dough up and over itself, flouring and turning the dough as you go, for 12 to 15 scrapes, or until the dough is soft and not sticky. Dust very lightly with flour.

3 Flour your hands and the rolling pin. Working the dough as little as possible and adding flour as necessary, roll the dough into a 14 by 12-inch rectangle. Arrange one-quarter of the onion filling on the upper half of the dough and press into the dough. Fold the other half of the dough over the filling. Turn the dough a quarter turn. Working the dough as little as possible and adding flour as necessary, roll the dough again into a rectangle. Again, arrange one-quarter of the filling on the upper half of the dough and press into the dough. Fold the other half over the filling. Turn the dough a quarter turn and roll into an oval. Let the dough rest for 5 minutes. Repeat the process with the remaining dough and onion filling.

4 Line 2 baking sheets with parchment paper. Form each oval of filled dough into a 16-inch-long cylinder. With a dough scraper, cut each cylinder into 8 (2-inch) pieces. Form each piece into a round roll. Lightly flour any sticky places on the dough. Pinch any seams together to prevent blowouts as the rolls bake. The dough should feel soft and smooth all over, like a baby's skin, but not at all sticky. Place the rolls about 2 inches apart on the prepared baking sheets.

5 Cover with a kitchen towel and let rest at room temperature for 45 minutes.

6 Meanwhile, preheat the oven to 450°F. Fill a spray bottle with water.

7 Bake for 15 to 17 minutes, spraying with water 3 times during baking, or until the crust is a blistered, medium dark brown and an instant-read thermometer inserted in the center of a roll registers at least 190°F. Transfer to wire racks to cool.

CHAPTER 4 | NIBBLE AND A SIP | APPETIZERS AND DRINKS

PERHAPS WE OWE OUR NATIONAL FONDNESS FOR NIBBLING to German immigrants. After all, when you drink a beer, you also want something crunchy and salty to go with it: potato chips, popcorn, or pretzels. Before Prohibition in the 1920s, the Midwest was dotted with beer gardens, shaded by hop bines or grapevines—even in Kansas. Almost every local burg had a tavern, which often specialized in sandwiches like the "pony shoe" from Springfield, Illinois—an open-faced sandwich with a special cheese sauce, the larger version called a "horseshoe."

Regional microbreweries made their way back to the Heartland in the 1990s, using breadbasket grains for lagers, ales, and wheat beers. Now those same grains are being distilled into fine vodkas and gins. Use a Midwestern spirit like Milwaukee's Rehorst to make a Farm Girl Cosmo (page 125) or a Garden Gimlet (page 125).

Hardy Heartland grape varieties, such as the Norton and Chambourcin, continue to produce wines that draw a loyal following and make a refreshing Summer Sangria (page 128).

Whether you entertain with a frosty mug of beer, a chic cocktail, or a glass of wine, there's a Heartland appetizer for the occasion. As an amuse-bouche, Chef Tory Miller of L'Etoile in Madison, Wisconsin, likes to offer guests rounds of toasted bread with an herbed local goat cheese topped by a roasted hickory nut. Andrew Zimmerman, chef at Sepia, as well as "Best Chef of the Great Lakes" Koren Grieveson of Avec, both in Chicago, top flatbreads with an array of regional, big-bang-for-your-taste-buck ingredients like lardo (cured pork fat scented with herbs and spices), stinging nettles, and homemade duck confit (see page 38). Across town, Susan Goss serves homemade potato chips her own way, as well as an addictive beer cheese, at West Town Tavern. Tim McKee at La Belle Vie in Minneapolis—another James Beard "Best Chef of the Midwest"—offers smoked trout with grilled salsify, an old-fashioned oyster-flavored vegetable once beloved in Midwestern gardens. From the white oak—fired oven at chef/owner David Falk's Boca in Cincinnati come roasted Brussels sprouts so divine that diners can't get enough—and eat them as an appetizer.

Appetizers don't have to be complicated, though. Herb and Kathy Eckhouse of La Quercia in Norwalk, Iowa, are correct when they say you can simply serve slices of their prosciutto and have your guests be happy. Likewise, you can set out a board of artisan and farmstead cheeses, choosing a variety from Midwestern cheesemakers. If you have a no-knead bread dough in the refrigerator, you can pat out one of the Four Seasons Flatbreads (page 116) in no time at all. In warm weather, Grilled Vegetable Bundles (page 122) make a delicious beginning to a meal. Give Heartland grocery store deli meats and cheeses an easy flair with Brewpub Cheese and Charcuterie on a Plank (page 108)—you'll be amazed at how wonderful they taste.

HOMEMADE CHIPS WITH CHAR-GRILLED ONION AND BLUE CHEESE DIP

SERVES 4

Although I grew up on Husman's and Grippo's potato chips in Cincinnati, Ohio, I like to make my own, sometimes using different kinds of root vegetables, for a hearty appetizer. I fry the chips a day or so before I entertain and store them in an airtight container. And instead of making a dip with dried onion soup, which first became popular in the 1950s, I use char-grilled red onion for a fresher flavor. I crumble in a good, blue-veined Maytag cheese from Newton, Iowa; BelGioioso gorgonzola from Denmark, Wisconsin; or Black River Blue from the North Hendren Co-op Dairy in Wisconsin. Although I always think this makes more than I think I'll need for four people, somehow it all disappears. If you spread the chips on a baking sheet and warm them in a 200°F oven for 15 minutes before serving, they'll disappear even faster.

Char-Grilled Onion and Blue Cheese Dip

1 cup Char-Grilled Onions (page 12), finely chopped

2 ounces blue cheese, crumbled (about ½ cup)

2 cups sour cream

Worcestershire sauce, for seasoning

Freshly ground white pepper

Chips

2 large baking potatoes

2 large sweet potatoes

2 medium beets

Canola oil, for frying

Kosher salt, for sprinkling

SUGGESTED VEGETABLE VARIETIES:
Irish Cobbler or Norcross potatoes, golden or Detroit Dark Red beets, Beauregard or Jewel sweet potatoes

1 For the dip, combine all the ingredients together in a medium bowl, cover, and chill until ready to serve.

2 For the chips, slice the vegetables paper-thin using a sharp knife or a mandoline and pat dry with paper towels. Heat the oil, to a depth of 4 inches, in a deep pan, electric skillet, or deep fryer until the oil reaches 350°F on a candy thermometer. Fry the chips in batches until they turn golden brown, 2 to 3 minutes, then remove with a slotted spoon and transfer to paper towels to drain. Sprinkle with salt. When cool, serve right away or store in an airtight container for up to 2 days.

SALTY. CRUNCHY. WAVY. MUNCHY.

In 1853, potato chips were created in Saratoga Springs, New York, and aptly dubbed "Saratoga Chips." By 1895, William Tappendon sold ready-made potato chips to stores in Cleveland, Ohio, converting his barn into a potato chip factory. Today, the Heartland has taken a big bite of the potato chip market. In Ohio alone, there are ten companies producing kettle-cooked potato chips, many of them mom-and-pop operations dating to the early 1900s (see Resources, page 266, for more information).

BETTER MADE POTATO CHIPS; DETROIT, MICHIGAN—Founded in 1930, this potato chip company now goes through 40 million pounds of potatoes a year to keep up with the cravings of the locals.

DE-LISH-US POTATO CHIPS; MILWAUKEE, WISCONSIN—The company began with a popcorn wagon during the Depression, but it is now famous for its Golden Potato Chips, made from regional Snowden potatoes.

MARCELLED ORIGINAL CHIPS; TIFFIN, OHIO—In 1920, Fred and Ethel Ballreich started cooking wavy potato chips in a copper kettle heated with wood scraps—in their garage! Made from Snowden, Atlanta, and Norchip potatoes grown in North Dakota, these wavy chips are often winners with celebrity taste panels—and northern Ohio snackers.

MIKE-SELL'S POTATO CHIPS; DAYTON, OHIO—Founded by Daniel Mikesell in 1910, Mike-sell's touts that it's the oldest potato chip company in the United States. Fried in peanut oil, the chips have a roasty-toasty flavor.

STERZING'S POTATO CHIPS; BURLINGTON, IOWA—Barney Sterzing started the business in 1933, and his potato chips are still made with only three ingredients: potatoes, oil, and salt.

BREWPUB CHEESE AND CHARCUTERIE ON A PLANK SERVES 8

Long known for oven-planked whitefish, Great Lakes–area chefs are taking planking in new directions. The Stonefly Brewing Company in Milwaukee, Wisconsin, offers an oven-planked appetizer of cheddar, pepper Jack, and gouda cheeses with deli meats like mortadella and prosciutto. I've taken this concept outdoors to give it yet another spin. Try this recipe first, and then use it as a blueprint and go with small wedges of Heartland cheeses and thin slices of charcuterie that *you* like. Shingle small slices of deli meats like coppa or salami; roll larger cuts like prosciutto into cigars. The more surface of the meat or cheese that touches the plank, the more aromatic wood flavor you will get in the food. I also like to add a handful (½ cup) of mesquite, hickory, or oak wood chips to the coals or to the smoker box of the gas grill for even more wood flavor. If you like, brush slices of country bread with olive oil and grill on the hot side of the grill before you plank, and then serve the grilled bread with the planked appetizer for a rustic—and easy—way to entertain. To oven-plank instead, preheat the oven to 400°F and oven-plank for 20 to 25 minutes.

1 (6-ounce) wedge blue cheese, such as Maytag Blue or Roth Kase's Buttermilk Blue

1 (6-ounce) wedge fontina cheese

1 (6-ounce) wedge Gouda cheese

16 slices (about 8 ounces) coppa

Crusty bread or crisp crackers, for serving

SUGGESTED PLANK:
2 cedar grilling planks or 1 baking plank, soaked in water for at least 1 hour

1 Prepare an indirect fire in your grill, with a hot fire on one side and no fire on the other.

2 Arrange the cheeses and meats on the plank(s).

3 If you are using wood chips, scatter them on the charcoal, or place them in a smoker box or an aluminum foil packet poked with holes near a gas burner. When you see the first wisps of smoke, place the plank(s) on the indirect side of the grill and close the lid. Cook for 15 to 20 minutes, or until the cheese is burnished and aromatic and has started to melt slightly. Serve right on the plank with bread alongside.

BEER HERE

Heartland brewing companies turn regional grains into pure liquid gold. Here are a few favorites (see Resources, page 266, for more information).

BOULEVARD BREWING COMPANY; KANSAS CITY, MISSOURI— Along with their Boulevard Wheat, Pale Ale, and Boulevard Pilsner, this local brewery also produces seasonal brews such as Boss Tom's Golden Bock and Nut Cracker Ale.

CAPITAL BREWERY; MIDDLETON, WISCONSIN—Sip a Supper Club Lager in their beer garden. As they say with classic Midwestern understatement, "Not bad."

HINTERLAND BREWERY; GREEN BAY AND MILWAUKEE, WISCONSIN—Cheeseheads flock to Hinterland pubs to knock down a Packerland Pilsner or two before hitting the "frozen tundra" of Lambeau Field.

NEW GLARUS BREWING COMPANY; NEW GLARUS, WISCONSIN— How can you resist a beer named Road Slush Oatmeal Stout? Or their Unplugged Cherry Stout made with Wisconsin Montmorency cherries?

THREE FLOYDS BREWING COMPANY; MUNSTER, INDIANA—A father and two sons (all with the surname Floyd) brew edgy Alpha King Pale Ale, Dark Lord Stout, and Gumballhead Wheat Beer.

GOOSE ISLAND; CHICAGO, ILLINOIS—Taking some of their names from the Chicago city map—Green Line Pale Ale and 312 Urban Wheat Ale—craft brews from the pioneering brewery have a devoted following.

BRANDING IRON BEEF WITH SMOKED TOMATO DRIZZLE **SERVES 8**

Kansas is, literally, "home on the range"—at least it was to Brewster Higley, the Smith County settler who wrote the song there in 1871. Today, there are still deer and even a few antelope, but mainly beef cattle in the Flint Hills and the western prairie. To make your taste buds sing, get your outdoor grill a-smokin' so you can rustle up this easy version of beef carpaccio. The beef gets a little tasty char around the outside, is very rare inside, and has a smoky sauce to finish. You can make the sauce and grill the beef a day ahead and then assemble the thin slices a few hours before your guests arrive. Keep them chilled until you're ready to serve.

Smoked Tomato Drizzle

1 cup mayonnaise

1 tablespoon smoked tomato puree (see page 16)

¼ cup chipotle hot sauce

Beef

1 pound boneless eye of round, top loin, or beef tenderloin

Olive oil, for brushing

Coarse kosher or sea salt and cracked black pepper

Drained capers, for garnish

Baby arugula, for garnish

1 For the drizzle, whisk together the mayonnaise, tomato puree, and hot sauce in a small bowl until smooth. Transfer to a plastic squeeze bottle and refrigerate.

2 Prepare a hot fire in your grill and place a cast-iron skillet or griddle on the grill grate to heat for 20 to 30 minutes.

3 Brush the beef with olive oil and season with salt and pepper. When the skillet is very hot, sear the beef on all sides until blackened, 1 to 2 minutes per side.

4 Let the beef rest until it is at room temperature. Cover with plastic wrap. To serve the same day, place it in the freezer for 30 minutes to firm up. To serve the next day, store in the refrigerator, then in the freezer for 30 minutes before serving. Chill the serving plates.

5 Using a mandoline or a very sharp knife, cut the beef into paper-thin slices and arrange on the chilled plates. Drizzle the sauce on each plate in a crosshatch pattern and scatter the capers and arugula over the top. Serve immediately.

SMOKED TROUT PÂTÉ WITH DILL AND LEMON

MAKES ABOUT ⅔ CUP

If you don't completely gorge yourself on all the delicious Apple-Smoked Trout (page 177), you can turn the leftovers into this delicious appetizer spread. This pâté can also be made with any tender type of hot-smoked fish, such as salmon, lake trout, chubs, or whitefish.

4 ounces smoked trout fillet

½ cup (1 stick) unsalted butter, cubed, softened

1 tablespoon chopped fresh dill, plus more for garnish

1 teaspoon freshly grated lemon zest

Fresh apple slices, sesame crackers, French bread, or pumpernickel rye bread, for serving

1 Remove any stray skin or bones from the trout fillet. Flake the fillet into the work bowl of a food processor. Add the butter, dill, and lemon zest and puree.

2 Serve the pâté in a crock or bowl, garnished with more dill and surrounded by its accompaniments.

GREAT LAKES SMOKEHOUSES
Scandinavians brought the practice of smoking lake fish to the Great Lakes, and they continue the savory tradition, usually over maple, hickory, or oak wood. Avid fishermen often convert an old refrigerator to smoke their catch in the backyard. See Resources, page 266.

CARLSON'S; LELAND, MICHIGAN—Over a century ago, Nels Carlson emigrated from Norway to the Upper Peninsula of Michigan to ply the waters of Lake Michigan. His family continues the business, offering maple-smoked lake fish.

JOHN CROSS FISHERIES; CHARLEVOIX, MICHIGAN—June Cross runs the family business, selling fresh whitefish and whitefish smoked over maple.

PORT CITY SMOKEHOUSE; FRANKFORT, MICHIGAN—fresh lake perch, trout, and whitefish and these fishes smoked over local maple wood.

CHARLIE'S SMOKEHOUSE; ELLISON BAY, WISCONSIN—chubs, trout, and whitefish smoked over local maple wood.

LA QUERCIA

"If salami is the blog of cured meats, then prosciutto is the great novel," writes Sarah Mulke in *The New York Times*. And if grocery store prosciutto is a cheap paperback, then La Quercia prosciutto is a hardback first edition, signed by the author.

That great prosciutto should come from Norwalk, Iowa, shouldn't really surprise us. After all, the raw materials are there in abundance—hogs that feed on corn and soybeans. It just took a while for the food artisan to show up.

"For a while, Iowa went away from making food for people to making food for animals or food for cars—ethanol," says Herb Eckhouse, co-owner of La Quercia with wife Kathy. When heritage pork came back in Iowa, "there was a great improvement in the quality of pork available to people," he says. And that made the lightbulb go off.

"There was already wine, cheese, bread, and chocolate" on the Midwest artisan scene, the couple thought. "We felt that cured meats could be the next step in American artisanal foods," says Herb.

Eckhouse, a Harvard grad, and Kathy, who grew up in Berkeley, California, had lived in Italy for a while, when Herb was an executive with Iowa-based Pioneer Seed. Both love good food and were intrigued with prosciutto. Their stay in Parma "evolved our way of eating," says Herb, to "ingredient-centered food."

When they returned to Iowa, they started experimenting with making "garage prosciutto," he laughs, using various cures and breeds of heritage pork, including Red Wattle, Duroc, and Tamworth. The couple eventually chose the Berkshire breed, raised by Eden Farms in State Center, and a Berkshire cross (with Chester White), which Becker Lane Farm in nearby Dyersville raises organically for them. Why Berkshire? "The enzymes that naturally occur in the meat produce the best taste and texture," Herb surmises. Kathy adds, "We do know that Berkshire meat is different from other breeds because the muscle fibers are shorter and there is more intramuscular fat (marbling)—these flavors create a more succulent and silky prosciutto."

To simulate traditional Italian prosciutto-making methods, which begin after hogs are killed in autumn, the rear legs spend some time hanging in a "winter" environment of 45°F and below, by which time the meat has lost 20 percent of its volume or moisture. Then, the pork moves onto more springtime-like temperatures before ending up in a "summer" room in La Quercia's spotless environment. "You have to control the variables of humidity and temperature. It's all happening deep inside the meat and you can only surmise what's going on," says Herb.

La Quercia also makes lardo, organic pork fat flavored with bay leaf, nutmeg, and coriander—a flavoring combination that Kathy developed. Kathy also renders lard to make wonderful pie crusts.

La Quercia, meaning "the oak" in Italian, is a fitting name for the company, as both Parma and the Des Moines area are situated on former oak savannahs. The Eckhouses also refer to the oak in their "Acorn Edition" Berkshire-cross subscription pork, in which subscribers receive "a pig's worth of participation," with fresh and frozen pork in the late fall and then prosciutto, guanciale, pancetta, and other cured meats later in the year. La Quercia is also experimenting with prosciutto crumbles or off cuts from sliced prosciutto, which are delicious on sandwiches or flatbreads or in eggs, as well as dry-cured Pancetta Americana—the most luscious American-style bacon you've ever tasted.

FOUR SEASONS FLATBREAD **EACH FLATBREAD SERVES 12**

With this master recipe, you can go through the seasons knowing you have at least one fabulous appetizer that looks as great as it tastes. Tangy Radish Rye Flatbread wakes up winter-dulled taste buds with snappy flavors and a pattern that looks midcentury modern. Make the most of your heirloom tomato harvest with a summer flatbread, and go all out for Oktoberfest smoked sausage, hearty cheese, and mustard—perfect with a craft beer. Celebrate the holiday season with a prosciutto and arugula flatbread that's ideal for a buffet or open house.

Tangy Radish Rye Flatbread

½ recipe prepared No-Knead Sour Caraway Rye Dough (page 96)

6 to 8 ounces fresh herb cheese, such as Green Dirt Farm Nettle, Arrowhead Herb from Blue Jacket Dairy, or Boursin

1 large and 1 small radish, trimmed and very thinly sliced

1 bunch chives, cut into 1-inch lengths or 2 cups sugar snap peas, thinly sliced

Coarse kosher or sea salt

1 Preheat the oven to 450°F. Place about 2 cups of hot water in a broiler pan on the lower rack. Line a baking sheet with parchment paper.

2 With wet hands, pat the dough into a 16 by 10-inch oval on the prepared baking sheet.

3 Bake for 20 to 22 minutes, or until risen, browned, and firm to the touch. Let cool on the baking sheet.

4 Spread the cheese over the flatbread. Arrange large and small circles of radish in a decorative pattern on top of the cheese. Arrange the chives on the diagonal over the radishes. Sprinkle with coarse salt. To serve, cut into slices.

Heirloom Tomato and Basil Flatbread

½ batch No-Knead Clover Honey Dough (page 80)

½ cup prepared basil pesto

12 fresh basil leaves

2 cups chopped heirloom or other fresh tomatoes (especially golden or orange)

1 cup grated Parmesan cheese (about 4 ounces)

2 tablespoons olive oil

1 Preheat the oven to 450°F. Place about 2 cups of hot water in a broiler pan on the lower rack. Line a baking sheet with parchment paper.

2 With wet hands, pat the dough into a 16 by 10-inch oval on the prepared baking sheet. Spread the dough with the pesto, then arrange the basil leaves and tomatoes on top. Sprinkle with the Parmesan and drizzle with the oil.

3 Bake for 20 to 22 minutes, or until risen, browned, and firm to the touch. Let cool on the baking sheet. To serve, cut into slices.

Continued on page 118

Continued from page 116

Sausage and Cheese Flatbread

½ batch No-Knead Sour Caraway Rye Dough (page 96)

¼ cup Dijon or whole-grain mustard

1 pound smoked sausage links, cooked and cut into ½-inch slices

2 cups shredded savoy cabbage

2 cups grated Gruyère or cave-aged Swiss cheese

1 Preheat the oven to 450°F. Place about 2 cups of hot water in a broiler pan on the lower rack. Line a baking sheet with parchment paper.

2 With wet hands, pat the dough into a 10 by 16-inch oval on the prepared baking sheet. Spread the mustard over the dough. Arrange the sausage, then the cabbage on the dough. Sprinkle with the cheese.

3 Bake for 20 to 22 minutes, or until risen, browned, and firm to the touch. Let cool on the baking sheet. To serve, cut into slices.

Winter Prosciutto and Arugula Flatbread

½ batch No-Knead Clover Honey Dough (page 80)

2 tablespoons olive oil

8 slices prosciutto

2 cups arugula

8 ounces goat cheese, crumbled

1 Preheat the oven to 450°F. Place about 2 cups of hot water in a broiler pan on the lower rack. Line a baking sheet with parchment paper.

2 With wet hands, pat the dough into a 16 by 10-inch oval on the prepared baking sheet. Brush the olive oil over the flatbread.

3 Bake for 20 to 22 minutes, or until risen, browned, and firm to the touch. Let cool on the baking sheet.

4 Arrange the prosciutto and arugula on top of the flatbread, then top with the goat cheese. To serve, cut into slices.

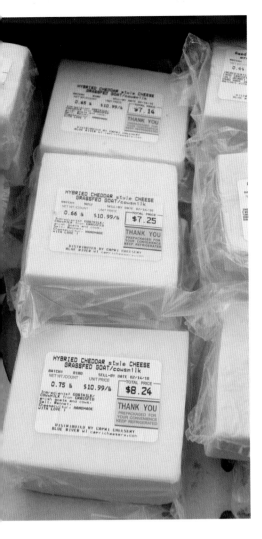

CAPRIOLE

It's quiet here in the rolling, wooded limestone bluff country of southern Indiana, rising above the Ohio River Valley. For cheese pioneer Judith Schad, each day means milking her herd of floppy-eared goats, and each week means making hundreds of pounds of the fresh and aged chèvre for which she is famous.

"I almost didn't become a cheesemaker," she says with a laugh. "In the late 1970s, I was studying for my doctorate in Renaissance literature. But my husband, Larry, and I wanted to raise our children in a more country lifestyle, so when we moved here, I put off doing my dissertation." She and Larry also discovered that the land they had bought had originally been in his family. They fashioned a house from two local log cabins, one of which was an old stagecoach station with a dogtrot. Locally made country antiques of bird's-eye maple, pine, and poplar, along with vases filled with cottage garden flowers, give the rustic interior a sophisticated polish—much the same thing that Schad does with her cheeses. Today, their farm is set like a triangle, with the log cabin house and herb garden across from the dairy and the goat barns.

A sense of humor is essential in her life, as well as an intuitive and flexible sensibility. "Goats are intelligent, inquisitive, and loving creatures, and you have to respond to them," says Judith. "It's the same thing with the curd. Curds can be really funny. They have their own agenda. You have to pay attention to when they're ready, and you have to make the chèvre right then."

Each morning, the goats are milked in the milking stall of the barn. A refrigerated, spotlessly clean stainless-steel holding tank keeps the goats' milk fresh until it's ready for the pasteurizer. Since the pasteurizer holds 400 gallons of milk, it will take several days' worth of milking to fill it. But once filled, the pasteurizer heats the milk to 145°F to kill bacteria. Once pasteurized, the milk flows into a bin to cool slightly, and Schad adds a beaker of rennet to the milk to create the curds. The milk is cooked briefly over low heat and then allowed to rest for an hour while the curds form. Then the curds are cut with a mesh screen, allowed to rest again, and scooped so that the whey drains out before being pressed into molds. After the cheese is drained and brined, it is either packaged fresh for chèvre, or aged for 5 to 9 months in temperature-controlled rooms to make cheeses like Wabash Cannon Ball, Old Kentucky Tomme, and Mont St. Francis.

POPCORN WITH SMOKED GOUDA   SERVES 4 TO 6

Instead of mindless snacking on foods with no nutritional value—or real flavor—why not make a batch of really, really good popcorn the old-fashioned way? You can find ready-to-pop unflavored popcorn in bags or jars. Of the five types of corn—flint for cornmeal, dent for hominy, sweet for eating fresh, pod, and popcorn—only popcorn dramatically pops. That's because it contains an inner starchy core that is moist; when the popcorn is heated, this moisture expands and explodes out of the hard surface of the kernel. North American Indians have been eating popcorn for thousands of years, and the habit has caught on with all Americans, who eat more popcorn than any other country—about 68 quarts per person per year. Most American popcorn is grown in Indiana, Illinois, and Nebraska. On the Saturday after Labor Day, the Popcorn Festival in Valparaiso, Indiana, salutes America's favorite snack food as well as its popcorn guru, Valparaiso native Orville Redenbacher. Thanks to Redenbacher, most popcorn today is free of "duds" or "spinsters," popcorn lingo for kernels that don't pop.

1 tablespoon canola oil

½ cup popcorn kernels

2 cups finely shredded smoked Gouda cheese

Garlic, celery, or onion salt

1   In a large saucepan with a handle and a lid, heat the oil over medium-high heat. Add the popcorn, cover the pan and hold the lid with one hand, and start shaking the pot with the other. Cook, shaking, until you hear the first popcorn kernel pop. Continue cooking and shaking until several seconds go by without a pop.

2   Remove from the heat and stir in the cheese until well blended. Add salt to taste, tossing well to blend. Transfer to a large bowl and dig in.

A SIGN FROM A SQUASH

When my sister and I were growing up in Reading, Ohio, we loved our copy of *The Golden Book of Nursery Tales*, now quite tattered. As I was writing this book, I reread the Carl Sandburg story about the popcorn-farming Huckabuck family: Jonas Jonas the father, Mama Mama, and Pony Pony the daughter. They each had two names because "If you call me by my first name Jonas and I don't hear you, then when you call me by my second name Jonas maybe I will," explains Jonas Jonas in the story.

When Pony Pony was getting ready to bake her first squash pie, she opened a squash with gold spots and found a silver shoe buckle inside. "It means our luck is going to change," said Mama Mama. And it did. A fire started in the night and popped all the popcorn they had "in the barns, cribs, sheds, shacks, cracks, and corners where the popcorn harvest was kept." Popcorn was everywhere.

The Huckabucks moved to Oscaloosa, Iowa, to get away from the flood of popcorn and said they'd come back to Nebraska when they got a sign and a signal.

Years went by in different places, but no signal. Finally, the Huckabucks were in Elgin, Illinois, where Jonas Jonas was a "watchman in a watch factory watching the watches." Pony Pony again made a squash pie from a squash with gold spots and found another silver shoe buckle inside—the mate to the one she already had. A sign!

So, the Huckabucks returned to Nebraska—not to farm popcorn anymore, but everything else, including rutabagas. And Pony Pony realized an important thing: "Squashes make your luck change good to bad and bad to good."

GRILLED VEGETABLE BUNDLES **SERVES 8**

When you want a fair weather appetizer that is not just mindless eating, grilled vegetable-wrapped bundles are just the ticket. These finger-food or knife-and-fork nibbles are easy to assemble, easy to grill, and delicious to eat. Judith Schad of Capriole in Greenville, Indiana, makes hers with Capriole goat cheese (what else?) wrapped in eggplant. Sanford D'Amato, chef-owner of Sanford in Milwaukee, Wisconsin, wraps Swiss chard from the West Allis farmer's market around smoked mozzarella and prosciutto, and grills and serves it with anchovy vinaigrette. The blueprint is this: You need something for a wrapper, something for an oozy filling, and something for big flavor. Mix and match at will. You just might decide to make these your meal and skip the steak.

Eggplant Bundles

3 to 4 small Japanese eggplants (about 6 inches long), ends trimmed and cut lengthwise into ½-inch-thick slices

10 ounces fresh goat cheese, cut into 8 slices

2 medium ripe tomatoes, cut into 8 slices

1 bunch Swiss chard, tough stems trimmed

8 (½-inch-thick) slices fresh or smoked mozzarella cheese, such as BelGioioso

4 slices prosciutto, halved lengthwise

Olive oil, for brushing

SUGGESTED VEGETABLE VARIETIES:
Ruby or rainbow chard, Diamond eggplant, Nebraska Wedding or Kellogg's Breakfast tomatoes

Anchovy Vinaigrette

2 tablespoons freshly squeezed lemon juice

2 teaspoons anchovy paste

1 teaspoon Dijon mustard

2 cloves garlic, minced

¼ teaspoon red pepper flakes

½ cup olive oil

Fine kosher salt and freshly ground black pepper

1 Prepare a medium-hot fire in your grill.

2 For the eggplant bundles, lay an eggplant slice on a clean, flat surface. Place a round of goat cheese and a slice of tomato in the middle and wrap with the eggplant, securing the bundle with toothpicks or small skewers. For the chard bundles, place a chard leaf on a clean, flat surface. Wrap a round of mozzarella with the prosciutto, then place in the middle of the leaf and fold in the sides, then the ends. Secure the bundle with toothpicks or small skewers. Repeat with the remaining ingredients. Brush the bundles with olive oil on all sides.

3 For the vinaigrette, whisk all the ingredients together in a small bowl.

4 Grill the bundles for 3 to 4 minutes per side, or until you have good grill marks and the cheese has softened and is beginning to ooze. Serve a bundle of each variety on each plate, drizzled with vinaigrette.

FARM GIRL COSMO SERVES 4

How you gonna keep 'em down on the farm after they've been to the Twin Cities and sipped Cosmopolitans, *Sex in the City* style? Maybe by serving a batch of these drinks, whose secret ingredient is a rosy syrup made from rhubarb, long a reliable staple of the farm wife's garden. Who knew that old-fashioned pie plant could be so hip? My thanks to daughter Sarah for creating this recipe. The cosmopolitan is thought to have been created by Neal Murray at the Cork & Cleaver steakhouse in 1975 Minneapolis, from whence it traveled to the fern bars of San Francisco and on to bigger fame after that. For a wonderful color contrast in the garnish, choose a stalk of rhubarb with a greenish cast.

¾ cup vodka

1 cup Rosy Rhubarb Syrup (page 34)

¼ cup freshly squeezed lime juice

1 teaspoon orange extract

Thin slices of lime for lime twists, for garnish

Combine the vodka, syrup, lime juice, and orange extract in a medium pitcher or cocktail shaker. Add ice and stir well. Strain or pour into 4 vintage jelly glasses. Garnish each drink with a lime twist.

GARDEN GIMLET SERVES 4

From garden to glass, this deliciously refreshing drink is just the thing on a hot day. In fact, it's so good that the Garden Gimlet could well become your household's signature drink. To be really authentic, use a Midwestern-distilled gin, such as Rehorst from Milwaukee, Wisconsin.

¾ cup gin

1 cup Fresh Herb Syrup (page 33)

½ cup freshly squeezed lime juice

8 sprigs basil

Combine the gin, syrup, and lime juice in a pitcher or cocktail shaker and stir well. Fill 4 highball glasses with ice, add a basil sprig to each, and muddle. Pour one-quarter of the gimlet mixture into each glass. Stir and serve each drink garnished with a basil sprig.

◀ Clockwise: Garden Gimlet, Farm Girl Cosmo, Summer Sangria

SIMPLE SIPS
Beat the heat with one of these wheat beers. If these beers are not available in your area, see if your local distributor can get them for you.

WHEACH—a peachy wheat beer from O'Fallon Brewery in O'Fallon, Missouri. Serve with a slice of fresh peach.

RASPBERRY WHEAT—from Free State Brewing Company in Lawrence, Kansas. Serve over ice with a few fresh raspberries.

BLACKBERRY WHEAT—from Town Hall Brewing Company in Minneapolis, Minnesota. Serve with a swizzle stick of lemon slices and blackberries.

VODKA IN THE HEARTLAND
While the 1990s brought a resurgence of microbreweries to the Midwest, which use regional grains, recent years have added small-batch craft distilling (see Resources, page 266, for more information).

REHORST VODKA FROM GREAT LAKES DISTILLERY IN MILWAUKEE, WISCONSIN—made from red winter wheat. Tasting notes include a sweet nose with a smooth, silvery texture and hints of roasted wheat.

PRAIRIE ORGANIC VODKA FROM PHILLIPS DISTILLING COMPANY—made from organic corn grown in Benson, Minnesota. Tasting notes include a sweet melon nose with a buttery texture and hints of roasted corn.

GRAND TRAVERSE TRUE NORTH VODKA FROM TRAVERSE CITY, MICHIGAN—made from rye. Tasting notes include a floral and fruity nose with a silken texture and hints of citrus.

DIVINE VODKA FROM ROUND BARN WINERY IN BARODA, MICHIGAN—made mainly from Ugni Blanc "cognac" grapes grown in the Lake Michigan Shore American Viticultural Area. Tasting notes include a floral and fruity nose with a smooth texture and hints of—what else?—grapes.

PORCH SWING LEMONADE SERVES 4 TO 6

Wouldn't it be nice to sit on the porch swing and visit with your neighbors, sipping a homemade lemonade? You really can sit back and relax if you make the syrups a few weeks or days ahead. Squeeze the fresh lemon juice right before you want to serve the drink. Stir it all together in a pitcher or portable container, and serve over ice.

1 cup freshly squeezed lemon juice (from about 7 large lemons)

1½ cups Rosy Rhubarb Syrup (page 34), Fresh Herb Syrup (page 33), or Blackberry-Lavender Syrup (page 32)

1½ cups water

Sugar, for sweetening

Fresh lemon slices, for garnish

Sprigs of lemon balm or rosemary, for garnish

Stir the lemon juice, syrup, water, and sugar together in a large pitcher. Add the lemon slices and herb sprigs. Add more sugar to taste, if desired. Serve cold.

SUMMER SANGRIA **SERVES 8**

Stir up a pitcher on a hot day, and sit back and relax. It's summer! Choose a semi-dry white wine from Heartland wineries and a triple sec made in Cincinnati, Ohio—perhaps Prairie Fumé from Wollersheim Winery in Wisconsin or Vignoles from Sainte Genevieve Winery in Missouri, and De Kuyper triple sec from Ohio.

2 (750-milliliter) bottles semi-dry white wine, chilled

⅔ cup Fresh Herb Syrup (page 33)

⅔ cup triple sec

1 liter sparkling water

½ cup freshly squeezed lime juice

2 cups fresh fruits in season (such as peach slices, strawberries, blackberries, blueberries, or gooseberries)

8 sprigs lemon balm or basil, for garnish

Combine the wine, syrup, triple sec, sparkling water, and lime juice over ice in a large pitcher. Add some of the fruit to the pitcher, and portion the rest among 8 glasses. Pour in the sangria, then garnish each glass with a sprig of lemon balm.

BACON BLOODY MARY **SERVES 1**

Bacon Bloody Marys often appear on Chicago bar menus. Because Bloody Marys are a classic brunch cocktail, this fusion makes perfect sense. If you want to evoke Heartland style, serve this chilled in a canning jar.

Bacon Swizzle Stick

1 slice bacon

1 yellow pear or red cherry tomato

Bloody Mary

2 tablespoons Bacon-Infused Vodka (page 37)

1 cup tomato juice (home-canned, if possible), chilled

1 teaspoon Worcestershire sauce

1 teaspoon freshly squeezed lemon juice

½ teaspoon chipotle hot sauce

¼ teaspoon hickory liquid smoke

¼ teaspoon celery salt

1 sprig basil, for garnish

1 For the swizzle stick, cut the bacon in half lengthwise and roll each piece into a spiral. Thread the spirals onto a wooden swizzle stick or short wooden skewer. Place on a doubled paper towel—lined plate and cover with another doubled paper towel. Microwave on high power for 2 minutes, or until the bacon curls are brown and crisp. Thread a tomato onto the skewer.

2 For the drink, stir together the vodka, tomato juice, Worcestershire, lemon juice, hot sauce, liquid smoke, and celery salt in a small pitcher or cocktail shaker. Serve straight up or on the rocks in a canning jar, garnished with the swizzle stick and basil sprig.

"IT WAS NO ORDINARY DAY when the wild ground gave birth to the first tame crop," thinks early Ohio settler Sayward Luckett Wheeler to herself in *The Trees*, by Conrad Richter. "The wind stood off. The clouds hung like summer. The tender sky came right down in the clearing, softening everything with a veil finer than spider skeins. A little ways there in the woods, Sayward knew the air still hung chill and dim. But here in the clearing, the four sides of the forest held summer in like the banks of a pond. Flies and beetles hummed in the bright warmth. The soil breathed up a sweet rank smell of sprouting and growing. And here and yonder the first tiny green shoots of the baby corn had pushed overnight through the black ground. You could just make out the faint, mortal young rows bending around the stumps."

This same story repeated itself as settlers moved westward from Ohio to Kansas and Nebraska, breaking up virgin soil and planting crops. In *Song of the Lark*, Willa Cather writes about a European immigrant's desire to have familiar plants in her Heartland garden. "The garden looked like a relief-map now, and gave no indication of what it would be in August; such a jungle! Pole beans and potatoes and corn and leeks and kale and red cabbage—there would even be vegetables for which there is no American name. Mrs. Kohler was always getting by mail packages of seeds from Freeport [Illinois] and from the old country."

The taste of a place often comes from what is gathered from the wild or grown in the garden. When I moved from Ohio to Kansas, I bemoaned the lack of the Silver Queen corn that I had loved, now that I lived in a drier climate not conducive to it. Others might cite Bibb or Limestone lettuce from Kentuckiana, the rolling terrain of southern Indiana that goes across the Ohio River into Kentucky. People in the Toledo, Ohio, area swear that their tomatoes taste best because they're grown on former black swampland. Michiganders know that there's nothing to beat a Harlayne apricot or sour cherry from the eastern shore of Lake Michigan.

Shoppers at the Dane County Farmer's Market in Madison, Wisconsin, or diners who attend farm dinners at Prairie Star Farm & Creamery in Champaign, Illinois, or Green Dirt Farm in Weston, Missouri, know exactly what garden to table tastes like, and they know there's nothing finer.

Capture the taste of the Midwestern garden at its peak in dishes like New Potato and Bitter Greens Salad (page 140) in spring, Prairie Panzanella (page 147) when summer tomatoes are at their peak, Minnesota Wild Rice Soup (page 163) or Roasted Butternut Squash Soup with Smoked Garlic Custard (page 167) in the fall, and Badlands Bison Chili (page 164) when the garden is but a dream in winter.

All the suggested fruit and vegetable varieties in this chapter are from the Seed Savers Exchange catalog in Decorah, Iowa (see Resources, page 266).

DANE COUNTY FARMER'S MARKET

The largest farmer's market in the country is neither in New York nor in California. It's on the town square, surrounded on either side by lakes, on the isthmus that is Madison, Wisconsin.

Since 1972, the market has run from 6 a.m. to 2 p.m. every Saturday, from mid-April to early November. Regular shoppers know that if you don't get there early—like dawn—you'll be disappointed as the 300 vendors sell out or you wait in lines six or seven people deep until it's your turn. Local chefs like Tori Miller of L'Etoile—who totes his purchases back to the restaurant in a kid's red wagon—look to see what's fresh or new, then create dishes around those ingredients. L'Etoile's founder and early local food champion, Odessa Piper, was also instrumental in founding the market.

All products must be Wisconsin-grown or -produced: heritage beef, pork, and chicken; farmstead cheeses; baked goods; morels and hickory nuts.

From spring greens and asparagus to summer vegetables and berries, and then on to autumn apples and wild mushrooms and winter root vegetables like celeriac and rutabaga—and always, rhubarb—there's something good goin' on.

"The Northern Spring proves worthy of our patience. In the beech/maple forests the wild leeks rise from matted leaves in lush green patches redolent of shallots. Then, the black morels form magically before our eyes like spectacular sculptures spawned of wood smoke and wild yeast. Verdant creeks come aglow with watercress and mint: trout lilies and then immaculate trilliums, with their languid grace, hypnotize everywhere. Finally, in the hilly orchards of the Fruitlands, above the cold blue lakes, the crystal air sings once again with honey bees, pollen and the reflected light of a million blossoms."

—JUSTIN RASHID, IN THE AMERICAN SPOON FOODS CATALOG

ORZO SALAD WITH CUCUMBER AND FETA **SERVES 4 TO 6**

Made from durum wheat grown in the Dakotas, teardrop-shaped orzo pasta is great to use in salads. With cool cucumber from the garden and tangy feta made in Wisconsin or Ohio, this salad is a delicious accompaniment to fish, chicken, beef, or pork—or it's just as good all by itself.

8 ounces orzo

1 bunch scallions, chopped

1 medium cucumber, diced

8 ounces feta or fresh goat cheese, crumbled (about 1 cup)

½ cup chopped, pitted kalamata olives

⅓ cup canola oil

⅓ cup freshly squeezed lemon juice

2 cloves garlic, minced

**2 tablespoons fresh dill, or
2 teaspoons dried dill**

¼ teaspoon dried oregano

Salt and freshly ground black pepper

**SUGGESTED CUCUMBER VARIETIES:
Bushy, a compact Russian cucumber, or
Japanese Climbing, which takes advantage
of vertical space**

1 Cook the orzo according to the package directions and let cool.

2 In a large bowl, combine the orzo, scallions, cucumber, feta, and olives. In a small bowl, whisk together the oil, lemon juice, garlic, dill, oregano, and pepper. Pour the dressing over the orzo and toss to blend. Cover and refrigerate until ready to serve.

NEW POTATO AND BITTER GREENS SALAD **SERVES 4**

If you think all potato salad is boring, then this recipe will change your mind. Hearty enough to be a main course but portable enough to take to a picnic, this salad is sure to please. Use any somewhat sturdy, bitter green, such as dandelion, escarole, Belgian endive, arugula, or radicchio—all of which appreciate the cool spring and autumn of the Heartland climate. The slight sweetness of the vinaigrette pulls the mellow potatoes, bitter greens, and smoky bacon flavors together.

1 pound baby or new potatoes

1 cup diced, thick-sliced smoked bacon or pancetta

3 small heads frisée or curly endive, torn into thin pieces

Cider Honey Vinaigrette

¼ cup cider vinegar

2 tablespoons clover honey

2 tablespoons finely minced shallot

2 teaspoons Dijon mustard

1 tablespoon rendered bacon or pancetta fat

½ cup canola oil

Fine kosher or sea salt and freshly ground black pepper

SUGGESTED VEGETABLE VARIETIES: Carola, Kerr's Pink, or All Red potatoes; Batavian Full Heart greens

1 Place the potatoes in a saucepan with enough water to cover. Bring to a boil and cook until tender when pierced with a knife, 12 to 15 minutes. Drain and rinse under cool water. Let cool to room temperature, then slice.

2 Cook the bacon or pancetta over medium-high heat in a large skillet until brown and crisp. Transfer to paper towels to drain. Reserve the fat in the pan.

3 In a large bowl, combine the potato slices, bacon, and greens. In a jar with a lid, combine the vinaigrette ingredients (including some of the rendered bacon fat from the pan), secure the lid, and shake to blend. Taste for seasoning and adjust if necessary. Pour the vinaigrette over the potato salad and toss to blend.

CANOLA
Behind every bottle of canola oil, there's a story.

Picture July in North Dakota, where brilliant yellow fields of blooming canola, a variety of rapeseed, blaze under a blue, blue sky. Many traditional wheat-growing farms are now including a rotation of canola, as health-conscious consumers buy more and more heart-healthy oil pressed from the ripe kernels.

Farmers plant canola in firm, moist soil in late April to early May, and then harvest it in August through early September. At harvest, farmers cut the tops of the canola plants when the seed heads are just starting to turn golden. If they cut too early, not enough seed heads will mature. If farmers wait too long, the seed heads will shatter and spill the seeds on the ground.

The cut heads of canola will then ripen for 10 to 14 days in windrows on the ground. Then the combine picks up the windrows, the seeds taken into the storage chamber and the chaff blown out on the field. The seeds continue to dry until they're crushed into oil at a canola plant.

WILD ABOUT RICE
Wild rice is neither rice nor necessarily wild. Wild rice—really an aquatic grass—is the only grain native to North America and was a staple food of the Sioux and Chippewa. True wild rice still grows in the lakes and rivers of Minnesota, upper Michigan, northern Wisconsin, and southern Canada. The Ojibwe called it manoomin or the good berry. French voyagers called it folle avoine or crazy oats.

Near Tower, Minnesota, Chippewa tribes still harvest rice from murky-bottomed Big Rice Lake and Lost Lake. With two people to a canoe, one person paddles to the plants and the other flails the ripened grains from the stalks with a cedar stick, and the grains fall into the canoe. When they get to shore, the harvesters spread the rice out on a tarp to dry or parch it over an open fire. Then it's winnowed, husked, and packaged.

Today, wild rice is also grown in artificial paddies, and only connoisseurs can tell the difference. Paddy development provides excellent breeding grounds and habitat for waterfowl and other wildlife.

Wild rice is a Midwestern pantry staple and can be stored indefinitely in tightly sealed containers. When it's cooked, 1 cup of raw wild rice makes 3 to 4 cups cooked wild rice. Because the cooking process takes about 45 minutes, many cooks keep frozen cooked wild rice in the freezer as a convenience food.

LOADED BAKED POTATO SALAD SERVES 8 TO 12

At a potluck dinner or a big family gathering, this dish never disappoints. Don't expect any leftovers. With sour cream and cheddar from Wisconsin, your favorite Heartland bacon, and scallions from the garden, this is an easy meal in itself.

5 pounds red potatoes

16 ounces sour cream

1 cup mayonnaise

2 teaspoons salt

1 teaspoon freshly ground black pepper

1 bunch scallions or baby leeks, trimmed and sliced

6 slices smoked bacon, cooked until crisp and crumbled

2 cups shredded mild cheddar cheese

SUGGESTED VEGETABLE VARIETIES:
German Butterball potato, baby Blue Solaise leeks

1   Preheat the oven to 350°F. Prick the potatoes all over with a fork and bake until tender, about 45 minutes. Let cool slightly, then slice as thinly as possible.

2   In a large bowl, whisk the sour cream, mayonnaise, salt, and pepper together until smooth. Gently stir in the potato slices, then the scallions, bacon, and cheese. Stir until well combined. Serve warm or chilled.

FEELING BLUE?
Heartlanders love their blue cheese, popular since the 1930s, when it was aged in stone wine cellars vacant because of Prohibition in Nauvoo, Illinois, right on the Mississippi River.

AMABLU; FARIBAULT, MINNESOTA—aged in caves carved out of glacial St. Peter sandstone.

CASTLE ROCK ORGANIC FARMS "SMOKEY BLUE"; OSSEO, WISCONSIN—hickory smoked.

MAYTAG; NEWTON, IOWA—from Holstein cows since 1941.

ROTH KASE BUTTERMILK BLUE; MONROE, WISCONSIN—creamy blue with tangy buttermilk.

SALEMVILLE AMISH BLUE AND AMISH GORGONZOLA; CAMBRIA, WISCONSIN—from cows milked by hand twice a day by eighty-five Amish families.

GRILLED PEAR SALAD WITH BLUE CHEESE AND HONEY **SERVES 8**

On the south side of my Kansas home, I have created an edible landscape with twin pear trees, tangled raspberry canes, fragrant roses and lavender, lemon balm, and whatever vegetables I can squeeze in. The Kieffer pears I grow are not good to eat fresh, but they are delicious poached or grilled; any ripe but somewhat firm pear will be fine in this recipe. Sweet pears cozy up to a Midwestern blue cheese like old flames at a high school reunion, made all the sweeter with a drizzle of local honey.

4 ripe but somewhat firm Bartlett or Bosc pears, cut lengthwise

Melted unsalted butter, for brushing

1 cup crumbled creamy blue cheese, such as Maytag, Salemville blue, or Roth Kase gorgonzola (about 8 ounces)

¼ cup canola or olive oil

2 tablespoons cider vinegar

1 teaspoon Dijon mustard

4 cups baby greens

Fine kosher or sea salt and freshly ground black pepper

Clover or wildflower honey, for drizzling

Toasted, chopped hickory nuts or pecans, for garnish

**SUGGESTED PEAR VARIETIES:
Golden Spice, Flemish Beauty, or Luscious**

1 Prepare an indirect fire in your grill, hot on one side and no fire on the other.

2 Use a melon baller to core and scoop out a small cavity in each pear half. Brush both sides of each pear half with melted butter.

3 Place the pears on the direct-heat side of the grill, cut side down, for 2 minutes, or until the fruit has blistered. Transfer to the indirect side and place skin side down. Mound tablespoon-size portions of cheese in the cavity of each pear. Cover and grill until the pears have blistered and the cheese has melted, about 8 minutes.

4 Whisk the oil, vinegar, and mustard together in a bowl large enough for the greens. Lightly toss the greens with the dressing and season to taste with salt and pepper. Divide the dressed greens among salad plates. Place a grilled pear on top of each mound of greens, drizzle with honey, and sprinkle with chopped nuts.

HEARTLAND FENNEL SLAW **SERVES 8**

Along with spring onions, rhubarb, and greens, bulb fennel is the pick of the Heartland garden in late spring. Its mild anise flavor and crunchy texture make it a natural with chicken, fish, or pork. Try this with Smoke-Roasted Pork Shoulder with Sooey Sauce (page 188). Mmmm.

2 fennel bulbs with fronds

1 bunch scallions, trimmed and sliced

3 tablespoons cider vinegar

½ cup mayonnaise

1 tablespoon sugar

2 tablespoons chopped fresh dill

1 teaspoon freshly grated lemon zest

½ teaspoon fine kosher or sea salt

1 teaspoon freshly ground black pepper

SUGGESTED FENNEL VARIETIES: plain green, Smokey Bronze, or Florence

1 Trim the fennel bulbs and cut off the stalks. Cut each bulb into quarters and cut out the core. Thinly slice the fennel bulbs and place in a large bowl with the scallions.

2 In a small bowl, whisk the cider vinegar, mayonnaise, sugar, dill, and lemon zest together. Whisk in the salt and pepper. Adjust the seasonings, if necessary. Pour the dressing over the fennel mixture and toss to blend. The salad will keep, covered, in the refrigerator for up to 3 days.

PRAIRIE PANZANELLA **SERVES 8**

When the garden is in full swing, make this luscious salad—inspired by a dish by Alabama chef Frank Stitt—which goes well with grilled foods of all kinds. Made with Missouri Skillet Cornbread, fresh garden herbs, and just-picked heirloom tomatoes, this could be a meal in itself.

1 red bell pepper

1 yellow bell pepper

3 tablespoons red wine vinegar

2 tablespoons sherry vinegar

Kosher salt and freshly ground black pepper

¾ cup extra virgin olive oil

6 large tomatoes, halved crosswise, seeded, and cut into 1-inch pieces

1 small red onion, quartered lengthwise and thinly sliced crosswise

½ cup kalamata olives, pitted and halved

2 small cucumbers, peeled, halved lengthwise, seeded, and cut crosswise into ¼-inch-thick slices

½ cup loosely packed fresh basil leaves

½ cup loosely packed fresh mint leaves

½ cup loosely packed fresh Italian parsley leaves

2 cups Missouri Skillet Cornbread (recipe and note, page 71) croutons or toasted sourdough croutons

SUGGESTED TOMATO VARIETIES:
Candy Stripe, Buckeye Yellow, Hazel Mae, Nebraska Mortgage Lifter, or Mr. Stripey

1 Under the broiler, on the grill, or over a gas flame, roast the bell peppers over high heat, turning with tongs, until the skins are blackened, 10 to 12 minutes. Transfer the peppers to a bowl and cover tightly with plastic wrap. Let them stand for 20 minutes.

2 When cool enough to handle, peel the peppers, discarding the stems and seeds. Cut the peppers into 1-inch pieces. Whisk the vinegars and salt and pepper to taste in a large bowl, then add the olive oil in a slow stream, whisking to combine. Add the tomatoes, onion, and olives to the vinaigrette, tossing to coat, and let marinate for 10 to 15 minutes.

3 Add the roasted peppers, cucumbers, basil, mint, parsley, and croutons to the bowl and toss. Taste and adjust the seasonings as desired. The salad should be bright with acidity from the vinegars and moistened well with olive oil.

ARUGULA and CHARD SALAD with BUTTERMILK DRESSING and CANDIED BACON SERVES 8

This hearty salad has it all—good-for-you greens, a family-pleasing buttermilk dressing, and the addictive crunch of candied bacon. I've adapted this from a recipe by Detroit-born Peter Golaszewski, who grew up on "city chicken, pierogies, kielbasa, sauerkraut, kischka, pickled herring, and so on." Translated from Midwesternese into American English, city chicken is pork and veal cubes on a skewer, fried like a chicken leg; pierogies are half-moon-shaped filled pasta; kielbasa is unsmoked Polish sausage; and kischka is a blood sausage made with barley or buckwheat. Golaszewski is now the chef at The Feed Store in Atlanta—"Don't ask how I started cooking southern food," he quips.

Candied Bacon

1 pound apple-smoked bacon, cut into ½-inch pieces

1 cup packed light or dark brown sugar

Buttermilk Dressing

1 cup mayonnaise

½ cup buttermilk (not low fat)

¼ cup sour cream (not low fat)

1 tablespoon chopped fresh cilantro

1 tablespoon chopped fresh oregano

1 tablespoon chopped fresh Italian parsley

2 cloves garlic, minced

Fine kosher or sea salt and freshly ground black pepper

1 Cook the bacon in a skillet until crispy, drain off the fat, and stir in the brown sugar until the bacon is well coated and candied, about 1 minute. Transfer to a baking sheet or paper towels to cool.

2 For the dressing, mix all the ingredients together in a bowl or a large jar with a lid. Whisk or shake to blend.

3 Heat the olive oil in a large skillet over medium heat and sauté the chard stalks and scallions for 2 minutes. Add the vinegar, sugar, and salt and pepper to taste, and bring to a boil. Add the chard leaves and stir until wilted. Let come to a boil again, then lower the heat and simmer for 2 minutes. Pour this mixture through a strainer, drain the liquid, and spread the mixture on a baking sheet to cool.

4 To assemble the salad, combine the arugula, chard mixture, candied bacon, and dressing in a large bowl and toss to blend.

Salad

1 tablespoon olive oil

2 pounds Swiss chard, leaves cut into 1-inch pieces, stalks diced

1 bunch scallions, trimmed and sliced

½ cup red wine vinegar

1 cup granulated sugar

Salt and freshly ground black pepper

1 pound baby arugula

SUGGESTED CHARD VARIETIES:
rainbow or Five Color Silverbeet

"Everything seems to be one piece. The air, our faces, all cool, moist and dark, and the ghostly sky. . . . All of a piece. . . . As if the sky were a pattern of nerves and our thoughts and memories traveled across it. . . . As if the sky were one gigantic memory for us all."

—LOUISE ERDRICH ON THE NORTHERN LIGHTS,
IN LOVE MEDICINE

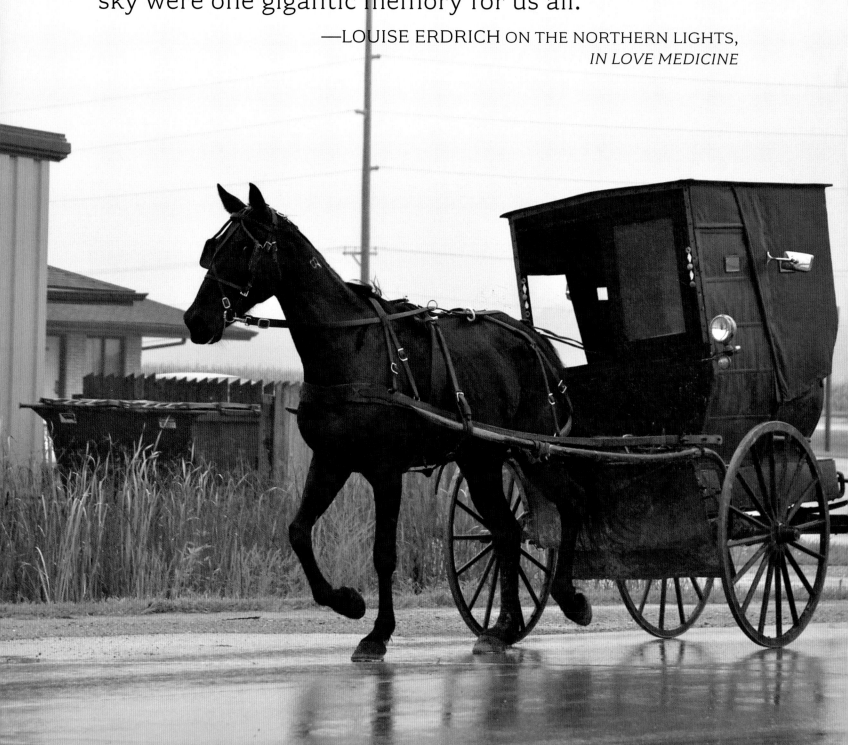

OVER THE RIVER AND THROUGH THE WOODS . . .

To great-grandmother's farm we go, now that the family farm of the nineteenth and early twentieth centuries has become a destination and living history museum.

AMISH FARM TOURS; HARMONY, MINNESOTA—
www.amish-tours.com

KAUFFMAN MUSEUM; NEWTON, KANSAS—
www.bethelks.edu/kauffman

KNIFE RIVER INDIAN (HIDATSA) VILLAGES; STANTON, NORTH DAKOTA—www.nps.gov/knri

LIVING HISTORY FARMS; URBANDALE, IOWA—
www.livinghistoryfarms.org

PROPHETSTOWN STATE PARK; WEST LAFAYETTE, INDIANA—
www.prophetstown.org

SAUDER VILLAGE; ARCHBOLD, OHIO—www.saudervillage.org

THREE SISTERS PARK; CHILLICOTHE, ILLINOIS—
www.threesisterspark.com

WELLINGTON FARM PARK; GRAYLING, MICHIGAN—
www.wellingtonfarmpark.org

WESSELS LIVING HISTORY FARM; YORK, NEBRASKA—
www.livinghistoryfarm.org

WESTON RED BARN FARM; WESTON, MISSOURI—
www.westonredbarnfarm.com

THE BEET QUEEN SALAD
WITH SMOKED GOAT CHEESE **SERVES 8**

I was struck by a photo of Alisa DeMarcov—the chef for Prairie Fruits Farm & Creamery's farm dinners—holding a platter of vibrantly colored beet salad. Not just ho-hum beet salad, but "gimme some of that" beet salad: a bed of fresh greens, sliced peaches, peppery nasturtium blossoms, all topped with a haystack of julienned red, striped, and golden beets. Oooh! So I set out to re-create it. As a salute to the fresh chèvre from Prairie Fruits Farm, I added a little crumble of goat cheese under the beets—but the goat cheese has a little smoke flavor. This salad goes well with anything, as far as I'm concerned, and could be a meatless entrée all on its own. Raw beets have a flavor similar to sweet corn and a texture like jicama, so prepare to be pleasantly surprised. I took a photo of my daughter Sarah, our family's Beet Queen, holding our salute to this great salad.

Orange-Tarragon Vinaigrette

Juice and zest of 1 orange

1 teaspoon Dijon mustard

1 clove garlic, minced

1 teaspoon tarragon vinegar

2 tablespoons fresh tarragon leaves

¼ cup canola oil

½ teaspoon fine kosher or sea salt

Salad

6 to 8 cups mixed greens

2 to 3 ripe peaches, peeled and sliced

½ cup crumbled Smoked Goat Cheese (page 14) or fresh goat cheese

1 medium striped or Chioggia beet, peeled, trimmed, and julienned

1 medium golden beet, peeled, trimmed, and julienned

1 medium red beet, peeled, trimmed, and julienned

1 For the vinaigrette, whisk all the ingredients together in a small bowl.

2 To assemble the salad, arrange the greens and peach slices on a large platter or serving plate. Sprinkle the goat cheese over the greens and peaches. Arrange the beets on top like confetti. Drizzle with the dressing and serve.

SUGGESTED BEET VARIETIES:
Detroit Red or Ruby Queen, Chioggia (striped), and Burpee's Golden

SUMMERTIME ZUCCHINI, YELLOW SQUASH, AND RED BELL PEPPER SALAD SERVES 8

Fresh from the garden and tossed with an old-fashioned celery seed dressing, this salad stays cool and crisp covered in the refrigerator for up to 3 days. Add a few sprinkles of blue cheese, feta, or Smoked Goat Cheese (see page 14) if you wish. For an easy hot weather meal, serve this with creamy cottage cheese, as they do at the Golden Lamb in Lebanon, Ohio.

2 medium zucchini, trimmed and cut into matchsticks

2 medium yellow summer squash, trimmed and cut into matchsticks

2 medium red bell peppers, cored, seeded, and cut into matchsticks

SUGGESTED VEGETABLE VARIETIES: Genovese zucchini, Scallop Yellow squash, and Round of Hungary red bell pepper

Celery Seed Dressing

¾ cup vegetable oil

⅓ cup cider vinegar

2 tablespoons sugar

1 teaspoon celery seeds

¼ teaspoon dry mustard

½ teaspoon kosher or sea salt

½ teaspoon freshly ground white pepper

2 cloves garlic, minced

8 ounces crumbled feta cheese, blue cheese, or Smoked Goat Cheese (page 14; optional)

1 Combine the zucchini, squash, and bell peppers in a large bowl.

2 For the dressing, combine the oil, vinegar, sugar, celery seeds, dry mustard, salt, white pepper, and garlic in a jar. Secure the lid and shake to blend.

3 Pour the dressing over the vegetables and toss to coat. Cover and refrigerate until ready to serve. Just before serving, top with the cheese.

HEARTLAND WEDGE SALAD SERVES 4

With a great grilled steak, this is all you need. A Heartland bacon and blue cheese make all the difference.

Blue Cheese Dressing

**4 ounces creamy blue cheese
(such as Maytag or Roth Kase)**

2 tablespoons heavy cream

2 tablespoons mayonnaise

**2 tablespoons buttermilk or sour
cream**

1 tablespoon canola oil

1 teaspoon Worcestershire sauce

**¼ teaspoon bottled hot sauce
(such as Tabasco)**

1 small shallot, finely chopped

**Kosher salt and freshly ground
black pepper**

Salad

**1 head iceberg or 4 heads butterhead
lettuce, cored and quartered
lengthwise**

**8 slices bacon, cooked until crisp
and crumbled**

12 cherry tomatoes, halved

**4 ounces crumbled blue cheese
(such as Maytag)**

½ cup chopped scallions

Freshly ground black pepper

1 For the dressing, combine the cheese, cream, mayonnaise, buttermilk, oil, Worcestershire, hot sauce, and shallot in the work bowl of a food processor and process until smooth and creamy, about 15 seconds. Season with salt and pepper to taste and transfer to a small bowl.

2 For the salad, arrange each lettuce quarter, cut side up, on a salad plate. Spoon the dressing over each wedge and garnish with the bacon, tomatoes, cheese, and scallions. Season with black pepper to taste.

CLAIM YOUR STEAK

MURRAY'S; MINNEAPOLIS, MINNESOTA—Murray's, started by Art and Marie Murray in 1946, is famous for their Silver Butter Knife Steak for two, a 28-ounce strip sirloin carved tableside.

THE PINE CLUB; DAYTON, OHIO—The Pine Club, so called because of its knotty pine paneling, still specializes in tender steaks with a charry crust—plus all the classic steakhouse fixings.

ITALIAN SAUSAGE AND ESCAROLE SOUP SERVES 6

One big-flavor ingredient like locally made Italian sausage can make all the difference in a soup. Italian families who emigrated to the Midwest in the early 1900s have left a legacy of wonderful salsiccia from makers like Graziano Brothers in Des Moines, Iowa; Mendolia's and Scimeca's in Kansas City, Missouri; Tenuta's in Kenosha, Wisconsin; and DiGregorio's in St. Louis, Missouri. Here, the sausage blends with tomatoes, herbs, and greens for a soul-satisfying dish.

2 tablespoons canola oil

1 medium red onion, diced

2 cloves garlic, minced

1 pound bulk sweet or hot Italian sausage

1 (28-ounce) can whole Roma tomatoes, with juice, cut into bite-size pieces

3 cups chicken broth

2 heads escarole, torn into pieces

1 teaspoon dried basil

1 teaspoon dried oregano

1 teaspoon fennel seeds

4 ounces penne (optional)

Shredded Parmesan cheese, for garnish

SUGGESTED LETTUCE VARIETIES:
Prizehead or Rossa di Trento

1 In a large saucepan, heat the oil over medium-high heat and sauté the onion and garlic until softened, about 5 minutes. Stir in the sausage and tomatoes with their juice. Pour in the chicken broth, then add the escarole, basil, oregano, and fennel seeds. Bring to a boil, then lower the heat to medium-low and simmer, uncovered, for 30 minutes.

2 Add the penne and cook until al dente, about 15 minutes more. Serve each bowl with a sprinkling of Parmesan.

VEGETABLE STEW WITH SMOKY CORNCOB SEASONING

In 1804, Meriwether Lewis and George Rogers Clark were traveling up the Missouri River, exploring the uncharted area that President Jefferson had bought from France. They spent the winter at a Mandan Indian village in what is now Mercer County, North Dakota, perhaps coming into contact with the ancestors of expert gardener Buffalo Bird Woman. "Kagohami or Little Raven brought his wife and son loaded with corn, and she entertained us with a favorite Mandan dish, a mixture of pumpkins, beans, corn, and chokecherries," they recorded on December 23, 1804.

Buffalo Bird Woman recounted a similar dish to Gilbert Wilson in the early 1900s: "Sunflower meal was used in making a dish that we called do'patsa-makihi'ke, or four vegetables mixed . . . our very best dish. . . . Into the pot I threw one double-handful of beans . . . dried squash . . . four or five double-handfuls of mixed meal, of pounded parched sunflower seed and pounded parched corn. The whole was boiled. . . ."

Buffalo Bird Woman's smoky seasoning was made from corncobs burned in a large pile after the harvest. Buffalo Bird Woman then gathered the ashes into balls. "We were so fond of seasoning our food with them that every family had used up its store before the autumn had passed," Buffalo Bird Woman recounted to Wilson.

HEIRLOOM BEAN RAGOUT IN AN ACORN SQUASH

SERVES 4

The Heartland—and especially the Dakotas—has long been a big producer of dried beans. In the early 1900s, Buffalo Bird Woman grew Shield Figure Beans in her garden along the Missouri River in North Dakota. Native American tribes also grew pale yellow–tan Arikara Yellow and Hidatsa Red beans there; these varieties were introduced to gardeners through the George Will Seed Company in 1915. Lina Sisco's Bird Eye beans, creamy tan and speckled with cranberry, were brought to Missouri by her grandmother in covered wagon days. Part soup, part stew, this vegetarian ragout celebrates the humble bean and looks festive served in half of an acorn squash. Use a Heartland port from St. James Winery in Missouri, Falconer Vineyards in Minnesota, or Wollersheim Winery in Wisconsin.

1 pound dried heirloom or pinto beans or a mix of several varieties

1 cup Caramelized Onions (page 37)

8 sprigs thyme

¼ cup port, sherry, or brandy

¼ cup clover or wildflower honey

½ cup sweetened dried cranberries or cherries

½ cup chopped dried apricots

Coarse kosher or sea salt and freshly ground black pepper

4 acorn squash

SUGGESTED VEGETABLE VARIETIES:
heirloom beans listed above, plus American Tonda, Amish Pie, or buttercup squash

1   Rise and pick over the dried beans, removing any debris. Place the beans in a large bowl and add cold water to cover. Let soak for 12 hours or overnight.

2   Drain the beans, then place them in a large saucepan with cold, fresh water to cover. Bring to a boil over medium-high heat, then lower the heat and simmer, covered, until tender, 1½ to 2 hours.

3   Stir in the caramelized onions, 4 of the thyme sprigs, the port, honey, cranberries, and apricots and bring to a simmer. Simmer for 30 minutes, then season to taste with salt and pepper. The ragout can be made to this point, covered, and refrigerated for up to 3 days.

4   When ready to serve, preheat the oven to 350°F. Cut the stem end of each squash all the way around, about 2 inches from the top, to remove it; reserve the tops. Remove the seeds and fibrous material. Trim away enough of the bottom of each squash so that it sits evenly on a large baking sheet. Fill each squash with the ragout. Bake, uncovered, for 25 minutes. Replace the tops and bake for 20 to 30 minutes longer, or until the squash are tender. Garnish each with a thyme sprig and serve with or without the tops.

SMOKE-ROASTED TOMATO SOUP **SERVES 4**

How can one soup hit so many flavor and texture notes—smoky, hearty, tangy, aromatic, rustic yet refined, and creamy? Serve this hot, with the bread crumb, goat cheese, and basil garnish, or serve cold with a dollop of Horseradish Crème Fraîche (page 177). With a stash of Smoke-Roasted Tomatoes, you can make this soup whenever the mood strikes. My thanks to friend and fellow BBQ Queen Karen Adler for this recipe.

2 cups smoke-roasted tomatoes (see page 16)

2 cups chicken or vegetable stock

1 cup heavy cream

2 tablespoons freshly squeezed lemon juice

Fine kosher or sea salt and freshly ground black pepper

2 tablespoons olive oil

1 cup fresh bread crumbs

1 cup crumbled Smoked Goat Cheese (page 14; optional)

8 large fresh basil leaves, cut into chiffonade or thin strips

SUGGESTED TOMATO VARIETIES:
Federle, Roma, or San Marzano

1 Combine the tomatoes, stock, and cream in a large saucepan over medium-high heat. Cook, stirring, until the soup bubbles around the perimeter of the pan but is not boiling. Remove from the heat and stir in the lemon juice. Season to taste with salt and pepper.

2 Meanwhile, heat the olive oil in a skillet and sauté the bread crumbs until golden.

3 Ladle the soup into bowls and top with the sautéed bread crumbs, crumbled goat cheese, and basil.

"Our horses picked their way along the edge of a prairie-dog town whose residents had disappeared down their holes, and all there was to see were earthen mounds and short clumps of buffalo grass. As we approached the valley, which was only a dozen miles from my home, I noticed taller grasses, stalks of bluestem and wheatgrass. The sun emerged from behind the clouds, and the landscape burst into color, dotted with sunflowers, bluebells, blazing stars, and purple sage."

—SUSAN POWER, *THE GRASS DANCER*

MINNESOTA WILD RICE SOUP **SERVES 8**

My great friend and barbecue co-author Karen Adler makes this soup every Christmas Eve for family and friends, and it always gets rave reviews. With much of American wild rice coming from Minnesota lakes, no wonder it has become a Twin Cities classic, as served at the St. Paul Grill or deconstructed at Porter & Frye. The rice is also a natural with duck—either in soup as at the Lake Elmo Inn, or topped with rich shreds of duck confit at Restaurant Max. Karen likes to sprinkle the cheddar in the bottom of each bowl or soup mug and pour the hot soup over it. For a somewhat smoky hit, you could omit the cheese and top with shredded Smoke-Roasted Pork Shoulder, as well as substitute it for the ham in the soup. Just don't expect any leftovers.

½ cup (1 stick) unsalted butter

½ cup chopped yellow onion

½ cup chopped celery

¾ cup unbleached all-purpose flour

3 cups chicken consommé or chicken stock

1 cup water

3 cups cooked wild rice

1 cup chopped cooked ham

1 cup chopped carrots

¼ teaspoon fine kosher or sea salt

1 teaspoon freshly ground white pepper

1¼ teaspoons curry powder

1 cup half-and-half or whole milk

½ cup dry white wine

1 cup shredded cheddar cheese (about 4 ounces), Smoke-Roasted Pork Shoulder (page 188), or Flyover Country Duck Confit (page 38)

1 Melt the butter in a large saucepan over medium-high heat and sauté the onion and celery until softened, about 5 minutes. Stir in the flour and cook, stirring, until the roux develops a nutty aroma, about 5 minutes. Stir the consommé and water together in a large glass measuring cup. Slowly add the liquid to the roux, stirring constantly, until well blended. Lower the heat and simmer for 20 minutes, or until thickened.

2 Stir in the rice, ham carrots, salt, white pepper, curry powder, half-and-half, and wine. Cook, stirring frequently, until warmed through.

3 To serve, ladle the hot soup into bowls or mugs and garnish with the cheese.

BADLANDS BISON CHILI **SERVES 4 TO 6**

American bison, once called buffalo, had quite a range over the broad swath of grassland from Ohio to Kansas until they were almost wiped out in the 1880s. Today, you can still see bison in the wild at Badlands National Park in South Dakota. At Sinte Gleska University in Rosebud, South Dakota, Lakota tribal students can study the way of the bison again—as their ancestors once did—at the research ranch in Mission. But what's really bringing these animals back is the demand for rich-tasting but low-fat, grass-fed bison meat raised on ranches. They drink 10 to 12 gallons of water a day and eat lots and lots of grass to reach 2,400 pounds (the males). Ranchers say, with a grin, that "you can get a bison to go anywhere it wants to go." The combination of bison and black beans is both regionally true to the Dakotas and simply delicious.

1 tablespoon canola oil

2 cloves garlic, minced

1 large yellow onion, chopped

½ cup chopped celery

1 pound ground bison

1 pound dried Black Turtle beans

1 red or green bell pepper, stemmed, seeded, and chopped

1 (15-ounce) can diced tomatoes, with juice

2 teaspoons dried thyme

1 teaspoon freshly ground black pepper

2 bay leaves

4 cups water

Sour cream, for garnish

Cornbread croutons (see page 71), for garnish

1 Heat the oil in a large saucepan over medium-high heat and sauté the garlic, onion, and celery until translucent, about 5 minutes. Stir in the bison, beans, bell pepper, tomatoes, thyme, black pepper, bay leaves, and water. Bring to a boil, then lower the heat and simmer for 1½ to 2 hours, or until the beans are tender.

2 Serve each bowl with a dollop of sour cream and a sprinkling of croutons.

"The buffalo wallows, perfectly round and set down into the prairie like a dish three or four feet deep, was solidly paved with violets."

—LAURA INGALLS WILDER IN *LITTLE TOWN IN THE PRAIRIE*, SET IN THE DAKOTA TERRITORY

GREAT LAKES "CHOWDA" SERVES 6 TO 8

While East Coast chowders feature clams, Midwest chowders go for what is plentiful in this region: bacon, corn, and freshwater fish. Kurt Steeber at Boulevard Blue offers a deconstructed "Cleveland Chowda" with a creamy, bacony sauce topped with turned potatoes and a pan-roasted freshwater fish fillet on top. This recipe, however, is your classic style of chowder, meant to fortify you when cold winds howl across the lake—or your street. More like a warm muffler than a silk scarf, this soup is a meal in itself.

6 slices apple-smoked or other good-quality bacon, diced

1 large yellow onion, diced

1 bunch scallions, chopped

1 red bell pepper, stemmed, seeded, and diced

1 yellow or orange bell pepper, stemmed, seeded, and diced

3 large red potatoes, peeled and diced

2 cups chicken stock or broth

8 ounces fresh or smoked whitefish or walleye fillet, chopped

3 cups fresh or thawed frozen corn kernels

1 cup half-and-half

Fine kosher or sea salt and freshly ground black pepper

1   In a large saucepan over medium-high heat, fry the bacon until crisp. Remove the bacon with a slotted spoon and transfer to paper towels to drain, but reserve the bacon drippings in the pan. Sauté the onion, scallions, and bell peppers in the bacon drippings until soft, about 5 minutes. Stir in the potatoes and stock and bring to a boil. Lower the heat and simmer for 15 minutes, or until the potatoes are tender.

2   Stir in the fish and 1½ cups of the corn and cook until the corn is tender, about 10 minutes. Meanwhile, place the remaining 1½ cups of corn and ½ cup of the half-and-half in the work bowl of a food processor and puree. Add this puree to the soup, stir in the remaining ½ cup half-and-half, and simmer until warmed through. Season to taste with salt and pepper.

ROASTED BUTTERNUT SQUASH SOUP WITH SMOKED GARLIC CUSTARD

SERVES 8

Winter squash, one of the "three sisters" of Native American agriculture (along with corn and beans), is now one of the bounties of the Heartland garden, prized for its long keeping qualities. Table Queen, a heart-shaped squash, was first introduced by the Iowa Seed company in Des Moines, Iowa, in 1913. Like acorn squash, Table Queen is deep orange with a sweet flavor and believed to be an offshoot of squash grown by the Arikara Indians along the Missouri River Valley in western North Dakota. Turk's Head Hubbard, a Mandan Indian heirloom from the Missouri River Valley in North and South Dakota, is dark green and mottled in appearance, with a sweet yellow flesh.

If your holiday guests aren't wowed by this soup featuring a scoop of garlic custard floated in the center of each bowl, something's wrong. To smoke 2 whole heads of garlic, follow the directions in the variation of Smoked Goat Cheese (page 14), or roast the garlic in the oven and add liquid smoke flavoring to taste when you puree it. You can make smoked garlic a few days ahead and the soup up to a week ahead, but serve the smoked garlic custard the same day you make it. Made with vegetable broth instead of chicken broth, this is a vegetarian dish.

4½ pounds winter or butternut squash, halved lengthwise

4 tablespoons (½ stick) unsalted butter

3 large leeks, trimmed and finely chopped

5 cups chicken or vegetable broth

1 teaspoon freshly ground white pepper

SUGGESTED SQUASH VARIETIES:
Turk's Head, Lakota, Sweet Meat, or Sibley

1 For the soup, preheat the oven to 350°F. Line a large baking sheet with aluminum foil. Scrape out the seeds and fibrous material from the squash. Place the squash, cut side down, on the baking sheet. Roast for 45 minutes, or until tender.

2 While the squash is roasting, melt the butter in a large saucepan and sauté the leeks over medium heat, stirring occasionally, until lightly browned, 20 to 25 minutes. When the squash is done, scoop the flesh into the leek mixture and whisk to blend. Discard the squash rinds. Add the broth and white pepper to the soup and bring to a boil. Lower the heat and simmer for 20 minutes. Transfer the soup, in batches, to a blender or food processor and puree. The soup can be made to this point, covered, and refrigerated up to 1 week ahead.

3 When ready to serve the soup, make the custard. Preheat the oven to 300°F. Butter the inside of an 8-inch round baking dish and place in a large pan filled with enough water to come halfway up the sides of the dish.

4 Puree the garlic cloves in the work bowl of a food processor. Add the milk, egg yolks, salt, and white pepper, and process until well blended. Strain the mixture into a 4-cup glass measuring cup. Fill the baking dish with the batter.

Continued on page 169

Continued from page 167

Garlic Custard

30 peeled cloves garlic from 2 bulbs of smoked garlic (page 14)

2 cups whole milk

7 large egg yolks

1 teaspoon fine kosher or sea salt

Freshly ground white pepper

Grated Parmesan cheese, for garnish

5   Bake for 55 to 60 minutes, or until set and a knife inserted in the center comes out clean. To serve, scoop a ball of custard into each bowl, pour the hot soup over, and sprinkle with the Parmesan.

"I'VE LANDED IN A PLACE you'd never think to go: a prairie mecca of sauerkraut pizza and buffalo hot dogs, of bull-a-ramas and pitchfork fondues; where sunshine and hailstorms take unpredictable turns blasting the fascinating but windswept landscape—and the fascinating but windswept people," wrote Adam Z. Horvath about North Dakota.

Heartlanders continue to joke that you can't be a wimp and live in the Midwest, where one day it starts out sunny and mild, and a few hours later you can have a combination thunderstorm/blizzard/tornado.

To live here, you have to be prepared for rapid change. Maybe that's why Heartland main dishes take their cues from comfort, add a side of ethnic heritage, and yet still celebrate what's fresh in the garden or produced regionally.

Grandma's pot roast has morphed into Heartland Daube with White Cheddar Polenta (page 198), with an added hint of smoky flavor. Those of Eastern European will love that you can now "schnitzel" any flat piece of pheasant, chicken, veal, or pork in Pheasant Schnitzel with Danish Red Cabbage (page 208), the red cabbage taking its slow-simmered flavor from tart red currant or lingonberry jelly. Bits and pieces of artisan cheese can get a delicious, final farewell in the can't-believe-this-is-thrifty Farmstead Cheese Soufflé (page 184), which is, I promise, no-fail. Even the most stalwart Heartlander, however, can go weak in the knees over Morel-Grilled Rib-Eye (page 195), with its deep-flavored grilling paste made with dried morels.

The resurgence of heritage breeds—which are more flavorful and worth the extra expense than their mass-produced kin—is perhaps the biggest thing to happen to the center of the Heartland plate in the past decade. Heritage breeds of beef, pork, and chicken not only appear on restaurant menus and in specialty meat lockers and suppliers but also are starting to arrive in the supermarket. Paradise Locker Meats (see Resources, page 266), just north of Kansas City and close to the airport, ships out heritage meats—from producers like Nathan Becker of Becker Lane Farm in Dyersville, Iowa—to the restaurants of Mario Batali, Lidia Bastianich, and Alice Waters on the East and West Coasts.

"Organic food started in 1971 in Berkeley," claims Patrick Martins, co-founder of Heritage Foods USA, which champions and markets heritage meats. "Heritage Foods started in 2005 in Kansas." (See Resources, page 266.)

Frank Reese of Good Shepherd Poultry Ranch in Lindsborg, Kansas, has made it his mission in life to bring back the full-flavored, heritage breeds of turkey and chicken that our grandparents and great-grandparents used to appreciate (see Resources, page 266).

One year, I made Thanksgiving dinner from local foods. The only ingredients not from Kansas were the after-dinner coffee and the spices for the pumpkin pie, and we all dined exceptionally well. Now that more and more Heartland farms are making the switch from emphasizing quantity to producing the best quality, that's the whole point.

ROASTED LAKE FISH WITH DILL PICKLE RÉMOULADE AND FRIZZLED TOMATOES SERVES 4

A fish fry is an integral part of the Heartland social scene. Whether it's a lawn fete, a church supper, or simply a casual Milwaukee Friday night, fried lake fish are on the menu. At home, however, it's easier—and less messy—to do fish in the oven. Slather fresh fish with this easy, tangy rémoulade and roast it surrounded by cherry tomatoes topped with fresh herbs. You can also do this recipe on the grill; arrange everything on a plank or two, place on the indirect side, close the lid, and plank-roast for 15 to 20 minutes, or until the fish is done.

Dill Pickle Rémoulade

1 cup mayonnaise

1 teaspoon Dijon mustard

¼ cup prepared dill pickle relish

Fish and Tomatoes

4 fresh fish fillets, such as lake perch, walleye pike, or tilapia

1 pint cherry tomatoes

1 pint yellow teardrop tomatoes

Olive oil, for drizzling

10 to 12 sprigs leafy herbs (such as a mix of basil, dill, tarragon, and/or Italian parsley)

Fine kosher or sea salt and freshly ground black pepper

1 For the rémoulade, mix the mayonnaise, mustard, and relish together in a small bowl. Cover and refrigerate until ready to serve.

2 Preheat the oven to 400°F. Slather the fish with half the rémoulade; reserve the rest to serve at the table. Arrange the fish on a baking sheet and surround with the tomatoes. Drizzle the tomatoes with olive oil and top with the herbs. Season everything with salt and pepper.

3 Roast for 15 to 20 minutes, or until the fish is beginning to flake in the thickest part when tested with a fork. Serve hot.

"Here in Minnesota, spring doesn't arrive for good until Mother's Day and the opening of walleye season, when men and their mothers go fishing and sit around the campfire afterwards and pass the whiskey bottle and she talks about her years traveling with the tent show before she met their father. . . ."

—GARRISON KEILLOR

HORSERADISH

The southwestern Illinois area including Collinsville, Illinois, just inland from the eastern bank of the Mississippi River north of St. Louis, is dubbed the Horseradish Capital of the World. Thanks to a glacial scouring that created the American Bottom Lands, the soil here is sandy and full of potash, a chemical nutrient that causes the root vegetable horseradish plant to thrive. More than 10 million pounds of horseradish root is grown in this region, about 85 percent of the world's market.

In addition to perking up the flavor of foods, horseradish also had a more practical function in nineteenth-century Midwestern kitchens. Horseradish added to vegetables preserved in vinegar kept a scum from forming on the top.

Maliner Kren, a large Bohemian horseradish variety sold in the Midwest since 1904, is the standard variety for condiment use because it's easier to grate. In the garden, it comes back every year like rhubarb and is ready for harvest after the first year. You simply dig up a root, clean and scrape it like a carrot, and then finely shred it by hand or in the food processor. Wear protective eyewear when you do, as horseradish fumes are worse than those of chopped onion. Freshly grated horseradish has the best flavor, but it can be placed in a jar, covered with cider or white vinegar, and refrigerated. Many Midwestern markets offer freshly grated horseradish.

APPLE-SMOKED TROUT WITH HORSERADISH CRÈME FRAÎCHE **SERVES 4**

From Clear Fork and Mad River in Ohio to the spring creek–fed Upper Midwest, the tributaries running to the Great Lakes, the Black Hills and Badlands of the Dakotas, and the Ozarks in Missouri, trout fishing is the Heartland fly fishermen's passion. When they come back with lots of fresh-caught fish, they need to preserve them. One way is to smoke the trout over hardwood, as do many Great Lakes fisheries. It's easy to smoke small fish like trout, as you'll see below, to eat right away or wrap and freeze for up to 3 months. Taking the skin off the trout first allows the smoke to penetrate more easily. Just about any fish can also be smoked this way. You will get about 8 ounces of fillet from a 14 to 16-ounce cooked whole trout. For a wonderful meal, serve the trout with Missouri Skillet Cornbread (page 71) and a fresh green salad. Any extra smoked trout can be used to make a fabulous Smoked Trout Pâté (page 112). You'll need 2 cups applewood chips for a charcoal grill and 1 cup for a gas grill.

½ cup sour cream

½ cup heavy cream

4 (14 to 16-ounce) whole trout, cleaned

½ cup unsalted butter, melted, for brushing

4 sprigs dill

4 sprigs tarragon

4 sprigs Italian parsley

Kosher salt and freshly ground black pepper

1 teaspoon prepared horseradish

Chopped fresh Italian parsley, for garnish

1 For the crème fraîche, combine the sour cream and heavy cream in a medium bowl, cover, and let sit at cool room temperature for several hours, or until thickened.

2 Prepare an indirect fire in your grill, with a hot fire on one side and no fire on the other side. For a charcoal grill, soak the wood chips in water first. For a gas grill, place the dry chips in a smoker box or an aluminum foil packet with holes poked through it.

3 Bring a large pot of water to a boil. Using tongs, dip each whole trout into the boiling water for 20 to 30 seconds. Remove the trout and peel off the skin. Brush each trout, inside and out, with the melted butter. Place a sprig of each herb in the cavity of each fish. Season with salt and pepper, and place in a disposable aluminum pan.

4 Place the pan on the indirect side of the grill, away from the fire. For a charcoal grill, drain the chips, then scatter them on the hot coals. For a gas grill, place the smoker box or packet over direct heat. When you see the first wisps of smoke, close the grill lid.

5 Smoke for 1 to 1½ hours, or until the flesh flakes easily with a fork. Stir the horseradish into the crème fraîche and serve each fillet with a dollop. Sprinkle chopped parsley over all.

CARAMELIZED CABBAGE ROLLS SERVES 4 TO 6

After a forced exile in Turkey, Sweden's King Karl XII returned home in 1715 without any of the traditional spoils of war. Instead, his entourage was joined by groups of creditors who patiently waited while the king paid off his debt. For years, these creditors lived in Sweden on a government allowance. Finally, however, the king paid up and the creditors departed. But not until the Turkish version of stuffed cabbage—using a syrup to help the cabbage rolls caramelize—had caught on. Through the years since, these delicate rolls filled with ground meat and rice have become a staple of Swedish home cooking, which then came to America. Cabbage rolls have traveled from the Middle East to the Balkans, Scandinavia, and western Europe, and from thence to the American Midwest, where each ethnic group has its favorite incarnation of cabbage, meat, rice, and sauce. Besides tasting good, this dish makes a lot out of a little. This version, somewhat elegant and spare, goes well with Buttery Mashed Potatoes (page 211).

1 medium head green cabbage

¾ cup plus ⅓ cup milk

¼ cup short-grain or Arborio rice

4 ounces ground beef

4 ounces ground pork

1 large egg, beaten

1 medium yellow onion, minced

2 tablespoons Rosy Rhubarb Syrup (page 34) or bottled lingonberry or other tart red fruit syrup

3 tablespoons unsalted butter, melted

¾ cup beef broth

1   Cut out the core of the cabbage. Bring a large pot of water to a boil and plunge the cabbage head into the water. Lower the heat and simmer, covered, for 20 minutes, or until the cabbage is tender and wilted.

2   While the cabbage is cooking, pour ¾ cup milk into a medium saucepan and bring to a boil. Add the rice, lower the heat, and simmer, covered, for 20 minutes, or until the rice is tender.

3   Preheat the oven to 425°F. Grease a rectangular baking dish. Transfer the cabbage to a draining board or colander until cool enough to handle. In a medium bowl, mix together the cooked rice, beef, pork, egg, onion, and the remaining ⅓ cup milk. Separate the cabbage leaves, pat dry, and trim away any thick parts with a paring knife. Place about 1 tablespoon of filling on the rounded bottom part of each cabbage leaf. Fold in the sides and roll up. Place each cabbage roll in the prepared baking dish. Drizzle the rolls with the syrup and the melted butter.

4   Bake for 20 minutes, then add the beef broth. Baste the rolls with the broth every 5 minutes for the next 15 minutes, or until the rolls are browned and caramelized. Serve hot.

MAKING SWEET SORGHUM

Two kinds of sorghum are grown in the Heartland. Grain sorghum is grown for animal feed and just recently has started being ground to make gluten-free flour. Sweet sorghum produces a sweet syrup that is milder than maple syrup but with more flavor than corn syrup.

In the Old Order Mennonite community of Rich Hill, Missouri, sweet sorghum is big business. The cycle begins in May, when sorghum cane seeds are planted. The Mennonites hoe the 30-acre sorghum fields by hand all summer, until the sorghum canes are 10 to 12 feet high. The harvest begins in late September and lasts through October. Workers use special cane knives to cut the leaves from the sorghum stalks. A horse-drawn implement cuts the stalks, which are then bundled and laid out to dry for several days. The bundles are then taken to the press shed above the mill. Farmers feed the dried cane into the sorghum roller press powered by huge Belgian and Percheron draft horses. Green sorghum juice trickles down a pipeline to the mill, where the juice will boil in a large pan, from which the foam and impurities are scooped away. When the juice looks right to the cooker, he lets it run into the next pan, where it cooks further.

Every year, the sorghum canes are different in composition, so the cooker's job is much like blending grapes for wine. When cool, the sorghum is poured into mason jars or plastic squeeze bottles.

Because sorghum is a pure food, pressed in small mills that process no other product, sorghum is often sold at health food markets. Sorghum can have citrus, spice, and caramel notes, so find one you like and use it as you would honey or molasses.

BATES COUNTY SORGHUM; RICH HILL, MISSOURI—dark and molasses-like, a very rich sorghum.

GOLDEN RUN SORGHUM; CAMDEN, INDIANA—a rich, brown, spicy sorghum.

MAASDAM SORGHUM MILLS; LYNNVILLE, IOWA—medium-spiced and citrus-like.

SANDHILL SORGHUM; RUTLEDGE, MISSOURI—mild-flavored, with just a hint of citrus and spice.

BUTTERNUT SQUASH, MOREL, AND SAGE BROWN BUTTER LASAGNE **SERVES 8**

These days, we always seem to need a vegetarian alternative for a big family meal. Here is one delicious way to celebrate culinary diversity with a dish that will please nonvegetarians, too. With butternut squash and fresh sage from the garden, regional butter, and morels from a forager (or the grocery store), you've got the taste of a Heartland autumn.

Besciamella

½ cup (1 stick) unsalted butter

⅓ cup unbleached all-purpose flour

2 cups whole milk

2 cups half-and-half

Ground nutmeg

Fine kosher or sea salt

Lasagne

½ cup boiling water

1 ounce dried morel or porcini mushrooms

4 cups butternut squash, cut into 1-inch cubes

2 tablespoons unsalted butter

28 fresh sage leaves (about 2 bunches)

½ of a 9-ounce box no-boil lasagna noodles

½ cup grated Parmesan cheese

1 For the Besciamella, melt the butter in a large saucepan over medium-high heat. Whisk in the flour to make a slurry, and stir for 2 minutes, or until the mixture has a somewhat nutty aroma. Whisk in the milk and half-and-half and cook, whisking, until the mixture thickens, 8 to 10 minutes. Season to taste with nutmeg and salt. Set aside.

2 Pour the boiling water over the dried mushrooms in a small bowl and let soften for about 15 minutes, then finely snip the mushrooms in the bowl with kitchen shears.

3 Cook the squash in a covered saucepan over medium-high heat with about ¼ cup water until tender, 10 to 15 minutes. Drain the water. Add the wild mushrooms with their liquid and lightly mash.

4 Melt the butter in a medium skillet and fry the sage leaves until they start to turn brown.

5 To assemble the lasagne, place a layer of uncooked noodles in the bottom of a rectangular baking dish. Spread with 1 cup of the squash filling. Arrange 7 fried sage leaves over the filling and top with 1 cup of the Besciamella. Repeat the process with a second layer of noodles, filling, sage, and Besciamella. For the third layer, arrange the remaining noodles and top with the remaining filling. Arrange another 7 fried sage leaves over the filling and top with the remaining 2 cups Besciamella. Arrange the remaining 7 fried sage leaves over the Besciamella and drizzle with the butter from the pan. Sprinkle the Parmesan over the lasagne. Bake right away, or cover with plastic wrap and refrigerate for up to 24 hours.

6   Preheat the oven to 350°F.

7   Bake the lasagne, uncovered, for 35 to 45 minutes, or until the sides are bubbling and the lasagna is heated through.

PASTA WITH FRESH TOMATOES, BASIL, AND SHEEP'S MILK CHEESE **SERVES 4**

Just reading the title of this recipe makes me hungry. I adapted it from one by Janice Cole, a Twin Cities editor of *Cooking Pleasures* magazine and a blogger about fowl escapades with Roxanne, Cleo, and Crazy Lulu, her three city chickens, at www.threeswinginchicks.blogspot.com. This one-dish meal is perfect for late summer/early fall, when tomatoes and basil are at their peak in the garden—and all your chickens have come home to roost, so to speak. I use our local sheep's milk cheese from Green Dirt Farm in Weston, Missouri, but you can also try Hidden Springs Creamery in Westby, Wisconsin, or Shepherd's Way Farm near Northfield, Minnesota—or use a good fresh chèvre. Enjoy this with a luscious Inland Sea Viognier from Amigoni Vineyards in Kansas City, Missouri.

3 large ripe tomatoes, chopped

½ cup slightly packed chopped fresh basil

½ cup extra virgin olive oil

3 medium cloves garlic, minced

¼ teaspoon fine kosher or sea salt

¼ teaspoon freshly ground black pepper

8 ounces linguine, fettuccine, or other pasta

8 ounces fresh sheep's milk or goat cheese or more, crumbled (about 1½ cups)

1 Combine the tomatoes, basil, olive oil, garlic, salt, and pepper in a large bowl. If possible, let marinate for 1 hour at room temperature to allow all the flavors to develop.

2 Meanwhile, bring a large pot of water to a boil and cook the pasta according to package directions; drain.

3 Gently stir the cheese into the tomato mixture. Add the cooked hot pasta and quickly toss with the tomato mixture until the cheese has melted to a creamy consistency. Serve immediately.

CRAZY FOR EWE

What's it like to be a sheep at Green Dirt Farm? Well, in summer, you spend your days grazing on prairie grasses—alfalfa, bird's-foot trefoil, and clover—until the alpha ewe leads you into the milking barn every so often, where you get a tasty treat—a shower of dried corn—while you're milked, all nice and relaxed. And those great big dogs keep the bad coyotes away.

Yep, it's a good life, and not just for sheep. Sarah Hoffman, a physician, and her husband, John Spertus, a research cardiologist, bought the 111-acre farm just outside Weston, Missouri. When they did a soil study, they realized that the rolling terrain was best suited for pasture. Hoffman had raised sheep as a child—"They are very comical animals, and they just make me laugh," she says—so they decided on East Friesian/Lacaune and Gulf Coast Native breeds, known for their milk. Along the way, the nanny for the couple's children—Jacque Smith—also began to "nanny" the sheep. Hoffman and her assistant Jana Loflin learned how to make fresh sheep's milk cheeses as well as the artisan Woolly Rind; Dirt Lover with its coating of ash; and Queen of the Prairie, a washed-rind Tomme.

Hoffman, very much at home in the stainless-steel cheese kitchen that is as sterile as an operating room, inoculates chilled fresh milk with bacteria that promotes the development of lactic acid. The next day, the milk gets heated to 145°F and held for 30 minutes, and then gets divided into portions—each getting a different type of bacteria, depending on the type of cheese desired. The milk cools to 80°F before rennet, an enzymatic substance that causes milk to form curds, is added. The curds then get ladled into molds, while fresh cheese is suspended in bags to drain out the whey.

Green Dirt Farm also hosts farm dinners celebrating the bounty of the pasture and local farms, transformed into contemporary fare by Kansas City chefs such as "Best Chef of the Midwest"—nominated by Colby Garrelts of Bluestem.

FARMSTEAD CHEESE SOUFFLÉ SERVES 8

Midwesterners grow up hearing their grandmothers say things like this: "Save it for a rainy day." "Stick close to home." "Be nice." Or from my grandmother: "The sun doesn't always shine on the same dog's back." That one took a while to decipher . . . but the basic message is about a way to live your life: Save so that you have plenty and be nice to people, because you never know what's going to happen. This recipe is the epitome of that message. It welcomes almost all hard grating-type cheeses, even the last bits left over from other recipes. Serving this soufflé is a great way to be nice to family and friends. And because you never know what's going to happen—they could be late or you could be busy checking e-mail when the oven timer goes off—this Heartland soufflé remains unruffled and doesn't deflate. Stick close to home by using Heartland cheeses and serve it with a green salad and crusty bread. Although unusual for a soufflé, this bakes best in an oblong pan.

6 tablespoons (¾ stick) unsalted butter

6 tablespoons unbleached all-purpose flour

2 cups milk

½ teaspoon fine kosher or sea salt

½ teaspoon freshly ground white pepper

5 large eggs

2½ cups grated Gruyère cheese (about 10 ounces; or a combination of hard grating cheeses)

3 tablespoons chopped fresh chives

1 Preheat the oven to 400°F. Butter the inside of a 2-quart oblong baking dish and set aside.

2 In a large saucepan, melt the butter and stir in the flour. Cook for 2 minutes, stirring, until a nutty aroma arises. Whisk in the milk and stir until you have a thick white sauce. Season with the salt and white pepper. Remove from the heat and whisk in the eggs, cheese, and chives. Spoon into the prepared pan.

3 Bake for 25 to 30 minutes, or until puffed and golden. To serve, spoon onto plates.

PLANKED ARTISAN SAUSAGES with BAKED KALE and HORSERADISH BUTTER **SERVES 4 TO 6**

When I was growing up, my mother made a savory cold weather dish of locally made German sausages, turnips, and kale. That's when people boiled things: vegetables, steamed puddings, and one-pot meals. Today, we don't boil as much as we roast, sauté, bake, grill, or zap in the microwave. Oven planked, these sausages take on the aromatic flavor of the wood plank. Slather a bakery bun (or a Golden Onion Sour Rye Roll, page 100) with horseradish butter, and you've got a sausage sandwich made in Heartland heaven. Serve the crunchy kale on the side, like potato chips, and watch it disappear. A Midwestern pale ale—such as Goose Island (Chicago, Illinois), Boulevard (Kansas City, Missouri), Free State (Lawrence, Kansas), or Great Lakes Brewing Co. (Cleveland, Ohio)—is the beverage of choice.

Horseradish Butter

6 tablespoons (¾ stick) unsalted butter, softened

3 tablespoons prepared horseradish

½ teaspoon kosher salt

Baked Kale

1 bunch kale (such as curly, Lacinato, or Russian)

2 tablespoons canola oil

6 artisan sausages, cut almost in half lengthwise

½ cup grated Asiago, Parmesan, or Gruyère cheese

6 kaiser rolls or ciabatta buns

SUGGESTED PLANK:
2 cedar grilling planks or 1 baking plank, soaked in water for at least 1 hour

1 Position racks in the upper and lower parts of the oven and preheat the oven to 350°F.

2 For the horseradish butter, combine the butter, horseradish, and salt in a small bowl with a fork until well blended.

3 For the kale, trim the tough ends from the kale and cut the leaves into 1-inch pieces. Arrange on a baking sheet, drizzle with the oil, and toss to blend.

4 Arrange the sausages on the plank(s), cut side down.

5 Place the sausage on the upper rack and the kale on the lower rack of the oven. Bake for 10 minutes, then stir the kale with a wooden spoon. Bake for 10 minutes longer, then sprinkle the kale with the grated cheese. Bake for 30 minutes longer, or until the sausages are done and the kale is crunchy. To serve, spread the horseradish butter on the rolls, place a sausage on the roll, and serve the kale on the side.

HEARTLAND SAUSAGES

Heartland butcher shops and smokehouses offer an astonishing array of homemade and smoked sausages, continuing the Old World customs today. Here is just a sampling.

BRATWURST—a pale German sausage made with veal (preferred) or pork, seasoned with nutmeg. Boil, broil, or grill.

JATERNICE—a Czech version of headcheese, spiced with paprika.

JELITA—a Czech blood and barley sausage. Boil.

KALBERWURST—a mild Swiss veal sausage made with cracker crumbs and milk. Boil, broil, or grill.

KIELBASA—a Polish pork and beef sausage that is spiced and smoked. Boil, broil, or grill.

KRAKOWSKA—Polish ham sausage that tastes like smoked ham and is delicious on sandwiches.

LANDJAEGER—a German long, thin beef and pork sausage that is cured, smoked, and then dried.

LIVERWURST—rich, spreadable ground liver sausage spiced with salt, pepper, and sometimes garlic; could be coarser ground or the smooth, creamy texture of Braunschweiger.

NADLAV—a Croatian Easter sausage made with cubed bread, bacon, green onions, ham, and beaten eggs stuffed into a casing and then baked.

POLTAVSKA—Russian-Ukrainian sausage studded with large squares of creamy white fat. Boil.

POTATISKORV—Swedish sausage of beef, pork, onion, potato, and seasonings ground together. Boil.

SALSICCIA—Italian pork sausage, seasoned with fennel seed, red pepper flakes, black pepper, and sometimes a dry aged cheese like pecorino. Sauté, bake, boil, or grill.

SCHWARTENMAGEN—a hearty mixture of beef heart, pork tongue, jowls, and skin that's still made locally in the Amana Colonies. Boil, broil, or grill.

SMOKE-ROASTED PORK SHOULDER WITH SOOEY SAUCE SERVES 12

I have fallen in love with smoke-roasted pork shoulder or butt. It's a dish that rewards in many ways. It's easy on the cook, as you can do the smoke roasting in late afternoon and then put the pork in a low oven overnight. The fat in the meat keeps it moist—even if you overcook it, which is difficult to do. You can slice and serve it on a platter or pull it apart to serve on sandwiches. The leftovers taste great in Haymaker's Hash (page 48) or as a topping for Minnesota Wild Rice Soup (page 163). And pork shoulder or butt is inexpensive. What more can we ask of a dish? The Sooey Sauce is equally rewarding. You simply thin a Kansas City–style barbecue sauce with a few ingredients and people will think you slaved all day. To be really savvy, freeze any leftovers. You will need 3 cups of hardwood chips, 3 wood chunks, or 3 (3-inch diameter) sticks for the grill (mesquite, hickory, or oak).

2 (3½-pound) boneless pork butts

1 cup mustard

¼ cup freshly ground black pepper

¼ cup smoked or sweet Hungarian paprika

2 tablespoons granulated garlic or garlic powder

2 tablespoons onion salt

2 tablespoons light or dark brown sugar

1½ tablespoons dry mustard

1½ tablespoons celery seeds

1½ tablespoons chili powder

1 Slather the pork butts with the mustard. Combine the pepper, paprika, granulated garlic, onion salt, brown sugar, dry mustard, celery seeds, and chili powder in a small bowl. Sprinkle this rub all over the pork butts. Place the pork in a disposable aluminum pan. Set aside for 15 to 30 minutes, or until the surface of the meat is tacky to the touch.

2 Prepare an indirect fire in your grill, with a hot fire on one side and no fire on the other. For a charcoal grill, scatter the wood chips on the charcoal. For a gas grill, place the wood chips in a smoker box or an aluminum foil packet poked with holes near a burner. When you see the first wisps of smoke, place the pork on the indirect side of the grill and close the lid. Smoke-roast for 2 to 3 hours, adding more charcoal as necessary, or until the pork has a darkened crust or bark and a good smoky aroma.

3 Meanwhile, preheat the oven to 250°F. Cover the pan loosely with foil and roast in the oven for 8 to 12 hours, or until you can insert a fork in the pork and easily twist it.

Sooey Sauce

1 cup spicy tomato barbecue sauce, such as KC Masterpiece or Whole Foods 365

1 cup apple cider

2 tablespoons clover or wildflower honey

4   For the sauce, whisk the barbecue sauce, cider, and honey together in a bowl until smooth. You can toss the pork with some of the sauce or pass it at the table—or both! The sauce will keep, covered, in the refrigerator for up to 6 months.

NOTE: In inclement weather, you can make this entirely indoors. Just start out with the pork in a 350°F oven for 2 hours, then lower the heat to 250°F and cook for another 8 to 12 hours, or until you can do the fork twist test.

HERITAGE PORK

In the early 1980s, when I lived in England, I was intrigued by specialty pork producer Anne Petch, who raised an old breed, Tamworth, at Heal Farm in Devon. No one at that point in America really talked about the provenance of your food, but here she was making a delicious case for pork raised in the traditional way. "The idea had a great deal going for it," she writes. "Old-fashioned breeds reared in a traditional farming system produce the best tasting pork." Pork from large-scale hog farms tends to be leaner, since the pigs are rushed to quickly achieve a certain weight before going to market. Pork raised the old-fashioned way has the time to marble the fat into the meat, not simply surround it.

Today, the Midwest is Heritage Pork Central. I can drive up to Paradise Locker Meats, near the Kansas City airport, and buy Berkshire, Duroc, Tamworth, or other heritage shoulder bacon, ribs, chops, and roasts. People in Des Moines, Madison, or the Twin Cities can easily find heritage pork in their areas too.

What's the big deal? Well, I put a Berkshire pork shank to the test. Conventional pork shanks need moist, low heat. I simply roasted the Berkshire in a hot oven with only salt and pepper. I brought it to my culinary book club—where it was promptly devoured. The shank was succulent and tender, with more flavor and a redder color than its mass-market counterpart.

Heritage breeds like the black Berkshire turn up on restaurant menus—from Chez Panisse in California to Lidia's in Kansas City and Babbo in New York City—and feature in La Quercia prosciutto and pancetta. They're raised mostly outdoors as the weather permits, with no growth hormones or routine antibiotics, at operations like Becker Lane Farm in Plainfield, Iowa; Willow Creek Farm in Loganville, Wisconsin; and Metzger Family Farms near Seneca, Missouri.

Heritage pork breeds take 6 to 8 weeks longer than the conventional Poland China to reach market weight. Heritage pork has a finer grain and more marbling. Says Mario Fantasma of Paradise Locker Meats, "That's where all the flavor comes from."

Today, "Kansas is the DOC of heritage foods," says Heritage Foods co-founder Patrick Martins, comparing it to Italy's *denominazione di origine controllata*, a designation that guarantees the origin and production standards of wine.

HOMEMADE NOODLES WITH PANCETTA, BLACK PEPPER, AND PECORINO OVER GREENS SERVES 4

At the end of a busy day—or a busy week—this one-dish meal is pure Heartland comfort. I like to use an artisan Heartland pancetta or guanciale (jowl bacon) from La Quercia, but any good bacon will also work well. Go for a good Wisconsin pecorino, such as the sheep's milk Marisa from Carr Valley. Serving this on top of greens is untraditional but delicious.

1 recipe Farmhouse Egg Pasta (page 24) or 1 pound dried pasta (such as fettuccine, egg noodles, or penne)

1 cup chopped pancetta, guanciale, or smoked bacon

¼ cup dry white wine

2 large eggs, beaten

1 cup grated pecorino cheese (about 4 ounces)

½ teaspoon freshly ground black pepper

4 cups baby spinach or arugula

1 Bring a large pot of salted water to a boil. Add the pasta and cook until al dente (the time will vary depending on what kind you are using). Drain the pasta, reserving 1 cup of the cooking water.

2 Meanwhile, cook the pancetta in a large skillet over medium heat until lightly browned but not crisp. Add the wine to the hot skillet and stir to deglaze. Remove from the heat. Add the hot, drained pasta to the skillet and toss with 2 forks to coat with the wine-pancetta mixture. Pour the eggs on top of the pasta and toss with 2 forks to coat it with the egg. Keep tossing and let the reserved heat of the pasta and skillet cook the eggs. Add the cheese and pepper and toss again.

3 To serve, place a cup of greens on each plate and top with the pasta.

HOG WILD

"I know of lots of people raising organic pork the way it should be done —from heritage breeds that live most of their lives outdoors—but few get results quite as delicious as yours," Michael Pollan (author of *Food Rules* and *In Defense of Food: An Eater's Manifesto*) wrote to Jude Becker, the newest generation of the Becker family to farm.

Becker is known for his "postmodern pigs"—organically raised heritage-breed porkers with "highly marbled meat with superior eating qualities" that have become the darlings of chefs and artisan cured-meat producers like La Quercia.

Some of Becker's Berkshire and Chester White pigs are fed almost entirely on Iowa acorns to develop flavor usually only found in similarly fed Italian and Spanish pork. The high-tannin acorn diet helps give the meat a sweet, nutty richness with a tender, lower-in-cholesterol fat that melts at room temperature, which makes acorn-fed heritage pork superb for making cured meats like prosciutto.

What's also unusual about Becker is that he is farming pretty much like his great-great-great-grandfather did. Christopher Becker emigrated from Oldenburg, Germany, to Ohio in 1850, then went on to Dyersville, Iowa, and purchased land, once given to soldiers for their service in the War of 1812, for $2.50 per acre. Before the chemical age, Christopher Becker farmed organically and then raised heritage breeds of livestock.

"As corn became a staple in the Midwest, it wasn't long until pig production evolved to be its alter ego," explains Jude Becker. "Pigs were a way for farmers to utilize the corn they produced on their farms by turning it into pork that could be shipped back east for consumption in the form of meat." Pork was the ultimate value-added product.

Today, the thirtysomething farmer has reached back to that tradition. He farms corn, soybeans, and oats organically. He rotates his fields. Straw from the cereal crops becomes bedding (and a plaything) for the pigs, and the pigs, in turn, help keep noxious weeds out of the fallow fields and fertilize them. And he keeps moving the pigs around. This is the time-tested way to keep the germs away so that you don't have to use antibiotics. "Livestock keeping through time has always been based on moving the animals and never making animals stay in one house forever," he says.

Chester White sows (they make better mothers) are bred to Berkshire boars. They give birth and nurse their young in individual, portable, insulated farrowing huts outdoors. The sows' body heat helps keep them all warm, so pigs can be farrowed all year long, a European practice that Becker studied. This also allows Becker to supply pork all year long, not just in the traditional fall and winter time frame.

When the piglets are old enough, they forage with their mothers in fallow grain, oat, or soybean fields and are also fed organic corn—or the acorns—until they're ready for prime time.

MOREL-GRILLED RIB-EYE **SERVES 4**

No matter if your steak is Hereford, Angus, Highland, Wagyu, or anonymous: Slather on this grilling paste that also functions as a marinade. Dried morel mushrooms—or other dried wild mushrooms like porcini, available in the produce section of better grocery stores or online—can make a very savory addition to the spice cupboard. Simply grind them into a powder in a clean coffee grinder or blender, and then use them in delicious concoctions like this one. Slather this paste on a big, thick sirloin, on smaller filets mignons, or on pork tenderloin destined for the grill. Marinate for at least 30 minutes, then sear. This paste gives foods a deep, complex, beefy flavor.

Morel Grilling Paste

2 tablespoons sugar

1 tablespoon kosher salt

5 large cloves garlic, minced

1 tablespoon red pepper flakes

1 tablespoon freshly ground black pepper

¼ cup dried morel mushrooms, ground to a powder in a coffee grinder

¼ cup canola oil

4 (1 inch thick) boneless rib-eye steaks

1 For the grilling paste, mix the sugar, salt, garlic, red pepper flakes, black pepper, morel powder, and oil together in a small bowl until it forms a paste. Slather the steaks with the paste and let marinate at room temperature for at least 30 minutes.

2 Meanwhile, prepare a medium-hot fire in your grill.

3 Grill the steaks for 3 minutes per side, turning once, for medium-rare.

HEARTLAND BEEF CATTLE BREEDS

Beef cattle can tolerate a dryer climate than dairy cattle, which need lots of rich green grass to make milk. That's why dairy cattle do better in the eastern Midwest, while beef cattle are perfectly at home in the Sandhills of Nebraska or the Flint Hills of Kansas, where cattle roam the rocky terrain in search of scrubby prairie grass.

AMERICAN SHORTHORN—brought from Yorkshire to America in 1783. Steers aged twelve months at slaughter weigh up to 1,200 pounds and produce reliably choice grade beef.

BELGIAN BLUE—a large-framed breed with superior beef flavor and texture, yet lower in fat and cholesterol. A recent arrival to the Great Plains.

BLACK ANGUS—Superior taste and texture makes marketing by the breed name easy.

HEREFORD AND POLLED HEREFORD—efficiently converts grass to meat; descended from eighteenth-century English cattle. Polled Herefords were developed by an Iowa rancher, who bred cattle born naturally without horns. Polled Herefords became a recognized breed in the early 1900s.

HIGHLAND—a light brown, shaggy-haired breed from the Scottish Highlands. Highland cattle can withstand the cold weather better than other breeds.

LIMOUSIN—a reddish gold French breed that first arrived in Kansas in 1971 from Canada.

MILKING SHORTHORN—a heritage breed that can be used for both dairy and meat, so a family farm favorite.

WAGYU—Wa translates as "Japanese" and gyū as "cow." A Japanese breed genetically predisposed to intense marbling, thus producing richer, juicier meat, even on grass. Five major breeds include Japanese Black, Japanese Brown, Japanese Polled, Japanese Shorthorn, and Kumamoto Reds. Sometimes, Wagyu are crossbred with Black Angus for a darker meat.

HEARTLAND DAUBE WITH WHITE CHEDDAR POLENTA

SERVES 12

When you're entertaining a crowd, as I do for my son Nick's birthday in the fall, this dish delivers. With just a touch of smoky flavor, it tastes like you simmered it slowly over a wood fire. Plus, you can take your time preparing it, if you like: marinate one day, slow-simmer the next, serve on the third day. And the leftovers? Fabulous. The cheddar polenta is a last-minute dish that stirs together easily. Prior to 1850, nearly all the cheese produced in the United States was cheddar. By 1880, Wisconsin took the cheddar-making lead. And today, Wisconsin is still the leading cheddar maker in the United States. Use an aged, sharp variety for the best flavor.

3 onions, thinly sliced

6 cloves garlic, chopped

3 medium carrots, peeled and chopped

4 pounds boneless chuck, cut into 1½-inch cubes

1 (750-milliliter) bottle full-bodied red wine

¼ cup Home-Rendered Lard (page 10) or canola oil

2 bay leaves

2 sprigs thyme, or ½ teaspoon dried thyme

1 cup pitted niçoise olives (preferably oil-cured)

Fine kosher or sea salt and freshly ground black pepper

1 tablespoon liquid smoke

1 Place the onions, garlic, carrots, and beef in a large nonreactive pan. Pour the wine over the mixture, cover, and refrigerate for 12 to 24 hours.

2 Preheat the oven to 325°F. Remove the beef from the vegetables with a slotted spoon (reserve the vegetable mixture) and pat the beef dry with paper towels. Heat the lard over medium heat in a large, heavy casserole with a lid. Brown the beef in batches in the hot oil. Remove the beef from the casserole, add the reserved marinade and vegetable mixture, and cook, scraping up the browned bits from the bottom of the pan. Return the beef to the pan with the liquid and add the bay leaves, thyme, and olives.

3 Cover and braise the beef over medium heat for 2½ to 3 hours, or until tender. If there is too much liquid in the pan about 2 hours into the cooking time, remove the lid to let some evaporate. Add the salt and pepper to taste and the liquid smoke. Remove the bay leaves and thyme sprigs. (The stew can be made a day or two ahead, covered, and refrigerated.)

4 For the polenta, bring the chicken broth and white pepper to a boil in a large saucepan over medium-high heat. Sprinkle in the grits and whisk to blend. Keep whisking until the grits thicken, 3 to 4 minutes. Stir in the cheese until it melts.

5 Scoop the polenta into shallow bowls and ladle the stew over the top. Serve hot.

White Cheddar Polenta

8 cups chicken broth

2 teaspoons freshly ground white pepper

2 cups quick-cooking hominy grits or polenta

4 cups grated aged white cheddar cheese (about 16 ounces; such as Widmer's)

HOME ON THE RANGE

Gone are the days of the open range, when cowboys could drive their herds of cattle across open country as Larry McMurtry immortalized in *Lonesome Dove*. Today, ranchers rarely see their cattle from birth to the stockyard. They usually specialize in one part of the whole process: buying and selling calves (from birth to weaning), pasturing, or putting the finishing touch on cattle before they go to the stockyard. Or they specialize in what ranchers call "boutique beef"—specialty breeds raised from start to finish, processed under the supervision of, and often dry-aged by, the rancher.

John and Dorothy Priske, who run a herd of 300 shaggy Highland beef cattle at their Fountain Prairie Inn and Farms near Fall River, Wisconsin, take one steer a week to be processed into grass-fed, dry-aged beef. Its full, beefy flavor has made it a favorite of chefs and shoppers at the Dane County Farmer's Market. Others, like Morgan Ranch in the Sandhills of Nebraska, specialize in Wagyu beef, the Japanese breed that produces extensively marbled meat. Regardless of the breed, however, the cycle remains the same.

In early spring, calves are born and enjoy their first few months of mother's milk and open pasture. When a calf is weaned, it usually weighs about 425 pounds. From the first of September until around April, calves pasture on green shoots of winter wheat, sugar beet greens, and hay, putting on about 125 more pounds. If calves stop pasturing on wheat in March, the farmer can still get in a good wheat crop. After the grasses green up again after the spring rains, the cattle are trucked from the ranch to open pasturage, often to places like the Flint Hills in east-central Kansas. During the summer, cattle will put on an additional 250 to 300 pounds. By the first of September, the eighteen-month-old "yearling" heifers and steers now weigh about 800 pounds, and the next stop could be a feedlot, many of which are in southwestern Nebraska and southwestern Kansas, or new pastures. When the cattle have added about 125 more pounds, they make the transition from stockyard to butcher shop.

THE ALL-AMERICAN HAMBURGER

Americans crave their hamburgers. Food historians credit mid-nineteenth-century German immigrants from Hamburg with introducing ground beef seasoned with onion and parsley, shaped into patties and pan-fried—the first hamburgers.

By the early 1900s, the chopped onion was starting to be grilled separately, and the unique American hamburger was born. America's oldest hamburger emporium, White Castle, began in Wichita, Kansas, in the early 1900s. Today, every small-town café in the Midwest has its own version of the hamburger, but none as tiny as the Cozy Burger, sizzled on a grill with butter and onions at the Cozy Inn in Salina, Kansas. Well-seared burgers on buttery buns are the calling card for Wisconsin-based Culver's, a current leader in the fast-food burger market.

Firmly established in the mainstream, burgers have now gone uptown, made with top cuts of juicy, grass-fed beef, ground-in-house and served on artisan ciabatta or brioche buns with chef-made condiments. From a trend started by New York chef Daniel Boulud in 2001, upscale burgers now invite Heartland chefs to get the most from a regional signature food. Try a to-die-for burger from dry-aged Highland beef, a heritage breed raised and processed by Fountain Prairie Inn and Farms near Fall River, Wisconsin (see Resources, page 266).

FIRE UP THE GRILL

Grilling and barbecuing, as cooking methods, owe much of their burgeoning popularity to three Midwesterners. In the 1920s, Detroit's Henry Ford recycled discarded wooden Model T frames into charcoal briquettes, which were sent in bags for Ford dealers to sell to customers, an unlikely but successful marketing method. Chicago's George Stephen invented the first kettle grill in 1951. President Dwight Eisenhower, born in Kansas, loved nothing better than "dirty steak"—a steak sizzled right on the charcoal in his grill at the 1950s White House.

Now there are various aromatic hardwoods available from Midwestern suppliers such as American BBQ Wood Products or Fairlane BBQ Wood (see Resources, page 266), for grilling with a kiss of smoke or slow smoking; hardwood lump charcoal, and every kind of barbecue sauce and spice imaginable. Weber-Stephen, based in Palatine, Illinois, is still the market leader in the ever-growing barbecue field.

GRILLED LAMB CHOPS and ASPARAGUS with ROSEMARY AIOLI SERVES 6 TO 8

Quick, quick, quick. With a hot fire, you'll get the flavor you need in just minutes, but you have to be vigilant and handy with the long-handled grill tongs. These lamb chops come off the grill succulently tender and the asparagus with just a little char. With a dollop of aioli made with regional canola oil and fresh rosemary, this is mighty fine eatin'—fast. Drink a lightly chilled, soft red wine such as Buffalo Red from Somerset Ridge in Kansas, Prairie Sunburst Red from Wollersheim in Wisconsin, or Big Red from Mackinac Trail in Michigan. For dessert, serve Summer in a Jar (page 261) made with rhubarb and strawberry.

2 pounds medium asparagus spears, trimmed

12 lamb chops, pounded to a ½-inch thickness

Canola oil, for brushing

Coarse kosher or sea salt and freshly ground black pepper

Rosemary Aioli

1 large clove garlic

1 to 2 tablespoons fresh rosemary leaves

1 teaspoon coarse kosher salt

2 large egg yolks

1⅓ cups canola oil

2 tablespoons freshly squeezed lemon juice

Sprigs of rosemary, for garnish

Lemon wedges, for garnish

1   Prepare a hot fire in your grill.

2   Brush the asparagus, then the lamb chops, with oil and season with salt and pepper.

3   Place the asparagus spears perpendicular to the grill grates, or use a perforated grill rack to keep them from falling through the grates. Grill the asparagus, turning as necessary, until the spears have good grill marks and a little char, 2 to 3 minutes. They will continue to cook off the grill. Grill the lamb chops for 1 to 2 minutes per side, turning once, or until an instant-read thermometer inserted in the thickest part registers 120° to 130°F for rare. Remove the lamb and let rest, tented with aluminum foil, for about 10 minutes (the internal temperature will continue to rise to 130° to 135°F).

4   For the aioli, place the garlic, rosemary, and salt in the work bowl of a food processor. Process until you have a fine paste. Add the egg yolks and pulse to blend. While the machine is running, slowly pour in half the oil, then the lemon juice, then the rest of the oil, until the mixture has emulsified like mayonnaise. Pulse in a little warm water (up to 2 tablespoons) if the mixture is too thick.

5   Arrange the lamb chops and asparagus on a platter and garnish with the rosemary sprigs and lemon wedges. Serve the aioli alongside.

PAN-ROASTED CHICKEN BREASTS WITH TARRAGON CREAMED CORN
SERVES 4

Free-range, organic chicken—a heritage breed, if you can find it—fresh sweet corn, and garden-grown tarragon provide the flavors in this new take on a farmhouse classic. A large cast-iron skillet, which can go from stovetop to oven, gives the crispest, most flavorful result. Cover the skillet with a lid or a sheet of aluminum foil to keep from making a big mess in your oven. Serve with a crisp green salad and Farmhouse Yeast Rolls (page 88).

4 bone-in, skin-on chicken breasts

2 tablespoons Home-Rendered Lard (page 10) or canola oil

Kosher salt and freshly ground black pepper

Tarragon Creamed Corn

4 cups fresh or frozen sweet corn kernels

½ cup chopped scallions

1 cup heavy cream

1 tablespoon fresh tarragon leaves

1 tablespoon tarragon vinegar

Kosher salt and freshly ground black pepper

Sprigs of tarragon, for garnish

½ cup dry white wine

1 tablespoon freshly squeezed lemon juice

SUGGESTED CORN VARIETIES:
Country Gentleman, Silver Queen, Boone County White, Butter and Sugar, Peaches and Cream

1 Preheat the oven to 475°F. On the stovetop, heat a large cast-iron skillet over high heat. While the pan heats up (this can take about 15 minutes), make sure the chicken is patted as dry as possible. Brush the skin side of the chicken breasts with the lard. When the pan is smoking hot, carefully place the chicken, skin side down, in the pan, and cover carefully with a lid or sheet of aluminum foil. With heavy-duty oven mitts, transfer the covered skillet to the oven. Roast for 10 minutes.

2 Carefully remove the hot pan from the oven and turn the chicken breasts. The skin should be beautifully golden and crisp. Generously season the skin side with salt and pepper. Cover and return the pan to the oven. Roast for 20 to 25 minutes longer, or until an instant-read thermometer inserted in the thickest part of a breast registers 160°F.

3 Meanwhile, make the creamed corn. In a nonstick skillet over medium heat, stir the corn, scallions, cream, and tarragon leaves together. Cook, stirring occasionally, until the corn is tender, about 5 minutes for fresh corn, 10 to 12 minutes for frozen. Stir in the vinegar and cook for 2 minutes longer. Season to taste with salt and pepper and keep warm.

4 Remove the chicken from the oven, transfer to a plate, and tent with foil to keep warm. Place the skillet over medium-high heat, whisk the white wine into the pan drippings, and let reduce by half, about 2 minutes. Stir in the lemon juice, then season to taste with salt and pepper. Place a chicken breast on each plate and drizzle with the pan sauce. Spoon the creamed corn onto the plate, garnish with the tarragon sprigs, and serve.

GRILLED DUCK BREAST WITH WILD RICE–DRIED CHERRY PILAF **SERVES 4**

The constellation of flavors in this dish comes from the Heartland larder: domestic duck, sorghum, wild rice, and dried cherries. If you buy whole ducks, make the legs and thighs into Flyover Country Duck Confit (page 38).

Sorghum-Lime Grilling Paste

2 cloves garlic, minced

Juice and grated zest of 1 lime

2 tablespoons sorghum syrup or dark brown sugar

4 domestic boneless duck breast halves

Fine kosher or sea salt and freshly ground black pepper

Wild Rice–Dried Cherry Pilaf

2 tablespoons Home-Rendered Lard (page 10) or canola oil

1 medium onion, chopped

1 cup wild rice

3 cups chicken broth

½ cup long-grain white rice

½ cup dried cherries

1 tablespoon sorghum syrup or honey

Fine kosher or sea salt and freshly ground black pepper

1 For the grilling paste, whisk the garlic, lime zest and juice, and sorghum together.

2 With a sharp knife, score the fat on each duck breast half, but don't cut through to the meat. Season the duck breasts with salt and pepper, then lightly paint the surface of each duck breast with the grilling paste. Let marinate at room temperature for 1 hour.

3 Meanwhile, prepare a medium-hot fire in your grill, and make the pilaf. In a large saucepan, heat the lard over medium-high heat and sauté the onion until translucent, about 4 minutes. Add the wild rice and chicken broth and bring to a boil. Lower the heat and simmer, covered, for 20 minutes. Add the white rice, dried cherries, and sorghum. Cover again and cook for 20 minutes, or until all the rice is tender. Season to taste with salt and pepper and keep warm.

4 Grill the duck breasts, fat side down, for 4 minutes, keeping a spray bottle filled with water handy in case of flare-ups. Turn and continue grilling for another 2 to 3 minutes, or until the duck reaches an internal temperature of 140° to 145°F for medium-rare. Transfer to a platter and let the duck breasts rest for 5 minutes.

5 To serve, slice the duck breasts on the diagonal, shingle them on each plate, and serve with the pilaf.

PECKING ORDER

The Heartland farm wife who kept heritage breed chickens in the farmyard had her own pecking order as to which breed fit which need.

Plymouth Barred Rocks grew fastest, so they were used for frying.

Dark Indian Game Cornish grew smaller, so they were poached for chicken salad and chicken and noodles.

Jersey Black Giants and New Hampshire birds grew slowest, so they were reserved for baking or roasting.

DUMB CLUCKS

In 1919, the Vermilion County Home Bureau in Illinois thought it wise to publish the following guidelines for farmers, so they could spot a slacker hen at a glance. (If it were only this easy for today's boss!)

"Fortunately, for the farmer, a hen can't refuse to lay and then lie about it. How to tell the slacker from the layer:

SLACKER (The hen to sell)	LAYER (The hen to keep)
1. Pale, shriveled comb	1. Large, red comb
2. Yellow ear lobe	2. Bleached white ear lobe
3. Deep yellow shanks	3. Pale yellow to white shanks
4. Early molter	4. Late molter
5. Exceptionally long toe nails	5. Short toe nails. . . .

Remember: The hen that lays is the hen that pays."

PHEASANT SCHNITZEL WITH DANISH RED CABBAGE SERVES 4 TO 6

With a mound of Buttery Mashed Potatoes (page 211) and a side of braised red cabbage, "schnitzelled" pheasant or chicken breast is just the kind of homemade meal I crave when the weather turns crisp. This sweeter, more aromatic version of braised red cabbage is our family's comfort food. Make it a day ahead, if you like, and then warm it on the stove while you sauté the schnitzel. Pounding the pheasant or chicken breast tenderizes it as well as lets it cook faster to a crisp and delicious finish. If you're using tougher wild pheasant, pound it to a ⅛-inch thickness. You can also use pork tenderloin or veal in this recipe.

Danish Red Cabbage

½ cup (1 stick) unsalted butter

1 head red cabbage, cored and thinly sliced

1 large red onion, chopped

2 red apples, cored and thinly sliced

½ cup tart red jelly (such as red currant or lingonberry jelly or preserves)

Fine kosher or sea salt

1 For the red cabbage, melt the butter in a large pot over medium-high heat. Stir in the cabbage and onion and cook, stirring, until the cabbage begins to wilt. Stir in the apple slices. Lower the heat and simmer, covered, for 2 hours, or until tender. Stir in the jelly until it melts and combines with the cabbage. Add salt to taste. (Cover and refrigerate if preparing this a day ahead, then warm over low heat.)

2 For the schnitzel, cut lengthwise through the thickest part of each breast so that you have 2 thinner breast pieces. Place the pieces between 2 pieces of waxed or parchment paper and pound until each is ¼ inch thick.

3 Combine the flour, salt, and white pepper on a small plate. Combine the eggs, 1 teaspoon lemon juice, and parsley in a shallow bowl. Arrange the bread crumbs on a second small plate. Dredge each breast piece, on both sides, in the flour mixture, then the egg mixture, then the bread crumb mixture. Place on a baking sheet and let the coating set for 15 minutes.

4 Heat the lard over medium-high heat in a large skillet. Sauté the pheasant, turning once, until golden brown on both sides, about 4 minutes total. Arrange the pheasant and red cabbage on plates, then add the white wine to the hot pan and let it bubble up for 2 minutes. Swirl the lemon juice and capers into the pan juices. Add enough butter to enrich the sauce as it melts and mixes in. Drizzle over the pheasant and serve.

Pheasant Schnitzel

4 boneless, skinless pheasant or chicken breasts

½ cup unbleached all-purpose flour

½ teaspoon fine kosher or sea salt

½ teaspoon freshly ground white pepper

2 large eggs, beaten

1 teaspoon freshly squeezed lemon juice or tarragon vinegar

1 tablespoon finely chopped fresh Italian parsley

1½ cups panko bread crumbs

2 tablespoons Home-Rendered Lard (page 10) or canola oil

¾ cup dry white wine

1 tablespoon freshly squeezed lemon juice

1 tablespoon capers, drained

2 to 4 tablespoons unsalted butter, softened

HUNTER'S PIE WITH BUTTERY MASHED POTATOES SERVES 8

With wild meat, you never know how old or tough the bird or beast was before you start cooking. With this recipe, it doesn't matter. Just chop the meat finely by hand or by pulsing it in a food processor and you're good to go. Obviously, a hunter's pie made with venison or bison will have a different flavor than the same recipe made with pheasant or duck, but it all works. Dried mushrooms add a deep, mysterious, woodsy flavor of their own. Even people who think they don't like game will like this hearty, one-dish meal, which can be made a day ahead and warmed in the oven. Serve this with a Heartland craft brew such as Goose Island's Nightstalker Stout or Hinterland Brewery's Packerland Pilsner, and be glad for leftovers.

1 ounce dried wild mushrooms (such as morel, porcini, or other)

1 cup boiling water

2 tablespoons Home-Rendered Lard (page 10) or canola oil

2 large onions, chopped

2 large carrots, peeled and chopped

2 cloves garlic, minced

8 ounces white mushrooms, sliced

1 pound finely chopped or ground pheasant, venison, bison, duck, wild turkey, or goose

1 pound ground pork

1 teaspoon fine kosher or sea salt

1 tablespoon unbleached all-purpose flour

1 (14-ounce) can chopped tomatoes, drained

½ cup dry white wine or port

1   Place the dried mushrooms in a medium bowl and pour the boiling water over them. Let steep for 15 minutes.

2   Meanwhile, heat the lard in a large pot over medium-high heat and sauté the onions, carrots, and garlic until the onions are translucent, about 5 minutes. Remove the softened wild mushrooms from their liquid, reserving the liquid, and chop. Add the wild and fresh mushrooms to the pot and sauté until the fresh mushrooms begin to give off their liquid, about 5 minutes.

3   Add the meats to the pot and cook, stirring, until they begin to brown. Stir in the salt and flour until well combined, then the tomatoes and wine. Bring to a boil, then lower the heat and simmer, covered, for 1 hour.

4   Meanwhile, make the mashed potatoes. Place the potatoes in a large pot with enough cold water to cover. Bring to a boil over medium-high heat and cook until the potatoes are tender, 15 to 20 minutes. Drain the potatoes. Transfer them back to the pot, mash them with the milk and butter, season with the salt and white pepper, and keep warm.

Buttery Mashed Potatoes

5 pounds red potatoes, peeled and cubed

¼ cup whole milk

4 tablespoons (½ stick) unsalted butter, plus more to dot on the top

½ teaspoon fine kosher or sea salt

½ teaspoon freshly ground white pepper

5   Preheat the oven to 400°F. To assemble the dish, spoon the meat mixture into a deep casserole dish, then top with the mashed potatoes. Dot the potatoes with tiny pieces of butter. (The pie can be prepared to this point 1 day ahead, covered, and refrigerated.)

6   Bake for 20 minutes, or until the potatoes have browned slightly and the filling is hot.

"Sweet corn was so delicious, what could have produced it except sex? . . . People have wanted sex to be as good as sweet corn and have worked hard to improve it, and afterward they lay together in the dark and said . . . 'That was so wonderful. . . . But it wasn't as good as fresh sweet corn.'"

—GARRISON KEILLOR

ALL EARS

The climate of the Midwest is ideal for growing corn, which needs hot, humid summers and rich bottomland soil to be "knee high by the Fourth of July" and then ripen to sugary goodness. When it's in season, people go nuts for it.

Festivals like the Sweet Corn Festival in Sun Prairie, Wisconsin, celebrate this delicacy every third week in August since 1953. Sure, there are the fire engine rides, a parade, a craft fair, and bingo. But generations of sweet corn lovers, from great-grandparents to the smallest child, grab the saltshakers suspended by strings from a clothesline and get down to business—gobbling ear after ear, right out of the pot.

Traditional sweet corn varieties like Silver Queen, Peaches and Cream, and Purdue Super Sweet barely make it in from the field before folks boil or grill it and devour it. Our collective love of sweet corn is also reflected in the names of new varieties: Temptation, Charm, Revelation, Sugar Pearl, Obsession, Passion, Gotta Have It, and Sweet Perfection. Who can resist?

ROAST HERITAGE TURKEY WITH PANCETTA-ROASTED BRUSSELS SPROUTS

SERVES 8 TO 10

"This is a truly American icon. This is the bird that fed Americans for 200 years," says Frank Reese about the American Bronze, Narragansett, and Bourbon Red heritage turkey breeds strutting around his Good Shepherd Turkey Ranch in Lindsborg, Kansas. More Marilyn Monroe than Dolly Parton, heritage birds are more proportioned, not overly endowed with dry, bland-tasting breast meat like mass-market birds. A heritage bird's dark meat is milder tasting than that of a conventionally raised bird; there is more fat, and so more flavor; and the texture is firmer too. "The smell of traditional turkey quietly roasting in the oven can bring a house to life," adds Reese. A heritage bird deserves an artisan accompaniment, so here's one that transforms a much-maligned vegetable into a holiday-worthy dish—with a little help from Pancetta Americano from La Quercia in Iowa. For Thanksgiving dinner, serve with Farmhouse Yeast Rolls (page 88), Cranberry-Pear Compote (page 51), and Fresh Pumpkin Pie (page 221).

¾ teaspoon fine kosher or sea salt

½ teaspoon freshly ground black pepper

½ teaspoon poultry seasoning

1 (12 to 16-pound) heritage turkey, giblets removed, rinsed, and patted dry

1 small yellow onion, quartered

8 sprigs tarragon

½ cup (1 stick) unsalted butter, melted

1 Preheat the oven to 325°F. Combine the salt, pepper, and poultry seasoning and season the bird on the outside. Stuff the cavity with the onion quarters and tarragon sprigs. Skewer the neck skin under the bird and arrange the wings akimbo against its back. Place the turkey, breast side down, on a roasting rack in a roasting pan with a cover. Pour about 2 cups water into the bottom of the pan and roast the bird, uncovered, for 30 minutes.

2 Baste the bird with the juices in the pan, tightly cover the pan, and continue roasting for 15 to 20 minutes per pound (4 to 5 hours), basting every hour, or until an instant-read thermometer inserted in the meatiest part of the thigh registers 180°F. During the last 30 minutes of roasting, remove the cover, baste again, brush generously with the melted butter, and let the bird brown. Remove from the oven, transfer the turkey to a cutting board or platter, tent with aluminum foil, and let rest for 15 minutes before carving.

3 When the turkey is out of the oven, increase the temperature to 450°F. Toss the Brussels sprouts, pancetta, shallots, oil, and salt and pepper to taste in another roasting pan and spread in one layer.

Pancetta-Roasted Brussels Sprouts

2 pounds Brussels sprouts, trimmed and halved

4 ounces pancetta, minced, or thick-sliced smoked American bacon

6 shallots, minced

1 tablespoon canola oil

Fine kosher or sea salt and freshly ground black pepper

½ cup water

½ cup dry white wine

½ cup heavy cream

Roast for 25 to 30 minutes, stirring halfway through. At the end of the roasting time, stir in the water, scraping up the browned bits in the pan. Season to taste with salt and pepper.

4   While the sprouts are roasting, make the sauce or "gravy." Place the roasting pan that held the turkey over medium-high heat on the stovetop and stir to loosen any browned bits. Bring to a boil and stir in the wine. Let the mixture reduce to about 1½ cups, then stir in the cream. Season to taste with salt and pepper and serve with the bird and Brussels sprouts.

"WE ALL HAVE HOMETOWN APPETITES.

Every other person is a bundle of longing for the simplicities of good taste once enjoyed on the farm or in the hometown left behind," writes Clementine Paddleford—food writer, tastemaker, and cookbook author—whose hometown was Stockdale, Kansas. That's especially true for desserts.

If there is a dessert that symbolizes the Heartland, it's homemade pie. Pie is friendly, unassuming, modest—you have to wonder what's under that crust. It welcomes a diversity of fillings and can be a common denominator. While cake usually means celebrating a special occasion, a homemade pie links people together on an everyday basis. When neighbors come to call, when business people need to talk over a deal, or when friends gather to gossip, it's pie and coffee. Slices of pie are sold at antique auctions, community events, and school functions.

While some Heartland pies are iconic—Hoosier Sugar Cream Pie (page 224), Fresh Pumpkin Pie (page 221), or Ohio Lemon Tart (page 227)—there's a new twist to them. Now that we're looking at lard in a different way—hydrogenated lard was bad, but Home-Rendered Lard (page 10) is good—the heartbreakingly flaky and delicious lard-and-butter pastry is back to envelop a berry, fruit, pumpkin, or cream filling. And the new darling of apples—the Honeycrisp from Minnesota—is worthy of its own special pie, Honeycrisp Apple Upside-Down Pie (page 222).

While pie is welcome-all democratic, cookies stay close to their ethnic roots. Every family has a certain holiday cookie that traces back to an ancestor's sweet tooth, such as Italian Fig Cookies (page 232), Lemon–Poppy Seed Whirligigs (page 231), or Espresso-Ginger Sandwich Cookies (page 229)—a traditional ginger cookie with a contemporary spin. You can reawaken memories of small-town bakeries with one bite of tender Bakeshop Butter Cookies (page 236).

Some desserts are just plain fun and evoke county fairs, but with delicious new flavors—Root Beer Funnel Cakes (page 259) or A Trio of Snow Cones (page 264), for example. And some desserts are simply irresistible. I feel that way about a Hot Fudge Sundae with Salted Caramel Sauce (page 248), especially when it's made with Jeni Britton Bauer's Vanilla Bean Ice Cream (page 247). Both the ice-cream cone (St. Louis World's Fair in 1904) and the ice-cream sundae (Green Rivers, Wisconsin, in 1881) were invented in the Heartland, but Jeni Britton Bauer has revolutionized ice-cream production by reinventing the dairy co-op, with 12 farms producing full-flavored, organic milk from grass-fed cows. I also find it difficult to stay away from Crackly-Top Hickory Nut Cake (page 252), so moist that it's almost fudgelike.

So many desserts, so little time. . . .

FARMHOUSE BUTTER-LARD PASTRY

MAKES ENOUGH FOR 1 (9-INCH) DOUBLE-CRUST PIE OR 2 (9-INCH) SINGLE-CRUST PIES

Heartland cooks swear by a butter and lard crust for flakiness and flavor. This type of crust also stands up to any filling. If you don't have good rendered lard made from leaf lard, substitute vegetable shortening instead. The extra step of smearing the dough helps distribute the fat through the flour and makes for an especially flaky pastry. Disks of this pie crust can be wrapped and refrigerated for up to 3 days or wrapped well and frozen for up to a year. Have several batches of this pastry made up, so that when you want to go berry picking, make potpies, or prepare for Thanksgiving, baking will be easier.

2 cups unbleached all-purpose flour

¼ teaspoon salt

½ teaspoon sugar

3 tablespoons Home-Rendered Lard (page 10), frozen and cut into small pieces

3 tablespoons unsalted butter, frozen and cut into small pieces

4 to 6 tablespoons ice water

1 Measure the flour by scooping it into a measuring cup, then leveling it with your finger. Pour the flour, salt, and sugar into the work bowl of a food processor. Pulse to blend. Add the lard and butter. Pulse quickly about 10 times, or until the mixture forms small crumbs. Drizzle 4 tablespoons ice water over the flour mixture. Pulse again several times, or until the dough starts to form medium crumbs. Test the dough by trying to gather it into a ball with your hand. If you can gather it into a rough ball, stop. If the dough is still too crumbly, drizzle another tablespoon or two of ice water over the dough and pulse again to blend.

2 Transfer the dough to a lightly floured surface. Gently gather the dough into a ball with your hand. Using the heel of your hand, smear one-quarter of the dough about 6 inches across the surface. Repeat until all of the dough is smeared in the same direction.

3 Using a dough scraper or pancake turner, gather the dough together into a rough cylinder. Cut the dough in half. Form each half into a ball, then flatten slightly into a disk. Wrap each disk in plastic wrap and refrigerate for 30 minutes before rolling out (or wrap and freeze for up to 6 months). Thaw frozen dough in the refrigerator for 24 hours before using.

NOTE: Freeze an unbaked, fruit-filled pie to bake later. Roll out the dough and fill double-crust pies with a fruit filling. Wrap well and freeze the unbaked pies for up to 1 year. Bake directly from the freezer in a 350°F oven for 1½ to 2 hours, or until the crust has browned and the filling is bubbling.

FRESH PUMPKIN PIE

MAKES 1 (9-INCH) SINGLE-CRUST PIE

When small sugar or pie pumpkins come on the market around Halloween, snap up a few to make a fresh pumpkin pie filling. When made from fresh pumpkin, the traditional Thanksgiving pie has a lighter and fresher flavor that may convert even those who think they do not like pumpkin pie. If you can, use a local honey. Good spices matter, too. Buy a whole nutmeg and grate some of it into the filling. Use Saigon or Vietnamese cinnamon for the strongest flavor. You can make and freeze the fresh pumpkin puree in 3-cup measurements ahead of time, so you're ready to bake in less time.

1 (3-pound) sugar or pie pumpkin

Pastry for a single-crust pie (see page 220)

4 large eggs, lightly beaten

¾ cup clover honey or other amber-colored honey

1 cup half-and-half

½ teaspoon ground nutmeg (preferably freshly grated)

½ teaspoon ground Saigon or Vietnamese cinnamon

1 teaspoon salt

1. Position an oven rack in the center of the oven and preheat the oven to 350°F. Line a baking sheet with parchment paper or aluminum foil and set aside.

2. Cut the pumpkin into large chunks and remove and discard the seeds and stringy matter. Place the pumpkin pieces, cut side down, on the baking sheet and roast for 45 minutes, or until the pumpkin is tender when pierced with a fork. Let cool.

3. Remove the rind with a sharp knife and place the cooked pumpkin in the work bowl of a food processor. Puree until smooth. Measure 3 cups of puree for the pie (reserve any remaining for another use).

4. When ready to bake, preheat the oven to 375°F. Line a 9-inch pie pan with the pastry and crimp the edges. In a bowl using a hand mixer, beat the pumpkin puree with the eggs, honey, half-and-half, nutmeg, cinnamon, and salt until smooth. Pour the filling into the pie shell. Place the filled pie pan on a baking sheet.

5. Bake the pie on the middle rack of the oven for 55 to 60 minutes, or until a toothpick inserted in the center comes out clean and the filling is glossy on top. Let cool before cutting and serving.

HONEYCRISP APPLE UPSIDE-DOWN PIE   **MAKES 1 (10-INCH) PIE**

How we have fallen in love with Minnesota's Honeycrisp apples, which *The New York Times* called the iPod of apples. Susan Goss at Chicago's West Town Tavern uses them to make turnovers served with caramel ice cream and caramel sauce. In Indianapolis, Ron Harris of Pink Pie Bakery—"I love pink. I love pie. And I can bake," he says— makes a mean Honeycrisp apple pie. The secret of success with this upside-down pie is a cast-iron skillet, which helps the apples caramelize evenly; the skillet goes right from the stovetop into the oven. Serve with Cinnamon Crème Fraîche (page 256).

6 tablespoons (¾ stick) unsalted butter

6 to 8 Honeycrisp or other sweet-tart apples (about 3 pounds), peeled, quartered, and cored

½ cup sugar

1 thawed frozen puff pastry sheet (keep it cold)

1   Preheat the oven to 425°F.

2   Melt the butter in a 10-inch cast-iron skillet over medium-high heat. Stir in the apples and sugar and cook, stirring occasionally so that the apples and sugar do not stick, until the apples turn a medium golden brown, 25 to 30 minutes. Remove the skillet from the heat.

3   Meanwhile, roll out the puff pastry sheet. Using a paring knife, cut a 10-inch circle to fit the skillet. Keep chilled.

4   Carefully turn the apples so the cut sides are facing up and they make an attractive pattern in the skillet. Place the pastry circle over the apples.

5   Bake for 35 to 40 minutes, or until the pastry has puffed and is a golden brown. Remove from the oven and place a large serving plate over the skillet. With oven mitts on both hands, invert the skillet onto the serving plate. Tap the bottom of the skillet to help release the tart, then slowly lift the skillet so that the tart falls, topping side up, onto the serving plate.

A HONEYCRISP APPLE A DAY

Bite into a Honeycrisp apple and you're hooked. Sweet/tart and almost explosively juicy, the Honeycrisp is "one in a million; the Einstein of apples," says David Bedford, the University of Minnesota's chief apple breeder. What's unique about Honeycrisp apples is that they have large cells with strong cell walls, so they hold a lot of juice. Great to eat fresh as well as bake and sauté, the Honeycrisp is now the most cultivated apple in Minnesota.

But the Honeycrisp almost didn't make it.

It started out as Number 1711, a stand of four hybrid apple trees cloned in the 1970s and due to be discarded. When Bedford went out to the test orchard in the spring of 1979, he decided to give them a reprieve, as the winters of 1978 and 1979 had been brutal—Midwestern states as far south as Ohio had endured extreme cold and howling blizzards in 1978; Lake Michigan completely froze in 1979.

A few years later, the Number 1711 trees bore their first fruits, and the rest, as they say, is history.

HOOSIER SUGAR CREAM PIE

MAKES 1 (9-INCH) SINGLE-CRUST PIE

"Sugar-cream pie, an Indiana signature dessert, is like cream candy in a savory crust," says Michael Stern of Roadfood fame. If Indiana had a state pie, this would be it. Not quite custard, sugar cream pie is a relative of chess and transparent pies that came from English settlers by way of Kentucky. The recipe probably came to Indiana through nineteenth-century Shaker communities that spread from New England to Ohio settlements near the Indiana border. Directions in the earliest "receipts" call for mixing the filling in the unbaked crust and then stirring it with the fingers as it baked. This contemporary version saves fingers from burning by combining the ingredients in a bowl and baking the filling without stirring.

Pastry for a single-crust pie (see page 220)

1 cup heavy cream

1 cup half-and-half

1 cup sugar

½ cup unbleached all-purpose flour

3 tablespoons unsalted butter, cut into small pieces

¼ teaspoon ground nutmeg

1   Preheat the oven to 425°F. Line a 9-inch pie pan with the pastry and crimp the edges.

2   In a medium bowl, combine the cream, half-and-half, sugar, and flour and mix well. Pour into the pie shell. Dot with the butter, then sprinkle with the nutmeg.

3   Bake for 15 minutes, then remove the pie and cover the edges with aluminum foil to prevent overbrowning. Lower the temperature to 350°F and bake for 45 minutes longer, or until a toothpick inserted in the center comes out clean. Let cool for 30 minutes before slicing and serving.

I'LL TAKE MY PIE WITH CREAM AND SUGAR

In 1944, Mr. and Mrs. "Wick" Wickersham began baking and selling sugar cream pies based on his great-grandmother's farm recipe. The sugar cream pies, and eighteen more varieties, were made by hand and delivered to customers in the family's 1934 Buick sedan. Milk, sugar, flour, shortening, vanilla, and nutmeg combined to form a single-crust pie with a sweet, custard-like filling subtly scented with spice. Wick's Pies, the bakery and restaurant in Winchester, Indiana, also has a bakery outlet, where you can buy "scratch and dent" pies with imperfect crusts but all the flavor (see Resources, page 266).

OHIO LEMON TART   MAKES 1 (8-INCH) TART

In the early 1800s, when Ohio was considered "the West," the communal Shaker sect established several villages—White Water near the southwestern Indiana border, Union near Lebanon, Watervliet near Dayton, and North Union in what is now the Cleveland area. The Shakers believed in "hands to work and hearts to God" as well as celibacy—maybe that's why they put so much love and attention into their food. For lemon lovers, there's nothing better than a warm slice of this rich and pucker-inducing tart, the filling made with paper-thin slices of whole lemons in the Shaker tradition. The Shakers would have eschewed the loop-de-loop meringue topping, and you can, too, but then you'd miss out on all the fun.

Crumb Crust

1¼ cups sugar cookie, gingersnap, or Bakeshop Butter Cookies (page 236) crumbs

6 tablespoons (¾ stick) unsalted butter, melted

2 tablespoons sugar

Filling

4 large egg yolks, beaten

2 cups sugar

2 large lemons, sliced paper-thin and seeded

Meringue

4 large egg whites

1½ cups sugar

2 teaspoons vanilla extract

1 Preheat the oven to 350°F. For the crust, combine the cookie crumbs, melted butter, and sugar in a bowl. Mix with your hands or a spatula until the mixture holds together. Pat the mixture into the bottom and up the sides of an 8-inch round or rectangular tart pan and bake for 10 minutes, or until very lightly browned.

2 Increase the oven temperature to 450°F. For the filling, whisk the egg yolks with ¼ cup of the sugar in a small bowl. Place the remaining 1¾ cups sugar with the sliced lemons in a medium saucepan over medium-high heat. Cook, stirring with a wooden spoon, until the sugar is moistened. Add a little hot sugar mixture to the eggs and whisk to temper the eggs. Slowly pour the egg mixture into the hot lemon mixture, stirring constantly with a wooden spoon. Cook, stirring, until the mixture thickens, coats the back of a wooden spoon, and creates a trail in the bottom of the saucepan when you drag the spoon across the bottom. The filling will continue to thicken as it cools. Transfer the filling to a food processor or blender and process or blend until the lemons are in very small pieces.

3 For the meringue, set a metal bowl over a saucepan of water and bring to a simmer. Whisk the egg whites and sugar together in the bowl over the simmering water. Whisk constantly for 3 to 4 minutes, or until the sugar has dissolved completely. Test by rubbing some of the mixture through your finger to make sure all sugar crystals have dissolved. Transfer the mixture to the bowl of a stand mixer and whip until soft peaks form. Add the vanilla and beat until stiff peaks form.

4 To assemble the tart, spread the filling into the crust. Top with the meringue and make loop-de-loops with a metal spatula or a piping bag fitted with a number 8 tip.

5 Bake for 4 to 7 minutes, or until the peaks of the meringue have browned. Let cool before serving.

PIE MARY

Holmes County, Ohio, is known for three reasons: stunningly graphic vintage Amish patchwork quilts from the 1930s and '40s, snapped up by New York City antiques dealers; the location of Winesburg, Ohio, the setting and title of the Sherwood Anderson novel; and the legacy of Pie Mary.

Mary Yoder started her adult life as an Amish farm wife in the 1940s. When one of her sons took over the family farm in 1973, she began her first cottage industry—quilting. When her fingers became too numb to quilt, however, she switched to baking pies. Known as Pie Mary, she and her husband, Andy, baked up to 100 pies a day, six days a week—cherry, apple, peach, pecan, raisin, peach pineapple, blueberry, black raspberry, elderberry, grape, Dutch apple, shoestring apple (a custard-style apple), ground cherry, banana, peanut butter, coconut cream, chocolate, butterscotch, pumpkin, and lemon. Some of the varieties, like elderberry in July, ground cherry in August, and pumpkin in November, were strictly seasonal.

"We make all the dough first," she used to say, "in four big batches. I put all my filling in hot, all from scratch. We never measure anything. We've done it so many times already." They didn't set timers or watch the clock while the pies were in the oven. "Just keep them in there until they're nice and brown. That's all," she advised.

"I just hardly ever use a recipe," Mary said. "I just know them by heart."

Today, a new generation operates Mary Yoder's Amish Kitchen in Middlefield, Ohio, but the pie tradition carries on (see Resources, page 266).

Chenango Strawberry
- Soft, snowlike apple
- Very fragrant flavor resembles the scent of roses
- 1800's, Chenango County, New York

Price:$___

ESPRESSO-GINGER SANDWICH COOKIES MAKES 12 TO 15 SANDWICH COOKIES

Ginger cookies—thin and crisp or soft and moist—are among the most beloved in the Heartland cookie jar. During the St. Lucia festival during mid-December, Swedish folk dancers pass them out to the crowds in Lindsborg, Kansas. Small-town bakeries always have them for sale. This crisp version with a frosting filling taps into our love of the richness of coffee, which deepens the spice flavors. This is adapted from a recipe in the late, lamented *Country Home* magazine.

2¼ cups unbleached all-purpose flour

2 tablespoons instant espresso powder

2 teaspoons ground ginger

1 teaspoon ground allspice

1 teaspoon baking soda

¾ cup (1½ sticks) unsalted butter, softened

½ cup packed dark brown sugar

1 large egg

¼ cup sorghum syrup or molasses

¼ cup raw or turbinado sugar crystals

Brown Sugar Frosting

½ cup packed dark brown sugar

2 tablespoons sorghum syrup or molasses

4 tablespoons (½ stick) unsalted butter, softened

1½ cups confectioners' sugar

2 to 4 tablespoons half-and-half or whole milk

1 In a medium bowl, combine the flour, espresso powder, ginger, allspice, and baking soda. In the bowl of a stand mixer, cream the butter until light and fluffy. Add the brown sugar and beat until light. Beat in the egg and sorghum until well blended. Add the flour mixture, one-third at a time, and beat until blended. Cover and refrigerate the dough for at least 30 minutes to make it easy to roll into balls.

2 Preheat the oven to 350°F. Line 2 baking sheets with parchment paper.

3 Place the raw sugar crystals on a small saucer. Scoop or shape the dough, a heaping tablespoon at a time, into balls. Roll in the raw sugar and place 2 inches apart on the baking sheets. You should have 24 to 30 balls of dough.

4 Bake for 13 to 15 minutes, or until the edges are firm and the tops are crackled. Let cool on wire racks while you make the frosting.

5 For the frosting, whisk the brown sugar, sorghum syrup, and butter together in a medium bowl until soft and creamy. Whisk in the confectioners' sugar. Add enough half-and-half to make a spreadable consistency.

6 Assemble the sandwich cookies by spreading about 1 tablespoon frosting on the bottom side of one cookie and placing another cookie on top, with the bottom facing inward.

SUNFLOWER COOKIE BRITTLE **MAKES ABOUT 36 PIECES**

Sunflowers, native to the Heartland, have become big business in the Dakotas—so much so that Fargo, North Dakota, is known not only as the setting for the quirky movie of the same name but also as the sunflower capital of America, while Kansas is known as the Sunflower State. A field of sunflowers in their neat rows, heads turned toward the sun, is quite a sight in late summer. They also provide quite a nutlike flavor and texture to this delicious, unleavened cookie that you just press into the pan and bake. A shorter baking time produces a chewier cookie; a longer baking time produces a crisper cookie. After the cookie has baked, you break it into irregular pieces like a nut brittle or a crazy quilt. Substitute slivered almonds or chopped walnuts or pecans for the sunflower seeds, as this recipe is very adaptable.

1 cup (2 sticks) unsalted butter, softened

1 cup sugar

1 teaspoon fine kosher or sea salt

1½ teaspoons almond or vanilla extract

2 cups unbleached all-purpose flour

1 cup salted roasted shelled sunflower kernels

1 cup semisweet chocolate chips

1   Preheat the oven to 350°F. Combine the butter, sugar, salt, and almond extract in a large bowl and beat until creamy. Stir in the flour gradually, beating until blended. Fold in the sunflower kernels and chocolate chips. Press the dough into a 16½ by 11½ by 1-inch jelly-roll pan.

2   Bake for 20 to 25 minutes, or until lightly browned. Let cool on wire racks. Break the baked cookie apart like peanut brittle. Store leftovers in an airtight container for up to 2 weeks.

LEMON-POPPY SEED WHIRLIGIGS MAKES 24 COOKIES

Heartlanders of Czech or Polish descent love the flavor combination of poppy seed and lemon. In small mom-and-pop Polish bakeries and grocery stores along Chicago's Milwaukee Avenue, you can buy a butter lamb as well as bags of ground poppy seeds, saving a step in making these cookies. The poppy seed filling makes a twirly center, like the whirligigs or windmills that are still common features on Heartland farms. If ground poppy seeds are not available in your area, grind your own poppy seeds in the food processor, blender, or coffee grinder. This slice-and-bake dough keeps in the refrigerator for up to a week, but the baked cookies might be gone in minutes. A dot or drizzle of lemon-flavored icing would be a fine addition.

Cookie Dough

½ cup (1 stick) unsalted butter, softened

⅓ cup granulated sugar

1 large egg

2 tablespoons sour cream

2 cups unbleached all-purpose flour

½ teaspoon salt

1 teaspoon freshly grated lemon zest

Filling

1 cup ground poppy seeds

2 tablespoons granulated sugar

1 teaspoon ground allspice

½ cup milk

1 tablespoon honey

Lemon Icing

1 cup confectioners' sugar

1 teaspoon freshly grated lemon zest or lemon extract

2 tablespoons half-and-half or whole milk

1 For the dough, beat the butter, sugar, egg, and sour cream together in a large bowl. Add the flour, salt, and lemon zest and blend together.

2 For the filling, bring all the ingredients to a boil in a small saucepan, then lower the heat and simmer for 5 minutes, stirring. Set aside to cool.

3 Preheat the oven to 350°F. Line a baking sheet with parchment paper. Roll out the dough to a rectangle ⅓ inch thick. Spread the filling on the dough and roll it up from the long side, like a jelly roll. Bake the roll on the prepared baking sheet for 45 minutes or until lightly browned. Let cool on a wire rack for 4 to 5 minutes, then slice the log, while still warm, into 24 cookies.

4 For the icing, whisk the confectioners' sugar, lemon zest, and half-and-half together in a small bowl until smooth. Dot or drizzle each cookie with the icing.

ITALIAN FIG COOKIES MAKES 48 COOKIES

The recipe for *cuccidati*, or Italian fig cookies, was one Sicilian immigrants clutched tightly to their collective bosoms on the journey west. No matter that fig trees struggle in the Midwestern climate—even as far south as Missouri, fig trees must be bundled up like toddlers in snowsuits to survive the seesaw extremes of winter weather—families of Sicilian origin want their fig cookies. So, bakeries like the newer Pasticceria Natalina in Chicago or the venerable Missouri Baking Company on "The Hill" in St. Louis, Missouri, oblige. One bite of this festive cookie and you'll see why. Make the filling a week or so in advance, if you wish, and keep it covered in the refrigerator until you're ready to bake.

Filling

1 cup dried figs (about 4 ounces)

⅓ cup dried pitted dates

⅓ cup dark raisins

1 tangerine or Satsuma orange, peeled, seeded, and sectioned (most membranes removed)

½ teaspoon ground nutmeg

½ teaspoon ground cinnamon

2 teaspoons freshly grated orange zest

¼ teaspoon fine kosher or sea salt

⅛ teaspoon freshly ground black pepper

1 tablespoon light corn syrup

1 tablespoon grappa, bourbon, or Cognac (optional)

1 For the filling, put the figs, dates, and raisins in a medium bowl and pour boiling water over the dried fruit. Let steep for 15 minutes, or until softened. Drain the fruit. Grind the figs, dates, raisins, tangerine sections, nutmeg, cinnamon, orange zest, salt, pepper, corn syrup, and grappa together in a food processor or in a food grinder until you have a moist paste. Cover and refrigerate for up to 2 weeks before baking.

2 For the pastry, sift the flour, baking powder, salt, and sugar together into the work bowl of a food processor. Add the butter and pulse until the mixture resembles small peas. In a small bowl, mix the eggs, milk, and vanilla together. Add this mixture to the flour mixture and pulse to form a mass. You will see small flecks of butter in the dough.

3 Preheat the oven to 400°F. Line 4 baking sheets with parchment paper and set aside.

4 Divide the dough into quarters. On a floured surface, roll a portion of dough into a 14 by 5-inch rectangle and position it so the long side is closest to you. Spoon or pipe one-quarter of the filling down the long center of the pastry strip. Bring the edges of the dough up and over each other and pinch them together with your fingers. Remove any excess flour with a pastry brush. Roll the strip gently to form a cylinder, then gently squeeze and stretch the cylinder to a length of 18 inches. Cut the cylinder into 1½-inch pieces. Place on one of the baking sheets, seam side down, about 1 inch apart. Repeat the process with the remaining pastry and filling.

Pastry

2¾ cups unbleached all-purpose flour, plus more for dusting

1 tablespoon baking powder

½ teaspoon fine kosher or sea salt

½ cup granulated sugar

1 cup (2 sticks) unsalted butter, chilled and cut into pieces

2 large eggs, beaten

2 tablespoons milk

2 teaspoons vanilla extract

Glaze

¼ cup milk

1 teaspoon vanilla extract

1½ cups confectioners' sugar

Colored sprinkles, for topping (optional)

5   Bake for 14 to 16 minutes, or until lightly browned.

6   For the glaze, whisk the milk, vanilla, and confectioners' sugar together in a small bowl. Brush the cookies with the glaze and sprinkle with colored sprinkles while still warm. The cookies will keep for up to 1 month in an airtight container.

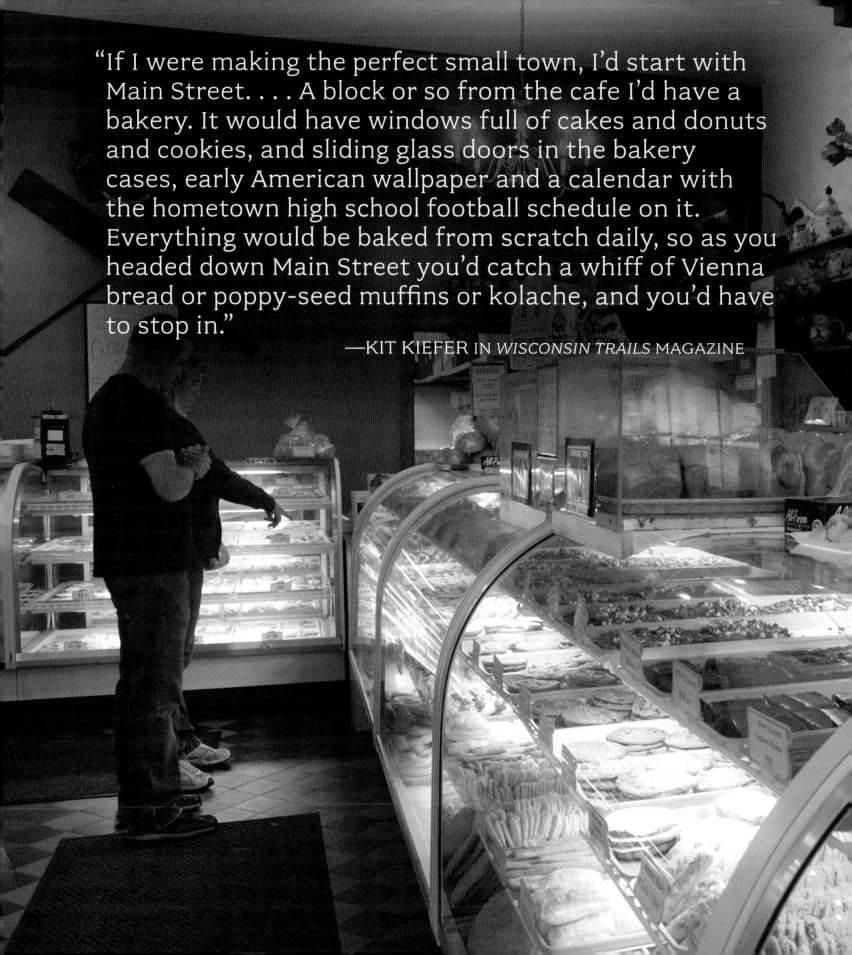

"If I were making the perfect small town, I'd start with Main Street. . . . A block or so from the cafe I'd have a bakery. It would have windows full of cakes and donuts and cookies, and sliding glass doors in the bakery cases, early American wallpaper and a calendar with the hometown high school football schedule on it. Everything would be baked from scratch daily, so as you headed down Main Street you'd catch a whiff of Vienna bread or poppy-seed muffins or kolache, and you'd have to stop in."

—KIT KIEFER IN *WISCONSIN TRAILS* MAGAZINE

BAKESHOP BUTTER COOKIES **MAKES ABOUT 36 COOKIES**

This is our family's favorite cookie—tender, irresistible, and rich with Heartland butter. It's so beloved by everyone, in fact, that even my childhood dog Jiggs had a thing for them. (He infamously snarfed a batch of these, leaving nothing but incriminating dog drool on the plate.) This versatile dough can be tinted and then pressed into any shape the occasion demands—flowers, Christmas trees, hearts, swirls; or roll it into a log and then in a bed of colored or chocolate sprinkles or poppy seeds, and finally cut it into rounds to bake. Add a little dot of confectioners' sugar icing, if you like. Store in airtight containers for up to 2 weeks.

1 cup (2 sticks) unsalted butter, softened

½ cup sugar

1 teaspoon almond or vanilla extract

Food coloring (if desired)

2½ cups unbleached all-purpose flour

½ teaspoon salt

1 Preheat the oven to 300°F. Line 2 baking sheets with parchment paper and set aside.

2 In a medium bowl of a stand mixer, cream the butter, sugar, vanilla, and food coloring together until light and fluffy. Sift the flour and salt into a bowl. Beat the flour mixture, ½ cup at a time, into the butter mixture until you have a smooth, thick dough.

3 Divide the dough in half. Place one-half in a cookie press. Press the cookies out onto a prepared baking sheet, about 1 inch apart. Repeat with the other half of the dough.

4 Bake for 25 to 30 minutes, or until slightly golden but not brown. Let cool on wire racks.

PRAISE AND PLENTY CUPCAKES MAKES 36 CUPCAKES

Sometimes dessert inspiration comes from surprising sources. When I was looking through the *Home for the Holidays* pattern book by Missouri quilt designers Linda Brannock and Jan Patek, I found the germ of an idea—even though I'm not a quilter. Their "Praise and Plenty" quilt in muted yellow, green, and orange on a creamy white background, surrounded by a border in homespun plaid, suggested a twist on traditional carrot cake to me. So here it is: cupcakes using garden plenty in a way that will garner praise—grated and spiced carrots, zucchini, and yellow squash. Use small, trimmed zucchini and yellow squash and grate them whole. If you like, spoon the batter into retro cupcake liners from Bake It Pretty (see Resources, page 266). Traditional cream cheese frosting and "garden confetti" are the crowning glories.

6 large eggs, at room temperature

3 cups granulated sugar

2 cups canola oil

3¾ cups unbleached all-purpose flour

1 tablespoon baking soda

1 tablespoon baking powder

1½ teaspoons salt

1½ cups grated zucchini

1½ cups grated yellow summer squash

1½ cups grated carrots

1 teaspoon ground coriander

1 teaspoon ground cinnamon

1 teaspoon ground ginger

1½ cups raisins

1½ cups chopped pecans or walnuts

1 Position an oven rack in the center of the oven and preheat the oven to 350°F. Line cupcake pans with 36 liners, and line a baking sheet with parchment paper, and set aside.

2 Beat the eggs with the sugar in a large bowl until light and frothy. Beat in the oil. Sift the flour, baking soda, baking powder, and salt together and add to the egg mixture, 1 cup at a time, beating well after each addition. Stir in the zucchini, squash, carrots, coriander, cinnamon, and ginger until well blended. With a rubber spatula, fold in the raisins and nuts until well blended. Fill the cupcake liners three-quarters full.

3 Bake, in batches, on the center rack for 20 to 25 minutes, or until a cake tester inserted in the center of a cupcake comes out clean. Let cool completely on wire racks, but keep the oven on and lower the temperature to 225°F.

4 For the frosting, beat together the cream cheese and butter in a large bowl using a stand mixer. Add the sugar and vanilla and beat until smooth. Frost the cupcakes after they have cooled and while the frosting is soft and spreadable.

5 For the garnish, combine the zucchini, squash, carrots, sugar, and water in a medium saucepan over medium-high heat. Cook, stirring, until the vegetables are translucent and you have a candied confetti. Spread the confetti in a thin layer on the prepared baking sheet and bake until crisp and dry to the touch, about 20 minutes. (This can be made a day or so ahead and kept in an airtight container.) When cool enough to handle, sprinkle the confetti on the top of each frosted cupcake.

Cream Cheese Frosting

2 (8-ounce) packages cream cheese, softened

5 tablespoons unsalted butter, softened

5 cups confectioners' sugar

1 tablespoon vanilla extract

Garnish

½ cup coarsely grated zucchini

½ cup coarsely grated yellow summer squash

½ cup coarsely grated carrots

¼ cup granulated sugar

2 tablespoons water

1 teaspoon freshly grated lemon zest

NOW, FORAGER!

Wild edibles were once a vital part of the diet for Native Americans in the Heartland—Shawnee, Miami, and Potawatomi in what is now Ohio, Indiana, and Michigan; Illini in Illinois; Ojibwe in Minnesota and Wisconsin; Sioux in the Dakotas; Kanza in Kansas; Ioway in Iowa; the Omaha in Nebraska; Osage and Missouria in Missouri. Early European settlers also foraged during lean times. After farms were established, however, gathering foods from the wild became a pastime, rather than a means of survival, says Roger Welsch, a Nebraska academic folklorist.

Welsch learned about foraging from friends in the Omaha tribe. But he also discovered that most folks dismissed elderberries, pawpaws, and wild greens as "poor people food."

In the 1980s, this mind-set began to change as chefs like Larry Forgione of the American Place in New York; Odessa Piper at L'Etoile in Madison, Wisconsin; and Harlan "Pete" Peterson at Tapawingo in Ellsworth, Michigan, began to buy from foragers and transform wild foods like ramps, morels, and hickory nuts into upscale fare.

The locavore movement has made foraging even more chic. You can't get much more local than a plant native to the immediate area. So, inventive chefs are putting foraged foods on their menus, from bland, sweet mulberries and tannic wild plums in desserts to elderflower foams and local honey infused with wild rose hips for entrées.

Foraging has also gotten high tech. Jonathan Justus, owner and chef at Justus Drugstore in Smithville, Missouri, uses a GPS navigation system so that he can identify and go back to the area where he finds his goodies—wild rose hips, black walnuts, and elderberries—or at night when their fragrance peaks, honeysuckle blossoms to distill for signature cocktails.

Foraging is also about nostalgia—a hankering for the seasonal dishes your grandma used to make with foods gathered from the wild. Retirees in Wisconsin and Indiana have their own cottage industries gathering labor-intensive hickory nuts (picking the nutmeats out of the shell) and persimmons (skinning, seeding, and pulping them), preparing them for sale each autumn.

SUMMER BERRY COBBLER WITH LEMON VERBENA WHIPPED CREAM **SERVES 8**

Deep blue sky, morning sun the color of lemons, warm air, fresh breeze. If a sunny summer day could be translated into a dessert, this would be it. Find fresh lemon verbena or lemon balm plants at a garden nursery, or just add lemon zest to taste. Make this after you go berry picking or come back from the farmer's market with the summer's best berries.

Lemon Verbena Whipped Cream

1 cup heavy cream

¼ cup packed fresh lemon verbena or lemon balm leaves, or 1 teaspoon freshly grated lemon zest

Cobbler

½ cup (1 stick) unsalted butter

1½ cups plus 1 cup sugar

1½ cups unbleached all-purpose flour

2 teaspoons baking powder

1 cup milk

1 teaspoon freshly grated lemon zest

4 cups mixed berries and cherries, such as blackberries, raspberries, blueberries, hulled and sliced strawberries, or pitted sour cherries

3 tablespoons sugar

1 For the whipped cream, place the cream and lemon verbena leaves in a saucepan to warm over medium heat for about 30 minutes. Do not boil. Strain the cream and chill for several hours or overnight.

2 For the cobbler, preheat the oven to 350°F. Melt the butter in a 13 by 9-inch baking dish in the oven. In a large bowl, whisk together 1½ cups of the sugar, flour, baking powder, milk, and lemon zest until you have a smooth batter. Pour the batter over the melted butter in the baking dish, but do not mix the two together. Sprinkle the berries in an even layer over the batter. Sprinkle the berries with the remaining 1 cup sugar. Bake for 35 minutes, or until a cake tester inserted in the center comes out clean.

3 Place the cream in a chilled bowl and beat until thickened. Gradually beat in the 3 tablespoons sugar until stiff. Serve the cobbler warm or at room temperature, with a dollop of whipped cream on the top.

INFUSIASM!
Heartland chefs infuse whipping cream with local garden aromatics for signature desserts. Former dessert chef—turned—chocolatier Christopher Elbow of Kansas City, Missouri, infuses cream with dried lavender buds. John Raymond of Roots in Milwaukee, Wisconsin, uses lilac blossoms. Jeni Britton Bauer of Columbus, Ohio, infuses spicebush berries, fresh mint, and sweet corn (paired with blackberries) to make her ice creams.

You can also infuse cream with organic peach leaves (almond flavor), vanilla-scented heads of elderflower (vanilla flavor), or even honeysuckle blossoms. Local flavor can be as close as your own backyard.

INDIANA MELON . . . INDIANA MELON . . .

According to novelist Henry James, the one perfect phrase in the English language is "summer afternoon, summer afternoon." When you say the words, they're like a murmur that conjures up sunny days with nothing to do but be lazy.

The taste that conjures up that same thought for me is the sweet flavor of a salmon-fleshed cantaloupe. Cool, juicy, and perfect by itself, melon stands alone like the ideal summer day. For me, the best melons are grown in southern Indiana, where the hot and humid summer climate and deep, sandy river bottom soil are optimal. And I'm not alone. As I looked through an old *Seed Savers Yearbook* from Decorah, Iowa, I saw a notation for a variety of oblong muskmelon called Indiana, and the gardener wrote beside it, "best I ever had."

Old Midwestern cookbooks recommend the Nutmeg melon, an heirloom variety still available from Seed Savers. This variety dates back to the 1830s, with green flesh and a distinctive spicy flavor and perfume. It's sometimes called Early Hanover or Green Nutmeg, and a Seed Savers gardener noted that its flavor was "ambrosial." Another antique melon, Jenny Lind, dating back to the 1830s with green flesh and a turbaned end, would also be a variety to try in your garden (see Resources, page 266).

RED HAVEN PEACH CRISP WITH ALMOND-OAT STREUSEL **SERVES 8**

A luscious dessert for summer, this recipe features oats in the streusel topping. The area around Cedar Rapids, Iowa, has been "sowing oats" for generations. Oats like a colder, moister climate, which this part of Iowa is happy to provide. Oat kernels, or groats, are treated in several ways; they are cut for steel-cut oats, which are used to make the scrapple-like "goetta," which is sliced and fried for breakfast in Cincinnati, Ohio. Steel-cut oats are also the gourmet's preference for making a slower-cooking but better-for-you oatmeal. Rolled flat, oat kernels become——you guessed it—rolled oats at the Quaker Oats plant in Cedar Rapids. Rolled oats give a little body to the streusel topping over luscious Red Haven peaches, a hardy variety that does especially well in Michigan's Upper Peninsula.

4 cups sliced fresh Red Haven or other ripe peaches (7 to 8 large)

½ cup sugar

½ teaspoon almond extract

2 tablespoons quick-cooking tapioca

1 tablespoon freshly squeezed lemon juice

Streusel

½ cup old-fashioned rolled oats

½ cup unbleached all-purpose flour

⅓ cup sugar

¼ teaspoon fine kosher or sea salt

½ cup crumbled almond paste

4 tablespoons (½ stick) unsalted butter, softened

1 Preheat the oven to 350°F. Spray a 2-quart baking dish cooking spray and set aside.

2 Combine the peaches, sugar, almond extract, tapioca, and lemon juice in a large bowl, then spoon into the prepared dish.

3 For the streusel, combine the oats, flour, sugar, and salt in a small bowl. Stir in the almond paste, then blend in the butter with your fingers until the mixture is lumpy. Drop the mixture onto the peaches until evenly covered.

4 Bake for 35 to 40 minutes, or until browned and bubbling. Serve warm.

FROM COW TO CONE

When pink-haired pastry chef Jeni Britton Bauer dreamed of making artisan ice cream using only organic milk from grass-fed cows, she thought it would be easy. After all, there were dairy farms all around Columbus, Ohio, where she lives. She was wrong.

"It took ten years to get together a group of twelve dairy farms in Wayne County that were 100 percent grass-fed and certified organic," she says. "I set out to change the dairy co-op system, and these farmers were willing to work with me."

Why specify milk from grass-fed cows? "The flavor is better in the milk when the cows eat grass," she explains. "We couldn't believe the difference in milk from grass- versus grain-fed cows."

On that milky canvas, she paints with regional flavors, some of which change throughout the year. She relies on Chris Schmiel of Integration Acres, a pawpaw grower and foraging company in nearby Albany, to supply her with spicebush berries, which have a lemon-rosemary flavor. Bauer also uses locally grown beets, carrots, cucumbers, celery, sweet corn, black raspberries, fresh mint, melons, and garden huckleberries for her summer collection, and spices and autumn fruits for the winter collection.

"Every season is a little bit different," she says. But the one constant is the line of customers snaking down the block all throughout the year (see Resources, page 266).

VANILLA BEAN ICE CREAM **MAKES 1 SCANT QUART**

Jeni Britton Bauer, artisan ice-cream maker in Columbus, Ohio, has been on the foodie radar for quite some time. She can even get Ohio and Michigan fans to deliciously coexist in her seasonal ice cream made with Blue Jacket Dairy goat cheese from Ohio and roasted Michigan cherries—"like a fluffy cherry cheesecake," she says. She formulated this recipe for the home cook, and each ingredient plays a part in getting the perfect taste and texture of a to-die-for vanilla ice cream. For the fullest flavor, use organic milk from grass-fed cows.

2 cups whole milk

1 tablespoon plus 1 teaspoon cornstarch

3 tablespoons cream cheese, softened

1¼ cups heavy cream

⅔ cup sugar

1½ tablespoons light corn syrup

1 vanilla bean, split and seeds scraped

⅛ teaspoon kosher salt

1 Fill a large bowl with ice water. In a small bowl, mix 2 tablespoons of the milk with the cornstarch. In another large bowl, whisk the cream cheese until smooth.

2 In a large saucepan, combine the remaining milk with the heavy cream, sugar, corn syrup, and vanilla bean and seeds. Bring the mixture to a boil and then cook over medium heat until the sugar dissolves and the vanilla flavors the milk, about 4 minutes. Remove the pan from the heat and gradually whisk in the cornstarch mixture. Return to a boil and cook over medium-high heat until the mixture is slightly thickened, about 1 minute.

3 Gradually whisk the hot milk mixture into the cream cheese until smooth. Whisk in the salt. Set the bowl in the ice-water bath and let stand, stirring occasionally, until cold, about 20 minutes.

4 Strain the ice-cream base into an ice-cream maker and freeze according to the manufacturer's instructions. Pack the ice cream into a freezer container.

5 Press a sheet of plastic wrap directly onto the surface of the ice cream and close with an airtight lid. Freeze the vanilla ice cream until firm, about 4 hours.

HOT FUDGE SUNDAE WITH SALTED CARAMEL SAUCE **SERVES 4**

The hot fudge sundae, like so many iconic American foods, was created in stages. In 1881, Ed Berner offered a special five-cent "sundae" (ice cream drizzled with chocolate syrup) at his ice-cream parlor in Two Rivers, Wisconsin, hoping to get folks to indulge on Sunday. Twenty-five years later, hot fudge sauce made the culinary scene—and voilà! A star was born.

Hot fudge sundaes brought my parents together. When my mother was a soda jerk in 1940s Lockland, Ohio, she was romanced by my father, who worked in the family butcher shop across the street and came over to show her his new shoes.

Today, the traditional hot fudge sundae is due for an upgrade. Once you've been spoiled by artisan chocolates from Vosges in Chicago and Christopher Elbow in Kansas City, the hot fudge sauce you find in most ice-cream parlors just won't do. Made with a little corn syrup for pourability and a final fillip of artisan chocolate, this hot fudge sauce (which makes about 1½ cups) takes on a more voluptuous flavor. The salted caramel that tastes so wonderful as a filling in a piece of dark chocolate is doubly decadent as a sauce (which makes about 1 cup) on a sundae. Both sauces are also perfect as holiday gifts from your kitchen.

Hot Fudge Sauce

¾ cup half-and-half

¼ cup light corn syrup

¾ cup sugar

¼ cup unsweetened cocoa powder

⅛ teaspoon fine kosher or sea salt

¼ cup chopped good-quality dark chocolate (such as Vosges or Christopher Elbow)

2 tablespoons unsalted butter, softened

1 teaspoon vanilla extract

1 For the Hot Fudge Sauce, bring the half-and-half, corn syrup, sugar, cocoa, and salt to a boil in a large saucepan over medium-high heat. Whisk until smooth. Lower the heat and simmer for 5 minutes. Remove from the heat and whisk in the chocolate, butter, and vanilla, and whisk until smooth and the butter has melted. Serve right away, or pour into a glass jar and refrigerate for up to 3 months.

2 For the Salted Caramel Sauce, combine the sugar and water in a 3-quart saucepan over medium-high heat. As the sugar begins to melt, stir with a whisk or long-handled wooden spoon. When the sugar comes to a boil, stop stirring. When bubbles that rise to the top get bigger and wider, the sugar is ready to turn color, usually in 10 to 12 minutes. Have oven mitts and the remaining ingredients ready. The sugar mixture will turn pale tan, then get browner. Remove the caramel from the heat when it turns dark amber.

Christopher Elbow's Salted Caramel Sauce

1 cup sugar

½ cup water

6 tablespoons (¾ stick) unsalted butter

½ cup heavy cream

½ teaspoon *fleur de sel* or fine sea salt

1 quart Vanilla Bean Ice Cream (page 247) or 1 quart premium vanilla or coffee ice cream

3   With oven mitts on, whisk in the butter until it has melted. The caramel will foam up, then subside. Wait for 30 seconds, and then whisk in the cream and salt until the caramel is smooth. Let cool in the pan for several minutes, then serve right away or pour into a glass jar and refrigerate for up to 3 months.

4   For the sundae, scoop ice cream into bowls. Drizzle with hot fudge, then warm salted caramel sauce.

INDIANA MELON SORBET **MAKES 1 PINT**

As a palate cleanser or a sweet treat, this sorbet is vividly flavored and colored and easy to make. Even served icy cold, this sorbet keeps its flavor. For a signature brunch cocktail, why not serve three tiny scoops in a champagne glass and top with chilled sparkling wine?

4 cups chopped cantaloupe or honeydew melon

½ cup Fresh Herb Syrup (page 33) or simple syrup

Freshly squeezed lime juice

SUGGESTED MELON VARIETIES:
Amish, Crenshaw, Ogen, Charentais, or Queen Anne's Pocket

1 Puree the melon and syrup together in the work bowl of a food processor. Put the mixture through a sieve into a medium bowl. Add lime juice to taste.

2 Pour the mixture into an ice-cream maker and freeze according to the manufacturer's instructions.

CRACKLY-TOP HICKORY NUT CAKE **SERVES 12 TO 16**

Traditional hickory nut cakes are layered extravagances with rich penuche frosting. This one is simpler, richer, and even more irresistible. It's a nutty, delicious, keeping cake with an almost fudgy texture—it's that moist. And it's a cake, like our family, that welcomes all nuts—hickory, pecan, almond, you name it. The crackly top is part of its quirky charm. I dreamed this up based on an almond cake that I love, which uses canned almond paste. No such thing as canned hickory nut paste, but it's easy to make your own in the food processor. A drizzle of Hot Fudge Sauce (page 248) over a piece of this cake, maybe even with a scoop of Vanilla Bean Ice Cream (page 247), and life is mighty fine!

Hickory Nut Paste

1 cup hickory nutmeats (or pecans or blanched slivered almonds)

1 cup granulated sugar

1 teaspoon vanilla extract

1 large egg white

Cake

1 cup (2 sticks) unsalted butter, softened

1 cup granulated sugar

1 large egg yolk

4 large eggs

1 cup cake flour

½ teaspoon fine kosher or sea salt

½ teaspoon baking powder

Confectioners' sugar, for dusting

1 Preheat the oven to 325°F. Spread the nuts in a single layer on a baking sheet and toast them in the oven until they have a somewhat toasty aroma, 10 to 15 minutes. Let cool.

2 For the paste, transfer the cooled nuts and sugar to a food processor or blender and grind to a fine paste. Add the vanilla extract and egg white and process for 2 to 3 minutes, until a soft paste forms. Store in an airtight container in the refrigerator until ready to use, for up to 1 week.

3 For the cake, butter and flour a 10-inch springform pan. In a large bowl using a stand mixer, cream together the butter and sugar until the mixture turns white, about 5 minutes. Add the nut paste and beat at low speed until well combined and smooth. Beat in the egg yolk, then the eggs, one at a time. Sift the cake flour, salt, and baking powder on top of the batter. With a rubber spatula, fold the flour mixture into the batter, going around the perimeter of the bowl with the spatula and then making several slices across it. Repeat the process until you can't see the flour. Spoon the batter into the prepared pan and smooth the top.

4 Bake for 65 to 70 minutes, or until the center is firm and a skewer inserted in the center comes out clean. Immediately run a knife around the perimeter of the pan and remove the sides of the springform pan. Invert the cake onto a wire rack, if the top is irregular, and let the cake cool. Dust with confectioners' sugar before serving.

GOING NUTS FOR HICKORY NUTS

Hickory nuts still bring to mind winter evenings by the fire, cracking the shells, and telling family stories.

Midwesterners use available hickory wood for smoking foods to a burnished deliciousness. But hickory nuts play hard to get. Like black walnuts, hickory nuts are more difficult to pry out of their hard shells, so they're not as commercially available as other types of nuts. They're smaller and paler than pecans but similar in flavor; the tastiest come from either shagbark or shellbark hickory trees.

George Blacksmith of Delafield, Wisconsin, believes his love of hickory nuts is genetic. As the son of Isabel Baxter Blacksmith, the onetime runner-up for Melon Queen in Mukwonago, George recognized the beauty of hickory nuts early on. When he was a little boy, he would gather them with his grandmother Sarah Baxter. After the first freeze in the fall, they would find shagbark hickories out in the woods. Sarah would sit beneath each tree, spreading out her long skirts and apron. George would shake the tree, and the nuts would come raining down to be caught up in her skirts and then gathered into a bag. Prying out the nutmeats was a task carried out over many evenings.

Mary Swan of Brunswick, Missouri—where there's a Hickory Street—recalls picking up hickory nuts and smaller northern native pecans. "When I was little, Granddad would hook up his horses, Troxie and Snip, and we'd take the wagon and gather the nuts that had fallen," she says. "Grandma had a wood stove, and we'd sit around the fire of an evening and pick out the nuts."

BLACK WALNUT–APPLE FANCY CAKE **SERVES 12**

Still the province of home cooks in the southern Midwest, where black walnuts abound, this regional cake won't be found in restaurants or bakeries. You will find it at community bake sales, church suppers, bed-and-breakfast inns, and country cafés. This three-layer cake gets a double dose of apple in its apple butter (pumpkin butter also tastes good) filling and cider frosting. You can make this as a layer cake, a loaf cake, or cupcakes. I think the taste marriage of apple and black walnuts is one made in heaven. In the Heartland, you can find black walnuts at the grocery store, but you can also order them from places like Hammons (see Resources, page 266).

1 cup (2 sticks) unsalted butter, softened

2 cups granulated sugar

5 large eggs, separated

1 teaspoon vanilla extract

1 cup buttermilk

1 teaspoon baking soda

2 cups unbleached all-purpose flour

1½ cups finely chopped black walnuts, pecans, or hickory nuts

½ teaspoon cream of tartar

1 Preheat the oven to 350°F. Butter and flour three 9-inch round cake pans.

2 In a large bowl using a stand mixer, cream the butter and sugar together on medium speed until the mixture turns white, about 3 minutes. Beat in the egg yolks, one at a time, and the vanilla. Combine the buttermilk and baking soda in a cup and mix into the batter, ⅓ cup at a time, alternating with the flour. With a rubber spatula, fold in the nuts until well blended.

3 In a separate bowl with a hand mixer, beat the egg whites with the cream of tartar on low speed until foamy. Then increase the speed and beat until stiff peaks form. With a rubber spatula, fold the egg whites into the batter, going around the perimeter of the bowl with the spatula and then making several slices across it. Repeat the process until you can't see the egg whites. Spoon the batter into the prepared pans.

4 Bake for 27 to 30 minutes, or until a toothpick inserted in the center comes out clean. Cool in the cake pans, then turn out onto wire racks.

Cider Frosting

½ cup (1 stick) unsalted butter, softened

1 (8-ounce) plus 1 (3-ounce) package cream cheese, softened

¼ cup apple cider

6 cups confectioners' sugar, or more if necessary

Filling

1½ cups apple butter or pumpkin butter

5   For the frosting, beat the butter and cream cheese together in a large bowl until smooth and creamy. Beat in the cider, then the confectioners' sugar a little at a time, until you have a smooth, fluffy frosting.

6   To assemble the cake, place one layer on a cake plate and spread with half the apple butter. Place the second layer on top and spread with the remaining apple butter. Place the third layer on top. Using a metal spatula, frost the top and sides of the cake.

VARIATION: For loaf cakes, butter and flour three 9 by 5-inch loaf pans. Fill each three-quarters full. Bake for 27 to 30 minutes. If you like, cut the cooled loaf cakes in half lengthwise, spread with apple butter, and sandwich together. Frost the top. For cupcakes, line cupcake pans with 36 liners. Fill about halfway full, then spoon a teaspoon of apple butter in the middle of the batter and fill with more batter until three-quarters full. Bake for 17 to 20 minutes.

BLITZ TART WITH CINNAMON CRÈME FRAÎCHE

SERVES 10 TO 12

When I was growing up, my favorite birthday cake—when I had outgrown the bakery type—was Blitz Torte. This German-style confection has two thin yellow cake layers topped with crunchy, cinnamon-pecan meringue, sandwiched together with vanilla pastry cream—three big steps and lots of cleanup afterward. This tart has the same mellow flavors but in an easier format—a pat-in-the-pan crust, a one-bowl cheesecake filling, and a simple no-cook topping. And I love it just as much. Northern pecans, native to the southern Midwest, are smaller and lighter in color than the Southern type but have more volatile oils for more flavor; Northern pecans are just a little larger than hickory nuts. Use Northern pecans for the best flavor.

Cinnamon Crème Fraîche

1 cup sour cream

1 cup heavy cream

2 tablespoons light or dark brown sugar

½ teaspoon ground cinnamon

Crust

1½ cups unbleached all-purpose flour

½ cup (1 stick) unsalted butter, melted

½ cup granulated sugar

¼ teaspoon ground cinnamon

¾ cup chopped, toasted Northern or other pecans, plus more for garnish

1 The night before or early in the day, whisk the sour cream, heavy cream, brown sugar, and cinnamon together in a medium bowl. Cover and let sit at room temperature until ready to serve.

2 Preheat the oven to 350°F. For the crust, combine the flour, butter, sugar, cinnamon, and nuts together in a medium bowl with a spatula or your hands. Pat the mixture evenly over the bottom and up the sides of a 10-inch springform pan. Bake until the crust is just beginning to brown, about 12 minutes.

3 For the filling, process the cream cheese, butter, sugar, eggs, and vanilla in the work bowl of a food processor until smooth. Pour the filling into the prepared crust. Bake for 22 to 25 minutes, or until the center is set and the edges are golden brown. Let cool on a wire rack.

4 When the tart is just warm, spread with the crème fraîche and garnish with pecans.

Filling

1 (8-ounce) package cream cheese, softened

½ cup (1 stick) unsalted butter, softened

½ cup granulated sugar

2 large eggs

2 teaspoons vanilla extract

ROOT BEER FUNNEL CAKES   **MAKES 4 MEDIUM FUNNEL CAKES**

Driving from Kansas City to Denver on I-70, I stopped in Hayes, Kansas—a town undergoing a renaissance. Late-nineteenth-century limestone buildings now house upscale boutiques and a spa. At Lb. Brewing Company/Gella's Diner, my eye was drawn to a root beer funnel cake on their menu. How fun! When I got home, I began to experiment with the recipe and found that the best flavor combination is bottled root beer in the batter and root beer extract in the glaze. This is not a recipe to serve a crowd at home—despite the funnel cake's popularity at county fairs—as you can only fry one at a time. You can find root beer extract at cake decorating shops.

Vegetable oil, for frying

1½ cups unbleached all-purpose flour

¼ teaspoon salt

¾ teaspoon baking soda

½ teaspoon cream of tartar

2 tablespoons granulated sugar

1 large egg

1 cup root beer

Root Beer Glaze

½ cup confectioners' sugar, plus more for dusting

¼ teaspoon root beer extract

1 tablespoon half-and-half or whole milk

Fresh berries of your choice, for garnish

1   In a large, deep skillet, pour in enough vegetable oil to reach 1 inch. Heat to 375°F over medium-high heat.

2   Meanwhile, mix the flour, salt, baking soda, cream of tartar, and sugar in a large bowl. Whisk the egg and root beer together in a cup, then whisk this mixture into the dry ingredients until smooth.

3   When the oil has reached the correct temperature, hold your finger over the bottom of a large kitchen funnel with a ½-inch diameter spout and pour ¾ cup batter into the funnel. Hold the funnel over the center of the skillet, remove your finger, and with a circular motion starting from a center point, let the batter create either a tight or freeform spiral in the hot oil. Fry until the funnel cake is light brown on one side, then carefully flip with a pancake turner and fry on the other side until golden brown. Remove with a slotted spoon and drain on paper towels. Let the oil come back to the correct temperature and repeat the process with the remaining batter.

4   For the glaze, whisk the confectioners' sugar, root beer extract, and half-and-half together in a small bowl. Drizzle over each funnel cake, then dust with more confectioners' sugar and garnish with fresh berries.

FOAM ON THE RANGE

After Prohibition began in 1920, Heartland breweries that had formerly made beer switched over, by necessity, to other beverages like root beer. Originally, root beer was made from the root of the sassafras tree, which was found, in 1960, to contain a potential carcinogen. Since then, artificial sassafras flavoring is the norm, often complemented by vanilla, wintergreen, cherry tree bark, birch, licorice root, sarsaparilla root, nutmeg, anise, molasses, cinnamon, clove, and/or honey. You'll still find artisan and mom-and-pop root beer companies all over the Midwest. Many craft breweries—like Lb. Brewing Company in Hayes, Kansas—also make their own nonalcoholic root beer as an extension of their product line. (See Resources, page 266, for how to order regional root beers and other beverages.)

BERGHOFF FAMOUS OLD-FASHIONED ROOT BEER; CHICAGO, ILLINOIS—smooth and crisp, with notes of birch.

CHICAGO ROOT BEER; CHICAGO, ILLINOIS—rich, creamy notes of caramel and wintergreen.

DAD'S ROOT BEER; CHICAGO, ILLINOIS—sharp-tasting, with hints of clove and cinnamon.

DOG 'N' SUDS; LAFAYETTE, INDIANA—mild, medium-spiced, slightly sweet.

FITZ'S; ST. LOUIS, MISSOURI—smooth, creamy, slightly anise-like.

FROSTOP; SPRINGFIELD, OHIO—vanilla-scented, creamy, spicy.

IBC; ST. LOUIS, MISSOURI—smooth, anise and molasses flavors, with a bit of a bite.

LOST TRAIL; LOUISBURG, KANSAS—smooth, vanilla-scented, medium-spiced, creamy.

STEVENS POINT; STEVENS POINT, WISCONSIN—honey-sweetened, medium-spiced, vanilla-scented.

SUMMER IN A JAR SERVES 8

"On a picnic morning, without a warning" goes the opening song of the 1955 film *Picnic*, which was filmed in the Hutchinson/Halstead area of south-central Kansas. When you're yearning for a little bit of summer or a bit of adventure, make this portable dessert that you can bring along to a potluck, a picnic, or an outdoor concert like the fabulous Symphony in the Flint Hills—an inspired pairing of big-sky prairie ranches and the Kansas City Symphony. This dessert tastes like those fresh cream desserts beloved of families with Norwegian or Swedish ancestry—but there's no baking. And it's adaptable to what you have on hand, fresh in the garden, or available at the farmer's market. Make a blackberry or a strawberry-rhubarb version. Assemble it in small canning jars or a trifle bowl to show off the layers.

2 cups cubed Crackly-Top Hickory Nut Cake (page 252) cubed pound cake, or crumbled Bakeshop Butter Cookies (page 236)

2 cups fresh blackberries or sliced strawberries

1 cup Blackberry-Lavender Syrup (page 32) or Rosy Rhubarb Syrup (page 34), plus more for drizzling

2 (8-ounce) packages cream cheese, softened

1 cup sour cream

¼ cup sugar

1 teaspoon vanilla extract

1   Divide the cubed cake or cookie crumbs among 8 half-pint canning jars, or place them in the bottom of a trifle bowl. Arrange the fruit over the cake or cookie crumbs. Drizzle the canning jars with 2 tablespoons syrup each or drizzle all of the syrup over the fruit in the trifle bowl.

2   Combine the cream cheese, sour cream, sugar, and vanilla in the work bowl of a food processor and process until smooth. Divide the mixture among the canning jars, spooning it over the fruit, or spoon it all over the fruit in the trifle bowl. (This can be made ahead, covered, and refrigerated for up to 24 hours before serving.) Serve chilled or at room temperature, drizzled with a little more syrup.

OLD-FASHIONED BUTTERMILK CHOCOLATE POUND CAKE

MAKES 1 BUNDT CAKE TO SERVE 24

Buttermilk was the Heartland farm wife's secret for high-rising, moist cakes. It's the secret ingredient in this one too. Tender and fudgy, this is the most delicious chocolate pound cake I have ever made. It's also versatile: It makes 1 large celebratory cake, 3 loaf cakes, or 3 dozen cupcakes. They all keep well and taste even better the day after baking. Don't skimp on the creaming step, as you're beating air into the batter for a lighter, more velvety texture. Simply dust a bundt cake with confectioners' sugar or use one of the two frostings on loaf cakes or cupcakes.

1½ cups (3 sticks) unsalted butter, softened

3 cups sugar

7 large eggs

2 teaspoons vanilla extract

2 cups unbleached all-purpose flour

¾ cup unsweetened cocoa powder

1 teaspoon baking powder

1 teaspoon fine kosher or sea salt

1 tablespoon instant espresso powder dissolved in ¼ cup hot water

1 cup buttermilk

Confectioners' sugar, for dusting

1 Preheat the oven to 325°F. Butter and flour a 10-inch bundt or tube pan and set aside.

2 Cream the butter and sugar together in a large bowl using a stand mixer until the mixture turns white, about 5 minutes. Beat in the eggs, one at a time, then the vanilla.

3 Sift the flour, cocoa, baking powder, and salt into a medium bowl. Mix the coffee mixture with the buttermilk in a cup. Alternate adding one-third of the dry ingredients with a portion of the buttermilk mixture to the butter mixture until you have a smooth, thick batter. Spoon the batter into the prepared pan.

4 Bake for 65 to 70 minutes, or until a cake tester inserted near the center comes out clean. Let cool on a wire rack for 20 minutes, then turn out of the pan and place on a serving plate. Dust with the confectioners' sugar after the cake has completely cooled.

VARIATION: For loaf cakes, grease and flour three 9 by 5-inch loaf pans. Fill three-quarters full. Bake for 65 to 70 minutes. Let cool, then frost with Cocoa Mocha or Peanut Butter Frosting. For cupcakes, line cupcake pans with 36 liners. Fill three-quarters full. Bake for 25 to 27 minutes. Let cool, then frost with Cocoa Mocha or Peanut Butter Frosting.

COCOA MOCHA FROSTING MAKES 3 CUPS

½ cup (1 stick) unsalted butter

¼ cup unsweetened cocoa powder

½ cup freshly brewed dark roast coffee, such as French roast or espresso

1 teaspoon vanilla extract

6 cups confectioners' sugar

Melt the butter in a large saucepan over medium heat. Whisk in the cocoa until you have a smooth paste. Whisk in the coffee and bring to a boil. Remove from the heat and whisk in the vanilla and confectioners' sugar, 1 cup at a time, until you have a smooth frosting.

PEANUT BUTTER FROSTING MAKES 3 CUPS

Peanuts may be a Southern crop, but artisan peanut butter has been a Midwestern product since the early 1900s. Krema in Dublin, Ohio, has been making peanut butter since 1908, after it was popularized at the 1904 World's Fair in St. Louis. Koeze in Grand Rapids, Michigan, is another small-batch peanut butter that's been going strong since the 1920s. Browning the butter first accentuates that wonderful roasty-toasty peanut flavor.

4 tablespoons (½ stick) unsalted butter

1 cup creamy peanut butter

1 teaspoon vanilla extract

4 cups confectioners' sugar

Melt the butter in a large saucepan over medium heat. Continue to cook until the butter starts to brown, about 5 minutes. Watch carefully and let the butter get to a medium brown color, then remove from the heat. Whisk in the peanut butter and vanilla until you have a smooth paste. Whisk in the confectioners' sugar, 1 cup at a time, until you have a smooth frosting.

A TRIO OF SNOW CONES **SERVES 4**

Lindsay Laricks, of Fresher than Fresh Snow Cones, is a graphic designer from 9 to 5. But on the weekends, she pulls her vintage Shasta trailer into the garden spot across from Bluebird Bistro in Kansas City, Missouri. There, she serves up summer's best refresher—gourmet snow cones in flavors from her homemade syrups: ginger-rose, blackberry-lavender, watermelon-basil, or green tea–pear. You can order a flight of five mini snow cones, served in small paper containers, or a big one all to yourself. If you're not fortunate enough to live in Kansas City, you can also make these at home for a fun dessert that will beat the heat. Follow Lindsay's blog at http://fresherthanfreshsnowcones.blogspot.com.

4 cups chopped or shaved ice (use a food processor or a stand mixer with an ice-crusher attachment)

½ cup Rosy Rhubarb Syrup (page 34)

½ cup Fresh Herb Syrup (page 33)

½ cup Blackberry-Lavender Syrup (page 32)

Mound ⅓ cup shaved ice in each of 12 small glass bowls or ramekins. Drizzle 2 tablespoons of Rosy Rhubarb Syrup over each of 4 bowls; 2 tablespoons of Fresh Herb Syrup over each of 4 bowls; and 2 tablespoons of Blackberry-Lavender Syrup over each of 4 bowls. Arrange one of each variety on 4 dessert plates and serve immediately.

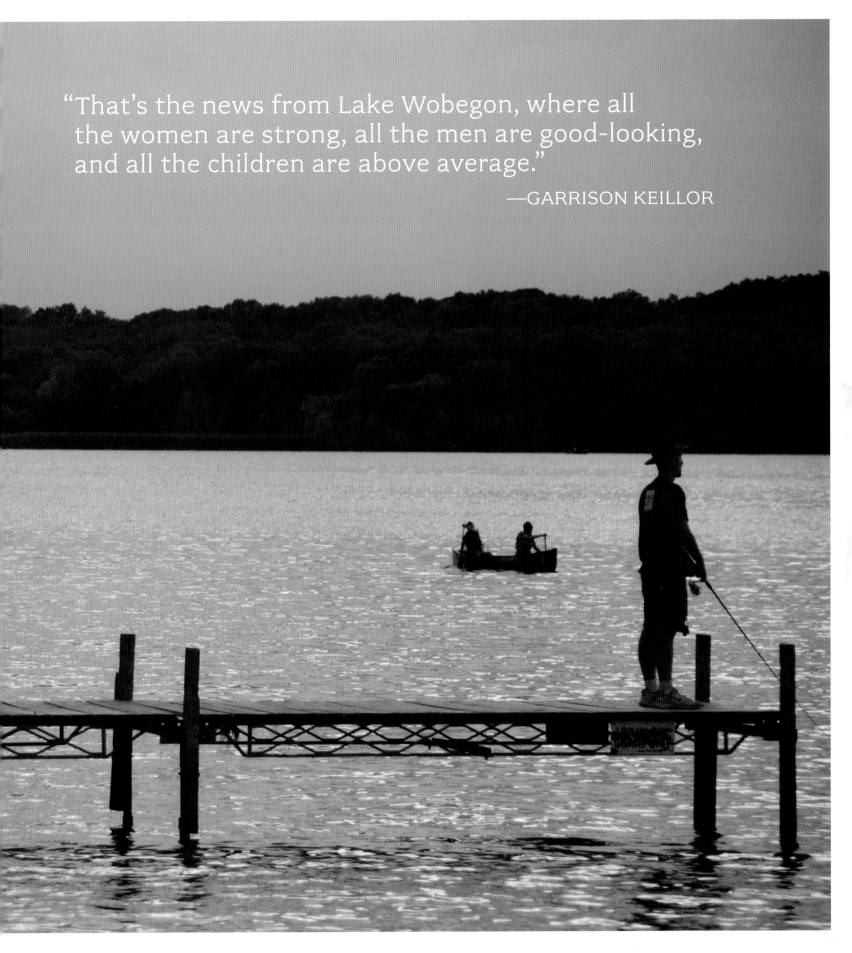

"That's the news from Lake Wobegon, where all
the women are strong, all the men are good-looking,
and all the children are above average."

—GARRISON KEILLOR

RESOURCES

AMERICAN BBQ WOOD PRODUCTS

(913) 648-7993

Suppliers of wood products from chips to logs in hardwoods such as apple, cherry, hickory, maple, pecan, and oak. No Web site.

AMERICAN SPOON FOODS

www.spoon.com

Since the 1980s, Justin Rashid and staff have made the exquisite stone fruits grown on Michigan's Upper Peninsula into fabulous jams, jellies, preserves, spoon fruits, and grilling sauces.

AMIGONI VINEYARDS

www.amigoni.com, www.inlandseawines.com

Inland Sea is an urban winery producing a wonderfully rich and aromatic Inland Sea Viognier from grapes grown in Centerview, Missouri.

BAKE IT PRETTY

www.bakeitpretty.com

Unusual and retro cupcake and cake liners and decorations are some of many baked goods decorations offered on this Web site.

BATES COUNTY SORGHUM

www.truefoodsmarket.com

Caramel-like sorghum from an Old Order Mennonite farm community in Bates County, Missouri, is also available at (877) 276-5303.

BECKER LANE ORGANIC

www.beckerlaneorganic.com

Jude Becker raises heritage pork on his organic farm in Dyersville, Iowa.

BELGIOIOSO CHEESE COMPANY

www.belgioioso.com

Since 1979, this Denmark, Wisconsin, cheesemaker, has been making classic Italian cheeses with Heartland dairy products.

BETTER MADE POTATO CHIPS

www.bmchips.com

Founded in 1930, this Detroit, Michigan, potato chip company now goes through 40 million pounds of potatoes a year to keep up with the cravings of the locals.

BEVNET

www.bevnet.com

Find out how to order your favorite root beers or other regional drinks at this site.

BLUE JACKET DAIRY

www.bluejacketdairy.com

This creamery in Bellefontaine, Ohio, makes delicious cheese curds, chèvre, quark, and their signature Gretna Grillin' halloumi.

BOULEVARD BREWING COMPANY

www.blvdbeer.com

Based in Kansas City, Missouri, this local brewery has a following for its Boulevard Wheat and Pale Ale, and seasonal brews.

CAPITAL BREWERY

www.capital-brewery.com

This brewery in Middleton, Wisconsin, produces "Supper Club" lager, Island Wheat, or Rustic Ale.

CAPRIOLE

www.capriolegoatcheese.com

In southern Indiana, Judith Schad led the Midwestern artisan charge in the 1970s, making her award-winning artisan goat cheese.

CHARLIE'S SMOKEHOUSE

www.charliessmokehouse.com

This small fish smokehouse on the tip of Door County in Ellison, Wisconsin, offers chubs, whitefish, and trout smoked with local woods.

CLAUS' GERMAN SAUSAGE & MEAT

www.clausgermansausageandmeats.com

Claus Muth's bacon is double-smoked over white oak, so people make a special trip to this Indianapolis, Indiana, store. If you don't get to his butcher shop early in the day, the double-smoked bacon could be sold out. Luckily, you can order it online.

CLOVER CLOVE DAIRY

www.clovercove.com

An organic ranch in the Nebraska Sandhills, this dairy emphasizes low-impact living and a "green" philosophy. Their organic milk from grass-fed cows is full of flavor.

DCI CHEESE COMPANY

www.dcicheeseco.com

Marketers of Salemville blue cheese made in a Wisconsin Amish community.

DE-LISH-US POTATO CHIPS

www.de-lish-us.com

The company began with a popcorn wagon during the Depression in Milwaukee, Wisconsin, but is now famous for its Golden Potato Chip made from regional Snowden potatoes.

DINKEL'S BAKERY

www.dinkels.com

When I was working on a strudel project, Dinkel's sent me some of theirs, and I was in strudel heaven. Their sweet and yeasty strudel dough is thicker than that made with filo pastry but is every bit as delicious. If you can't get to Chicago, you can order online.

EARTHY DELIGHTS
www.earthy.com

This DeWitt, Michigan, business links foragers with chefs and home cooks who want the best of the Heartland's wild bounty: fresh morels, ramps (wild leeks), pawpaws, and chokecherry or shagbark hickory syrup.

FAIRLANE BBQ WOOD
(816) 761-1350

Supplier specializing in hardwoods for barbecue, such as pecan, oak, hickory, sassafras, and apple. No Web site.

FOUNTAIN PRAIRIE INN AND FARMS
www.fountainprairie.com

When you see shaggy Highland cattle on this Fall River, Wisconsin, farm, you're not seeing things. This hearty, heritage breed produces superior beef, which is managed from beginning to end by the Priske Family.

FREE STATE BREWING COMPANY
www.freestatebrewing.com

Named for the early moniker for Kansas, this microbrewery/restaurant pioneered a return to local beer and local food in Lawrence, Kansas.

FRESHER THAN FRESH SNOW CONES
www.ftfsnowcones.com

Lindsay Laricks serves all-natural iced treats from her vintage mobile trailer in Kansas City, Missouri.

GOLDEN RUN SORGHUM
www.prophetstown.org/farmproduce.html

This rich, brown sorghum made in Camden, Indiana, is offered for sale by Prophetstown, a historic, nonprofit working farm near Brookston, Indiana.

GOOD SHEPHERD POULTRY RANCH
www.goodshepherdpoultryranch.com

Frank R. Reese, Jr., produces historically authentic Heritage Poultry.

GOOSE ISLAND BREWING COMPANY
www.gooseisland.com

This Chicagoland brewery is known for their Night Stalker stout, 312 Urban Wheat Ale, and Green Line Pale Ale.

GRAND TRAVERSE DISTILLERY
www.grandtraversedistillery.com

Located in Traverse City, Michigan, this is known for its True North vodka distilled from rye. They also have, of course, a sour cherry vodka. Salut!

GRASS POINT FARMS
www.grasspoint.com

This dairy farm in the rolling hills of Thorpe, Wisconsin, offers full-flavored, grass-fed milk, butter, and cheeses.

GREAT LAKES DISTILLERY
www.GreatLakesDistillery.com

This small distillery crafts Rehorst vodka from hand-selected hard red winter wheat and a fabulous gin, made with Wisconsin ginseng, in Milwaukee, Wisconsin. Order from your local distributor or from Binny's Beverage Depot (888) 942-9463 (www.binnys.com).

GREEN DIRT FARM
www.greendirtfarm.com

A sheep farm and cheesemaker, "up to their elbows in curds and whey" in the hilly country near Weston, Missouri. They also sell grass-fed lamb.

HAMMONS PRODUCTS COMPANY
www.black-walnuts.com

All things native, hand-harvested black walnut from this Stockton, Missouri, business.

HERITAGE FOODS USA
www.heritagefoodsusa.com

This organization, founded as the marketing and sales arm of the nonprofit Slow Food, champions heritage breeds, traceability, sustainability, diversity, and flavor.

HICKORY WORKS
http://hickoryworks.homestead.com

Gordon James makes lightly smoky and nutty-tasting syrup from the bark of the shagbark hickory in Brown County, Indiana. On their Web site, you can watch the syrup being made.

HINTERLAND BREWERY
www.hinterlandbeer.com

These Green Bay and Milwaukee, Wisconsin, brewers make Packer-land Pilsner and Hinterland Pale Ale to enjoy with the German sausage platter or honey wheat—battered fish and chips at their pubs.

HOOK'S CHEESE COMPANY, INC.
www.hookscheese.com

Tony and Julie Hook have been making delectable cheese for over thirty-five years in Mineral Point, Wisconsin.

HUDSON CREAM FLOUR
www.hudsoncream.com

The last sifting of this premium all-purpose flour, made by Stafford County Flour Mills, is done through a skein of silk so fine that water can't drip through it.

INTEGRATION ACRES
www.integrationacres.com

These Ohio Valley foragers sell ramps (wild leeks), spicebush (Lindera benzoin, a fragrant native bush), and pawpaws (wild bananas) in season. Integration Acres also farms goats and makes their own goat cheese.

JENI'S SPLENDID ICE CREAMS

www.jenisicecreams.com

From cow to cone, says this Columbus, Ohio, maker of signature ice creams.

JOHN CROSS FISHERIES

(231) 547-2532

A Charlevoix, Michigan, institution since 1945, this is the place to get Great Lakes whitefish from Lake Michigan, fresh and smoked, plus whitefish sausage and smoked fish salad.

KING ORCHARDS

www.KingOrchards.com

In Michigan's Upper Peninsula, the King family's orchards are bursting with fruit—from sour cherries to apricots and apples.

KOEZE

http://koeze.com

This Grand Rapids, Michigan, company, founded in 1910 by Sibbele Koeze, specializes in fresh-roasted nuts and an addictive all-natural peanut butter made with just peanuts and a pinch of salt.

KREMA NUT COMPANY

www.krema.com

Since 1898, Krema has been roasting and toasting nuts for all-natural nut butters—no sugar, salt, or preservatives—in Columbus, Ohio.

LA QUERCIA

www.laquercia.us

Herb and Kathy Eckhouse in Norwalk, Iowa, make fabulous prosciutto, pancetta, coppa, speck, guanciale, and more.

LUCY'S SWEET SURRENDER

www.lucyssweetsurrender.com

Famous in Cleveland, Ohio, for both sweet and savory strudels.

MAASDAM SORGHUM MILLS

www.maasdamsorghum.com

Since 1926, this family-owned mill has been making sorghum in Lynnville, Iowa.

MARCELLED ORIGINAL CHIPS

www.ballreich.com

In 1920, Fred and Ethel Ballreich started cooking wavy potato chips in a copper kettle heated with wood scraps—in their Tiffin, Ohio, garage. Their wavy chips are still popular with northern Ohio snackers.

MARY YODER'S AMISH KITCHEN

www.maryyodersamishkitchen.com

"Pie Mary's" family now continues her legacy of making pies, along with traditional Amish fare at their Middlefield, Ohio, restaurant. You can eat there and take pies out, but no mail order.

MAYTAG DAIRY FARMS

www.maytagdairyfarms.com

Since 1941, this cheesemaker in Newton, Iowa, has been making a blue cheese from the milk of black and white Holstein cows. It's now an American classic.

MIKE-SELL'S POTATO CHIPS

www.mike-sells.com

Founded by Daniel Mikesell in 1910, Dayton, Ohio's Mike-sell's touts that it's the oldest potato chip company in the United States.

NEW GLARUS BREWING COMPANY

www.newglarusbrewing.com

Tiny New Glarus, Wisconsin, features a Swiss bakery, dairy farms, and its own craft brewery with a sense of humor. Try their Road Slush Oatmeal Stout as well as Unplugged Cherry Stout made with Wisconsin Montmorency cherries.

NORTH HENDREN CO-OP DAIRY

www.northhendrenbluecheese.com

Famous for their Black River Blue cheese, this tiny Wisconsin cheesemaker has been making local cheeses since 1923.

NUESKE'S

www.nueskes.com

Since 1933, the Nueske family has been selling applewood-smoked meats from their farm in Wittenberg, Wisconsin. Their apple-smoked, dry-cured bacon—a favorite of chefs—has an irresistible aroma and flavor.

O'FALLON BREWERY

www.ofallonbrewery.com

Owners Fran and Tony Caradonna brew signature beers with a local stamp in the St. Louis area.

ORGANIC VALLEY FAMILY OF FARMS

www.organicvalley.coop

This cooperative of family farmers in La Farge, Wisconsin, produces wonderful, seasonal, organic Pasture Butter, which is made when the cows graze on the pasture at its spring/summer peak.

PARADISE LOCKER MEATS

www.paradisemeats.com

This Trimble, Missouri, processor offers a wide array of heritage, game, and smoked meats.

PENZEYS SPICES

www.penzeys.com

In a no-frills but big-flavor sort of way, Bill Penzey has traveled the world to bring home the herbs and spices that Heartlanders love back to Milwaukee, Wisconsin, and Penzeys stores all over the country.

PERSIMMONS

www.persimmonpudding.com

Check out this Web site for all things native persimmon. Watch Dymple Green (who used to own Dymple's Delight cannery for native persimmons) talk about them at http://www.youtube.com/watch?v=29N3kgiVpPY.

PORT CITY SMOKEHOUSE

www.portcitysmokehouse.com

Get your fresh lake perch, trout, and whitefish or smoked over local maple wood at this fish smokery in Frankfort, Michigan.

POWELL GARDENS

www.powellgardens.org

The twelve-acre Heartland Harvest Garden in Kingsville, Missouri, shows what "bounty" is all about.

PRAIRIE FRUITS FARM & CREAMERY

www.prairiefruits.com

Wes Jarrell and Leslie Cooperband raise goats, make artisan goat cheese, grow organic fruits and vegetables, and host farm dinners at their Urbana, Illinois, farm.

PRAIRIE ORGANIC VODKA

www.prairievodka.com

From Phillips Distillery in Minneapolis, Minnesota, this smooth, buttery vodka is distilled from organic corn.

RADIANCE DAIRY

(641) 472-8554

This grass-fed dairy near Fairfield, Iowa, prides itself on its sustainable approach to agriculture and its full-flavored, organic milk. No Web site.

RAY'S HICKORY NUTS

www.rayshickorynuts.com

Ray Pamperin of Juneau, Wisconsin, started the foraged hickory nut/butternut business now run by daughter Linda M. Schaalma.

ROTH KASE

www.rothkase.com

Makers and marketers of Buttermilk Blue, Raclette, Gruyère, and other European-style and farmstead cheese, Roth Kase is located in Monroe, Wisconsin

ROUND BARN WINERY

www.roundbarnwinery.com

This Michigan distillery uses mainly Ugni Blanc grapes (the same used for Cognac) to craft DiVine Vodka, "the vodka for wine lovers."

RUHLAND'S STRUDEL

www.thestrudelhaus.com

"Have strudel, will travel" could be the motto of this mom-and-pop business based in Eagan, Minnesota, which makes the rounds of Heartland festivals. Puff pastry encloses homemade fillings made with local Haralson apples and rhubarb as well as with brats and sauerkraut.

SANDHILL SORGHUM

www.sandhillfarm.org

This organic, communal farm in Rutledge, Missouri, grows, presses, and produces a fine sorghum.

SEED SAVERS EXCHANGE

www.seedsavers.org

In northern Iowa, this charming farm (open to visitors) champions heirloom seeds and is the headquarters for Seed Savers, a network of gardeners who preserve them. Their yearly catalog will make your green thumb itch.

SHATTO MILK COMPANY

www.shattomilk.com

This family dairy farm in Osborn, Missouri, offers bottled milk (with graphics that say "Yummy" or "Fresh" or "Family"), butter, ice cream, and cheese curds with a devoted following.

STERZING'S POTATO CHIPS

www.sterzingchips.com

Barney Sterzing's potato chips are still made in Burlington, Iowa, with only three ingredients: potatoes, oil, and salt.

SUTTER'S RIDGE FAMILY FARM

www.suttersridge.com

Matt and Julie Sutter are the third generation to run the family farm in Mt. Vernon, Wisconsin.

THREE FLOYDS BREWING COMPANY

www.3floyds.com

A father and two sons (all with the surname Floyd) brew edgy beers like Alpha King pale ale and Calumet Queen in Munster, Indiana.

TOWN HALL BREWING COMPANY

www.townhallbrewery.com

A Minneapolis, Minnesota, brewpub noted for their summertime Blackberry Wheat Beer and casual food with a local twist.

TRADERS POINT CREAMERY

www.tpforganics.com

This Zionsville, Indiana, creamery is known for its organic, grass-fed milk and European-style, drinkable yogurt.

TWO COOKIN' SISTERS

www.bigsistersalsa.com

Kristi Robinson Rensberger and Kim Robinson are the two cookin' sisters who make jams, jellies, salsas, and condiments in Brookston, Indiana.

UPLANDS CHEESE COMPANY

www.uplandscheese.com

The Uplands Cheese Company makes Pleasant Ridge Reserve, an artisan cheese from Dodgeville, Wisconsin.

WICK'S PIES

www.wickspies.com

Sugar Cream, Peanut Butter, German Chocolate, Peach . . . the list goes on of Wick's Pies from this well-known Winchester, Indiana, bakery.

WILD RICE

www.manoomin.com

Find Wisconsin, Minnesota, and Michigan distributors of authentic wild rice at this Web site.

PERMISSIONS

Grateful acknowledgment is made for permission to reprint excerpts from the following works:

Enemy Women by Paulette Jiles (Harper Perennial Library, 2002). Reprinted by permission of HarperCollins.

The Midwestern Country Cookbook: Recipes and Remembrances from a Traditional Farmhouse by Marilyn Kluger (Prima Publications, 1993). Reprinted by permission of Marilyn Kluger.

Nothing to Do But Stay: My Pioneer Mother by Carrie Young (University of Iowa Press, 1991). Reprinted by permission of University of Iowa Press.

Lake Wobegon Days by Garrison Keillor (Viking Penguin, 1985). Reprinted by permission of Penguin (USA).

"The Circus That Is Life Blooms Fully in Spring" by Garrison Keillor (*Kansas City Star*, March 28, 2009). Reprinted by permission of Tribune Media Services.

White Ladies and Naked Gardens by Justin Isherwood (Cornerstone Press, 1991). Reprinted by permission of Justin Isherwood.

Loving Frank by Nancy Horan (Ballantine Books, 2007). Reprinted by permission of Random House, Inc.

Shoeless Joe by W. P. Kinsella (Houghton Mifflin Company, 1999). Reprinted by permission of Houghton Mifflin Harcourt.

The Trees by Conrad Richter (Ohio University Press edition, 1991; originally published by Alfred A. Knopf, 1940). Reprinted by permission of Alfred A. Knopf.

Love Medicine by Louise Erdrich (Holt, Rinehart and Winston, 1984). Reprinted by permission of Henry Holt and Company.

The Grass Dancer by Susan Power (G. P. Putnam's Sons, 1994). Reprinted by permission of Penguin Group (USA).

Little Town on the Prairie by Laura Ingalls Wilder (Harper Collins, 1941). Reprinted by permission of HarperCollins.

"North Dakota Has Room for the Mind to Wander" by Adam Z. Horvath (*Newsday*, November 5, 1995). Reprinted by permission of *Newsday* and PARS International Corporation.

Leaving Home by Garrison Keillor (Viking Penguin, 1987). Reprinted by permission of Penguin (USA).

PHOTO LOCATIONS AND CREDITS

page 192 a: Becker Lane Organic Farm, Dyersville, Iowa; b: Berkshire (black) Chester White, Becker Lane Organic Farm, Dyersville, Iowa; c: Feeding organic corn mash, Becker Lane Organic Farm, Dyersville, Iowa; d: Jude Becker, Berkshire boars, Becker Lane Organic Farm, Dyersville, Iowa; e: Chester White sow and piglets, Becker Lane Organic Farm, Dyersville, Iowa

page 196 a: Lange Farms, Platteville, Wisconsin; b: Hereford (whiteface) Angus (black) cattle, Lindsborg, Kansas

page 197 Beef cattle, Amana, Iowa

page 199 Chef Tori Miller, Brunkow Cheese Stand, Dane County Farmers' Market, Madison, Wisconsin

page 200 Dorothy Priske, Fountain Prairie highland cattle, Fall River, Wisconsin

page 201 a: Tallgrass prairie, Fountain Prairie, Fall River, Wisconsin; b: Highland calf, Fountain Prairie highland cattle, Fall River, Wisconsin

page 202 a: Brown steer, Green Dirt Farm, Weston, Missouri; b: Fountain Paradise highland cattle, Fall River, Wisconsin

page 207 a: Barred Plymouth Rock heritage rooster, Good Shepherd Poultry Ranch, Tampa, Kansas; b: White Cornish heritage chickens, Good Shepherd Poultry Ranch, Tampa, Kansas; c: Good Shepherd Poultry Ranch, Tampa, Kansas

page 209 Tietz Family Farm Stand, Dane County Farmers' Market, Madison, Wisconsin

page 211 Gourmet Delight Mushrooms Stand, Dane County Farmers' Market, Madison, Wisconsin

page 212 Corn fields, Mt. Horeb, Wisconsin

page 213 a: Corn on the stalk; b: Alsums Sweetcorn Stand, Dane County Farmers' Market, Madison, Wisconsin; c: Corn fields, Blue Mounds, Wisconsin

page 215 White Holland and Slate Grey heritage turkeys, Good Shepherd Poultry Ranch, Tampa, Kansas

CHAPTER 7

pages 216—217 D.H. Day Farm, Sleeping Bear Bay, Lake Michigan, Glen Haven, Michigan

page 219 Hickory nut tree, Juneau, Wisconsin

page 223 a: Powell Gardens, Kingsville, Missouri; b: Weston's Antique Apple Orchard Stand, Dane County Farmers' Market, Madison, Wisconsin; c: Powell Gardens, Kingsville, Missouri

page 225 a: Friske Orchards Farm Market, Atwood, Michigan; b: Holstein cow, Iowa; c: Late Victorian Queen Anne house, Lindsborg, Kansas

page 228 a: Raspberries, Sutter's Ridge, Mt. Horeb, Wisconsin; b: Sweet cherries, King Orchards, Central Lake, Michigan; c: Weston's Antique Apple Orchard Stand, Dane County Farmers' Market, Madison, Wisconsin

page 230 Sunflowers, Kennebec, South Dakota

page 233 Sleeping Bear Dunes National Lakeshore, Michigan

page 234 Jaarsma Bakery, Pella, Iowa

page 235 a: Vermeer Mill, Pella, Iowa; b: Jaarsma Bakery, Pella, Iowa; c: Vermeer Mill, Pella, Iowa

page 239 Against the Grain Gallery, quilts, Mineral Point, Wisconsin

page 240 a : Jonathan Justus, Justus Drugstore, Smithville, Missouri; b: Copper alembic still, Justus Drugstore, Smithville, Missouri; c: Jonathan foraging for honeysuckle flowers at night, Missouri; d: Camille Eklof sorting honeysuckle blossoms, Justus Drugstore, Smithville, Missouri; e: Honeysuckle flowers, Smithville, Missouri

page 241 a: Honeysuckle distillate, Justus Drugstore, Smithville, Missouri; b: Chris Conatser, the botanist bartender at Justus Drugstore in Smithville, Missouri

page 244 a: Wildflowers, Wisconsin; b: Luck's Produce, Dane County Farmers' Market, Madison, Wisconsin

page 246 a and c: Holstein cows, Juneau, Wisconsin

page 249 Celeste Murdick's Fudge, Charlevoix, Michigan

page 253 a: Hickory nuts on the tree, Juneau, Wisconsin; b: Linda Schaalma, hickory nuts, Juneau, Wisconsin; c: Ray's Hickory Nuts, Juneau, Wisconsin

page 255 The Nut Factory, Dane County Farmers' Market, Madison, Wisconsin

page 257 Harrowing, Reliance, South Dakota

page 261 Symphony in Flint Hills 2008, White Ranch, Morris County, Kansas

page 264 Lindsay Laricks, Fresher Than Fresh Snow Cones, Kansas City, Missouri

page 265 Fishing on Lake Mendota, Madison, Wisconsin

Thanks to the following people and organizations for their help with the location photography for *Heartland*: Herb and Kathy Eckhouse at La Quercia, Jude Becker at Becker Lane Organic Farm, Sarah Hoffman and Jacquie Smith at Green Dirt Farm, Powell Gardens, Lindsay Laricks at Fresher than Fresh Snow Cones, Jonathan Justus at Justus Drugstore, Laura Christensen at Blue Door Farm, Farmers' Community Market at Brookside, Danny Williamson at Good Shepherd Poultry Ranch, Inc., Powell's Pumpkin Patch, Kauffman Museum, Allen and Paul Schrag at Silver Creek Farm, Matt and Julie Sutter at Sutter's Ridge Family Farm, John and Dorothy Priske at Fountain Prairie Highland Cattle, Chef Tori Miller at L'Etoile, Against the Grain Quilts by Joey Mahieu, Mike Gingrich at Uplands Cheese, Willi Lehner at Bleu Mont Dairy Company, Little Norway, Tony Hook at Hook's Cheese Company, Inc., Dane County Farmers' Market, Justin Rashid at American Spoon Foods, Jim and Rose King at King Orchards, Celeste Murdick's Fudge, Bill and Jennifer Carlson at Carlson's of Fishtown, and Martin and Marty Jelinek at Jelinek Orchards.

METRIC CONVERSIONS AND EQUIVALENTS

METRIC CONVERSION FORMULAS

TO CONVERT	MULTIPLY
Ounces to grams	Ounces by 28.35
Pounds to kilograms	Pounds by .454
Teaspoons to milliliters	Teaspoons by 4.93
Tablespoons to milliliters	Tablespoons by 14.79
Fluid ounces to milliliters	Fluid ounces by 29.57
Cups to milliliters	Cups by 236.59
Cups to liters	Cups by .236
Pints to liters	Pints by .473
Quarts to liters	Quarts by .946
Gallons to liters	Gallons by 3.785
Inches to centimeters	Inches by 2.54

APPROXIMATE METRIC EQUIVALENTS

VOLUME

¼ teaspoon	1 milliliter
½ teaspoon	2.5 milliliters
¾ teaspoon	4 milliliters
1 teaspoon	5 milliliters
2 teaspoons	10 milliliters
1 tablespoon (½ fluid ounce)	15 milliliters
¼ cup	60 milliliters
⅓ cup	80 milliliters
½ cup (4 fluid ounces)	120 milliliters
⅔ cup	160 milliliters
¾ cup	180 milliliters
1 cup (8 fluid ounces)	240 milliliters
2 cups (1 pint)	460 milliliters
3 cups	700 milliliters
4 cups (1 quart)	.95 liter
1 quart plus ¼ cup	1 liter
4 quarts (1 gallon)	3.8 liters

WEIGHT

¼ ounce	7 grams
½ ounce	14 grams
¾ ounce	21 grams
1 ounce	28 grams
2 ounces	57 grams
3 ounces	85 grams
4 ounces (¼ pound)	113 grams
5 ounces	142 grams
6 ounces	170 grams
7 ounces	198 grams
8 ounces (½ pound)	227 grams
16 ounces (1 pound)	454 grams
35.25 ounces (2.2 pounds)	1 kilogram

LENGTH

¼ inch	6 millimeters
½ inch	1¼ centimeters
1 inch	2½ centimeters
2 inches	5 centimeters
6 inches	15¼ centimeters
12 inches (1 foot)	30 centimeters

OVEN TEMPERATURES

To convert Fahrenheit to Celsius, subtract 32 from Fahrenheit, multiply the result by 5, then divide by 9.

DESCRIPTION	FAHRENHEIT	CELSIUS	BRITISH GAS MARK
Very cool	200°	95°	0
Very cool	225°	110°	¼
Very cool	250°	120°	½
Cool	275°	135°	1
Cool	300°	150°	2
Warm	325°	165°	3
Moderate	350°	175°	4
Moderately hot	375°	190°	5
Fairly hot	400°	200°	6
Hot	425°	220°	7
Very hot	450°	230°	8
Very hot	475°	245°	9

COMMON INGREDIENTS AND THEIR APPROXIMATE EQUIVALENTS

1 cup uncooked rice = 225 grams
1 cup all-purpose flour = 140 grams
1 stick butter (4 ounces • ½ cup • 8 tablespoons) = 110 grams
1 cup butter (8 ounces • 2 sticks • 16 tablespoons) = 220 grams
1 cup brown sugar, firmly packed = 225 grams
1 cup granulated sugar = 200 grams

Information compiled from *Recipes into Type* by Joan Whitman and Dolores Simon (Newton, MA: Biscuit Books, 2000); *The New Food Lover's Companion* by Sharon Tyler Herbst (Hauppauge, NY: Barron's, 1995); and *Rosemary Brown's Big Kitchen Instruction Book* (Kansas City, MO: Andrews McMeel, 1998).

INDEX